Vanessa Freerks

Baudrillard with Nietzsche and Heidegger:
Towards a Genealogical Analysis

STUDIES IN HISTORICAL PHILOSOPHY

Editor: Alexander Gungov

Consulting Editor: Donald Phillip Verene

ISSN 2629-0316

1   *Dustin Peone*
        Memory as Philosophy
        The Theory and Practice of Philosophical Recollection
        ISBN 978-3-8382-1336-1

2   *Raymond Barfield*
        The Poetic Apriori: Philosophical Imagination in a Meaningful Universe
        ISBN 978-3-8382-1350-7

3   *Jennifer Lobo Meeks*
        Allegory in Early Greek Philosophy
        ISBN 978-3-8382-1425-2

4   *Vanessa Freerks*
        Baudrillard with Nietzsche and Heidegger: Towards a Genealogical Analysis
        ISBN 978-3-8382-1474-0

5   *Thora Ilin Bayer and Donald Phillip Verene*
        Philosophical Ideas
        A Historical Study
        ISBN 978-3-8382-1585-3

Vanessa Freerks

BAUDRILLARD WITH NIETZSCHE AND HEIDEGGER:
Towards a Genealogical Analysis

Bibliografische Information der Deutschen Nationalbibliothek
Die Deutsche Nationalbibliothek verzeichnet diese Publikation in der Deutschen Nationalbibliografie; detaillierte bibliografische Daten sind im Internet über http://dnb.d-nb.de abrufbar.

Bibliographic information published by the Deutsche Nationalbibliothek
Die Deutsche Nationalbibliothek lists this publication in the Deutsche Nationalbibliografie; detailed bibliographic data are available in the Internet at http://dnb.d-nb.de.

Cover image: ID 147633071 © Mariia Domnikova | Dreamstime.com

ISBN-13: 978-3-8382-1474-0
© *ibidem*-Verlag, Stuttgart 2021
Alle Rechte vorbehalten

Das Werk einschließlich aller seiner Teile ist urheberrechtlich geschützt. Jede Verwertung außerhalb der engen Grenzen des Urheberrechtsgesetzes ist ohne Zustimmung des Verlages unzulässig und strafbar. Dies gilt insbesondere für Vervielfältigungen, Übersetzungen, Mikroverfilmungen und elektronische Speicherformen sowie die Einspeicherung und Verarbeitung in elektronischen Systemen.

All rights reserved. No part of this publication may be reproduced, stored in or introduced into a retrieval system, or transmitted, in any form, or by any means (electronical, mechanical, photocopying, recording or otherwise) without the prior written permission of the publisher. Any person who does any unauthorized act in relation to this publication may be liable to criminal prosecution and civil claims for damages.

Printed in the EU

Acknowledgements

The reworking of my PhD thesis for this book was done while I was a post-doctoral fellow at the University of Sofia and I wish to acknowledge the kind support of Alexander Gungov for making this possible.

I am most indebted to my PhD supervisor, Rafael Winkler, who has consistently supported me to pursue my projects amidst adversity and who now named me his research associate at the University of Johannesburg. The exchanges and rich conversations with him helped to clarify a number of issues regarding Nietzschean genealogy and the intricacies relating to Heidegger's conception of death.

This book would not have seen the light of day without Douglas Kellner, whose work on Baudrillard has accompanied me throughout my research. He has continuously given me important questions to reconsider, especially surrounding the relation between Baudrillard and Nietzsche. I am honoured that he also agreed to further contribute to this book by writing the Preface.

I am especially thankful to 福文心, who tirelessly read, edited, and commented on early drafts of this book.

I would also like to thank Frank Chouraqui who encouraged me to research the associations between Baudrillard and Nietzsche's *On the Genealogy of Morals* and Thaddeus Metz for sharing his experience and insights concerning the reworking my book.

Abstract

In this study, I seek to show how Baudrillard reactualizes Nietzsche's *On the Genealogy of Morals*. To my knowledge, no scholar has specifically tried to reconstruct how certain critical elements, strategies and figures within Nietzsche's *On the Genealogy of Morals* are mobilized in Baudrillard's work.

I first deal with Baudrillard's genealogy of consumer society. I argue that both Nietzsche and Baudrillard are interested in analyzing the power structures and differential relations upholding moral systems. Baudrillard applies the critical tools of genealogy to Saussurean linguistics and he analyzes concepts as symptoms of the powers and forces that have become dominant. For Baudrillard, Saussurean linguistics presents us with a theory of language and it describes the consumer "morality" of late modernity.

Nietzsche's *On the Genealogy of Morals* anticipates the general outline of Baudrillard's critique of the morality of consumption, but Baudrillard also transforms certain Nietzschean positions, processes, practices and figures. I show how the Nietzschean figure of the "ascetic priest" is turned into the modern advertiser in Baudrillard's works on consumer society. In addition, I discuss whether the "ascetic ideal" lives on in consumer society, despite the "end of transcendence".

After tackling Baudrillard's consumer society, I scrutinize his genealogy of the orders of simulacra in relation to Nietzsche's "reversal of Platonism". In addition, I deal with Baudrillard's genealogy of death and in the process, I examine Baudrillard's (problematic) relation to Heidegger, which I do to accentuate Baudrillard's closeness to Nietzsche.

Contents

Acknowledgements v

Abstract vii

Introduction 1
    Chapter Outline 10

1. **The Morality of Consumption: Reading Baudrillard's *Consumer Society* with Nietzsche's *On the Genealogy of Morals*** 19
    Introduction 19
    1.1 Baudrillard Reading Nietzsche 21
    1.2 Baudrillard's critical semiology 24
    1.3 Aristocratic and Slave Narratives 32
    Conclusion 42

2. **Processes of Subjection and the Figure of the Ascetic Priest** 43
    Introduction 43
    2.1 The Genesis of the Subject 44
    2.2 Economies of Debt and Exchange in Nietzsche and Baudrillard 50
    2.3 The "Liturgy of Solicitude" 55
    2.4 Ascetic ideals and consumer society 61
    Conclusion 64

3. **The End of Transcendence in *Consumer Society*** 67
    Introduction 67
    3.1 Wasteful Expenditure 68
    3.2 Ascetic consumption 75
    3.3 Pseudo-Events in Consumer Society 82
    Conclusion 93

4. **The Reversal of Platonism** 97
   Introduction 97
   4.1 The Reversal of Platonism 99
   4.2 The Simulacrum and the Motivation for Plato's Method of Division 106
   4.3 Baudrillard's Simulacrum 112
   Conclusion 119

5. **Hyperreality of Simulation** 121
   Introduction 121
   5.1 Genealogy of Simulacra 122
   5.2 The Hyperreal Structural Law of Value 130
   5.3 The Causes of Simulation 145
      5.3.1   Simulation as an economic effect 146
      5.3.2   Simulation as media effect 147
      5.3.3   Simulation and the Death of God 150
   Conclusion 152

6. **Baudrillard and Heidegger: Towards a Genealogy of Death** 155
   Introduction 155
   6.1 Death and Subjectivity 157
   6.2 Baudrillard (Re-)socializing Death 164
   6.3 Beyond death as natural fatality 168
   6.4 (Re-) Situating Heidegger and Baudrillard 175
   Conclusion 181
   Concluding Remarks and Summary of the Study 185

7. **Bibliography** 194

   Index 208

Introduction

This study seeks to bring to light how Baudrillard reconstructs certain critical elements, strategies and figures in Nietzsche's *On the Genealogy of Morals*. To my knowledge, no scholar has specifically tried to show how Nietzsche's *On the Genealogy of Morals* is remobilized in Baudrillard's work. [1]

In chapters 1, 2 and 3, I deal with Baudrillard's genealogy of consumer society as outlined in *Consumer Society* (1970; 1998).

In chapter 4 and 5, I go through his genealogy of the image and of simulation, as analyzed in the books *Simulacra and Simulations* (1981; 1994) as well as *Symbolic Exchange and Death* (1976; 1993).

In chapter 6, I tackle Baudrillard's genealogy of death as sketched in his book *Symbolic Exchange and Death*. In this final chapter on Baudrillard's genealogy of death, I discuss Baudrillard's (problematic) relation to Heidegger, which as we shall see, further underlines Baudrillard's closeness to Nietzsche.[2]

I will start the following introduction to my study with some comments made by Baudrillard regarding his relation to Nietzsche. This serves as a background to clarify why I find it important to focus on certain elements within Nietzschean genealogy to better understand Baudrillard.

Baudrillard's direct and explicit references to Nietzsche are rare but comments he has made in interviews show the importance of Nietzsche to his thought. In the following excerpt

---

[1] For a general overview of the influence of Nietzsche on Baudrillard see Lepers (2009); Pawlett (2007, 112-113) and interviews between François L'Yvonnet and Baudrillard (2001; 2004).

[2] In the following excerpt from an interview collected as *D'un fragment l'autre* Baudrillard discusses his philosophical trajectory and he mentions Heidegger: "my philosophical background is shaky, particularly where the classical philosophers are concerned, such as Kant and Hegel or even Heidegger. I have read Heidegger of course, but not in German, and fragmentarily. Perhaps one only ever studies one philosopher seriously, just as one has only one godfather, as one has only one idea in one's life. Nietzsche is, then, the author beneath whose broad shadow I moved, though involuntarily and without really knowing what I was doing" (Baudrillard 2004, 2).

from an interview collected as *D'un fragment l'autre* Baudrillard says:

> "I read [Nietzsche] very early ... I held him in a kind of quasi-visceral memory, but I'd retained only what I wanted to" (Baudrillard 2004, 1).

Baudrillard, in the footsteps of Nietzsche, advocates an "interpretative violence" at the heart of his approach and it is in *On the Genealogy of Morals* that Nietzsche suggests that interpretation is always a matter of "forcing, adjusting, shortening, omitting, filling-out, inventing, falsifying and everything else *essential* to interpretation" (Nietzsche 2007, 112; italics in the text). In addition, Baudrillard follows Nietzsche in regarding all interpretation as polemical: to support one view is to combat another view. The subtitle of Nietzsche's *On the Genealogy of Morals* is *A Polemic* and a characteristic of Nietzsche's genealogical study is that it combats interpretations which claim to be self-evident, beyond dispute, necessary and eternal.

In interviews, Baudrillard admits that he indirectly extends Nietzsche's work and creates an afterlife for Nietzsche's ideas. Baudrillard says:

> "I find it curious, all those people who've read Nietzsche ... but nothing has rubbed off on them. How can you go on doing your own thing in your own little discipline as though nothing had happened?" (Baudrillard 2004, 56).

Here we see how Baudrillard highlights the transformative effect of Nietzsche's writing. For Baudrillard, it is only possible to study a single philosopher seriously and he claims that the one philosopher he did study was Nietzsche.[3] Engaging with Nietzsche's thought, in Baudrillard's eyes, does not entail explicit interpretation and detailed analysis of Nietzsche or becoming involved in the debate regarding (the value of) Nietzsche's philosophy.

---

[3] In the collection of interviews *D'un fragment l'autre*, Baudrillard says: "Perhaps one only ever studies one philosopher seriously, just as one has only one godfather, as one has only one idea in one's life. Nietzsche is, then, the author beneath whose broad shadow I moved, though involuntarily and without really knowing what I was doing" (Baudrillard 2004, 2).

Baudrillard does not follow Nietzsche in any systematic way but secondary critics often underscore (without systematic, in depth or prolonged analysis, however) the clear and "profound influence" (Pawlett 2007, 3) of Nietzsche on Baudrillard. Holger Zapf (2010, 12; my translation) claims that Baudrillard can be regarded as the "Nietzsche of social scientific theory" (he does not go into further detail on this, however).

Baudrillard is constantly in search of radical otherness and seeks to lift any anchors that fix thoughts or the world. He disputes the meaningfulness of the fundamental concepts of the social sciences as well as the appropriateness of social scientific methods; he throws out normative orientations and declares many theoretical enterprises (from Marxism, Positivism up to "Post Modernism") as redundant. He thereby constitutes the degree zero of theory.

Baudrillard disputes in a certain sense that social reality can be grasped within theoretical statements and even denies the existence of "the social" and "the political" as categories that pick out their corresponding referent. When he does provide a description of social reality, he uses neither a rigorous conceptual set of instruments nor an explicit theory that clearly states its epistemological premises. Rather, according to the Baudrillard critic, Peter W. Zima (2010, 104), Baudrillard makes use of alarming metaphors to create a conceptual fog and shows no interest in theoretical coherence.

One of Baudrillard's sharpest critics, Alex Callinicos, claims that in Baudrillard's work all that is left are *"belles lettres"*, where unsubstantial theoretical propositions encounter "banal aperçus" (Callinicos 1989, 147). This is a valid criticism and Baudrillard indeed has more in common with a novelist than with a theoretician. For King (1998, 99; italics in the text), Baudrillard's

> "writing is merely an earnest but stripped form of academic writing, which moves from *asserted* claim to claim, rather than from *sustained* claim to claim for the slow but rigorous building of an argument".

The building of arguments indeed does not interest Baudrillard as much as the stylistic figures that make up the literary and rhetorical charge of a text. It is obvious, however, that behind his literary mediated perspective there lies an indirect semiology (such as that of Ferdinand de Saussure), anthropology (such as that of Marcel Mauss), philosophy (such as Nietzsche) and theology, in short a 'theory', which can be made explicit by the secondary literature (for instance Gary Genosko's (1994) *Baudrillard and Signs. Signification Ablaze,* Holger Zapf's (2010) book on *The Radical Thinking of Jean Baudrillard as a Political Theory,* James Walters's (2012) book on *Baudrillard and Theology* and Charles Levin's (1996) book on Baudrillard's *Cultural Metaphysics.*

What differentiates Baudrillard from a literary figure is his heterodox notion of theory. With no evident method, with no explicit premise, Baudrillard only equips himself with a set of arbitrary hypotheses and theorems which most of the time contradict each other and make a coherent theory impossible. For example, he claims "All things," (including statements on these things) "are ambivalent and reversible" (Baudrillard 1993 TE, 77). Regarding political facts, he says "this confusion of the fact with its model...allows each time for all possible interpretations, even the most contradictory" (Baudrillard 1981, 32; 1994, 17).

Baudrillard's work can by no means comply with theoretical standards, because he himself declares these standards inadequate. As a result, his thinking cannot qualify as theoretical. Critics of Baudrillard do mostly agree, however, that he has many important insights.

How does Baudrillard come to these perspectives and what scope do they have? To investigate this, one would have to reconstruct a theory from his fragmented insights, as one does with works of literature.

Perhaps there is a theory in Baudrillard's work, which he himself eliminated. For Baudrillard, a good theory is "reversible"; it eliminates itself. Reversibility is in tune with Baudrillard's rejection of any notion of linear progress and his Nietzschean view[4]

---

[4] As Nietzsche puts it in the Third Essay, paragraph 27 of *On the Genealogy of Morals*: "the law of *necessary* 'self-overcoming' is the essence of life" (Nietzsche 2007, 119).

that systems have a built-in obsolescence.[5] Baudrillard's own work follows a strategy of reversibility, which according to Rex Butler means that the "basic axioms of the system" under examination must be pushed "to the point where they begin to turn upon themselves, to produce the opposite effects from those intended" (Butler 1997, 52).

For Baudrillard, the rationality of the Enlightenment produces "the orders of simulacra" that destroy it (chapter 4 and 5). 'Reality', in Baudrillard's eyes, has become hyperreal. A central Baudrillardian concept I will study is hyperreality (chapter 5), which is the new ruling linguistic condition of society. Hyperreality puts an end to distinctions between object and representation, thing and idea. It is a world composed of models or simulacra, which have no referent or ground in any 'reality' except their own, and I will show how this parallels Nietzsche's definition of nihilism: the highest values cannot resist their own reversal and devaluation.

Generally speaking, nihilism takes two forms in Nietzsche. The first is when life is judged lacking in relation to something super-sensuous beyond it, as in the case of Platonism or Christianity. In this case, truth, meaning and value is derived from a transcendent origin. The second form of nihilism is when these higher values are devalued, as in the case of the Enlightenment. In this case, meaning and value are questioned. For Nietzsche, any philosophy must decide how to deal with these two problems, which are integral to thought. According to Nietzsche, passive nihilism remains locked within the recognition that the world is without true foundation, ground and meaning. Active nihilism, on the other hand, arises from the general insight that "the meaning and value of life depend on fictions that we must accept as true" (Winkler 2018, 105).

---

[5] In his entry "Nihilism" in *The Baudrillard Dictionary*, Rex Butler (2010, 139) says: "Nietzsche is one of Baudrillard defining influences. He is one of the few thinkers whose presumptions are not turned against them" as Baudrillard did with Marx in *The Mirror of Production* (1975) and Saussure as well as Freud in *Symbolic Exchange and Death* (1993).

In chapter 4, I show how Nietzsche problematizes the value of truth (without simply overturning the super-sensuous Platonic value structure, for instance, by privileging appearances). Nietzsche's early essay "On Truth and Lying in a Non-Moral Sense" (1873; 1999) overcomes the dualistic and hierarchical ordering between sensuous and super-sensuous, illusion and reality, appearance and essence. This is because, for Nietzsche, the production of truth is itself an illusionary process. I will start chapter 4 (section 1) by discussing Nietzsche's reversal of Platonism and I do so by examining Nietzsche's early text "On Truth and Lie in the Non-Moral Sense" as well as his later text *Twilight of the Idols*.[6]

Christopher Norris (2000, 364) regards Baudrillard's own project as "a species of inverted Platonism". For Norris,

> "Baudrillard's …discourse… systematically promotes the negative terms (rhetoric, appearance, ideology) above their positive counterparts. It is no longer possible to maintain the old economy of truth and representation in a world where 'reality' is entirely constructed through forms of mass media feedback, where values are determined by consumer demand (itself brought about by the endless circulation of meanings, images and advertising codes), and where nothing could serve as a means of distinguishing true from merely true-seeming (or logical) habits of belief. Such is the world we inhabit, according to Baudrillard" (Norris 2000, 364).

Norris does not mention, however, the extent to which Baudrillard, like Nietzsche, breaks down privileged hierarchical relations altogether. In my view, Baudrillard does not triumph the rise of the simulacrum nor does he lament a loss of the real in simulation, rather, Baudrillard's work seeks to challenge processes of simulat ion that try to bring about a real, that create effects of the real ("hyperreality", as we shall see in more detail in chapter 5).

Rex Butler (1997, 54) rightly claims that "Baudrillard's point is that each system he analyses (and the work of any great thinker) creates its own reality, sets out the very terms in which it must be understood". Yet, in Baudrillard's work, as Butler also points out,

---

[6] I follow R.L. Anderson (2005, 185) in this regard.

there is another side to any attempt to create the real in simulation, a side which resists any method of simulation. [7]

Baudrillard's reversible and "anagrammatic"[8] theory is necessarily radical and aims straight at its own roots. For Baudrillard, the real joy in writing is to sacrifice a whole chapter for a sentence, a whole sentence for a word. A theory that destroys itself is not merely something that has vanished to nothing. After the anagrammatic "implosion", (Nietzsche's "Twilight of the Idols", dealt with in chapter 4) there remains a moment of silence, uncertainty and doubt. The theory ends as it started: with "wonder". In this sense, Baudrillard's crime was almost perfect: he managed to erase the theoretical traces of his enterprise and he transformed his theory into an uncomfortable but surprising story, with many insights (Zapf 2010, 13).

One should not be swayed by rhetorical strategy; one must (while keeping in mind Baudrillard's assertion regarding the connection between thought and event) suspend one's own judgment when the text's theses collide. Only then perhaps is it possible to glimpse Baudrillard's theory.

The Baudrillard critic, Charles Levin (1996), prefers to speak of a "metaphysics" rather than "theory" in Baudrillard's work. Instead of "post-modern," Levin opts for the label "cultural metaphysics" because metaphysics has relinquished its demand for seriousness and legitimacy (Levin 1996, 15). Theory is associated with intellectual seriousness and involves "academic responsibility" (Levin 1996, 15) even though Baudrillard uses the word himself and plays with its seriousness. Levin's study seeks to emphasize the non-systematic aspects of Baudrillard's work, and how Baudrillard strips his work to referentiality and practicality (espe-

---

[7] "It is this real, excluded by any attempt to speak of it, that is the limit to every system – it is the Platonic paradox that Baudrillard means by the real" (Butler 1999, 53). The paradox first raised by Plato in his dialogue *Cratylus* (1875, 257) has been treated by Derrida in his essay *Plato's Pharmacy*.

[8] Baudrillard's chapter "The Extermination of the Name of God" in *Symbolic Exchange and Death* starts with a section on 'The Anagram'. In his book on Baudrillard entitled *Baudrillard's Bestiary*, Mike Gane (1991b, 118-121) discusses the intricacies of the anagram in his chapter "Anagrammatic Resolutions".

cially the case in Baudrillard's later work)⁹ and the importance it places on the power of criticism to actually end up making reality (Levin 1996, 15). Among other cultural metaphysicians Levin includes Nietzsche, Bataille and Deleuze (Levin 1996, 16) who also have a prominent place in my study.

According to Rex Butler (1999, 15), Levin's approach does not provide examples of exactly how Baudrillard avoids referentiality and practicality or how Baudrillard transforms them in his work. This means that Levin does not focus systematically enough on Baudrillard's writing and how its inner logic functions. For Baudrillard, writing is always in the process of being formed and literature becomes the avatar of philosophical renewal. Literature challenges philosophy and in so doing, it triggers the creation of new perspectives, as well as new modes of thinking and writing.

As Rex Butler (1999, 5; italics in the text) explains:

> "Criticism or theory understands itself no longer as responding to or explaining a previous real, but as bringing about its own real. Or Baudrillard's work engages with the real, but not in the way this is usually understood. It is a real not external but *internal* to the work. The model for Baudrillard's writing, though he rarely mentions him by name, is…Nietzsche."

The position Baudrillard reaches towards the end of his work is that writing creates its own reality. Writing redirects and transforms external circumstances. For Baudrillard, the distinctive aspect of significant thought is that it overhauls the influences upon it and makes something else of them.

Philippe Lepers (2009, 337-350) in his article "Baudrillard und Nietzsche: vademecum, vadetecum" provides a general overview of the relationship between Baudrillard and Nietzsche, and he investigates to what extent Baudrillard moves under Nie-

---

9   *Symbolic Exchange and Death,* published in French in 1976, is the most all-encompassing exposition of Baudrillard's ideas and it is the last of his works that proceeds in an overall systematic and scientific style. Here, Baudrillard provides a "genealogy" of death, but death is here already a figure of speech for the more general notion of symbolic exchange. After this book, Baudrillard steadily leaves the conventions of academic writing behind and he attempts to critique all systematic thought (by delving into the 'simulations' he describes).

tzsche's shadow, as well as how Nietzsche's work serves as a platform for Baudrillard's own projects. Baudrillard is loyal to Nietzsche's adage "vademecum, vadetecum" (Lepers 2009, 349), and in his conclusion, Lepers questions to what extent Baudrillard's reception of Nietzsche can bring forth new interpretations of Nietzsche's philosophy, specifically whether Nietzsche can now be regarded (after Baudrillard) as a philosopher of "alterity", which in Baudrillard's work encompasses all that which challenges the homogeneous and universal discourse or code (Lepers 2009, 350). This transformative aspect of Baudrillard's reading of Nietzsche will also be important for my study. Nietzsche can be seen to anticipate many of Baudrillard's ideas, but this study will also emphasize how Baudrillard transforms Nietzschean concepts.

Lepers (2009, 344; my translation) identifies certain areas of Nietzschean critique that may have influenced Baudrillard. Below are the ones he identifies that are also important to bear in mind for my study.

- Nietzsche's allergic reaction to any form of Socialism;
- Nietzsche's critique of Utilitarianism;
- Nietzsche's rejection of any objective meaning that is natural or free of human involvement;
- Nietzsche critique of the autonomous rational subject. The human being is the result of a constant struggle of forces and everything the human does is symptomatic, a sign of sickness or health; and
- Nietzsche's critical position towards any idea of continuous progress of European culture.

In my own study, relating Nietzsche to Baudrillard (and making explicit what Baudrillard left implicit), I will try to reveal the subtle 'genealogical foundation' that is hidden behind Baudrillard's disturbing yet brilliant rhetoric. Baudrillard must be regarded as an intellectual who decides to present his political and social interventions in a disturbing and provocative way. As Anthony King puts it:

> "[t]he importance of Baudrillard lies in the fact that he both demonstrates the most extreme symptoms of contemporary intellectual malaise and simultaneous provides the cure for that disease" (King 1998, 106).

Baudrillard, in the footsteps of Nietzsche does not read philosophical truth claims according to their alleged accurate reflection of reality (as it is in-itself), but as symptoms of a certain form of life.[10] Nietzsche and Baudrillard use genealogy to undermine modern moral practices expressing a "will to truth". In *On the Genealogy of Morals,* Nietzsche rejects the idea that there can be one account of truth that corresponds with the way things are in themselves, "independently of the mediation of perspectives by relations of willing" (Allsobrook 2009, 703).

A central claim in *On the Genealogy of Morals* is that our unconditional will to truth has brought us to the point of nihilism. An unconditional commitment to the value of truth disempowers us as agents. Truth can never be above our interest in truth and our perspectives (from which truth claims are made) are affected by the things we value. Baudrillard, I argue, follows Nietzsche in emphasizing the importance of exploring different perspectives, drives, affects or passions.

Genealogy, as practiced by Nietzsche and Baudrillard, reminds readers not only of the contingency of their perspectives but proposes different perspectives. It motivates readers to assess the value of their perspectives in relation to other perspectives.

Chapter Outline

In chapters 1, 2 and 3, I investigate to what extent Nietzsche's *On the Genealogy of Morals* anticipates the general outline of Baudrillard's critique of the morality of consumption, which Baudrillard develops in his first two published works, *The System of Objects* (1968; 2005) and *Consumer Society* (1970; 1998).

---

[10] For an analysis of Nietzschean symptomatology see for example van Tongeren (2000, 7,9,140-141).

In chapters 4 and 5, I go through Baudrillard's genealogy of the image and of simulation. In the final chapter 6, I deal with Baudrillard's genealogy of death.

In chapter 1, I show that both Nietzsche and Baudrillard are interested in analyzing the power structures and differential relations upholding moral systems. Baudrillard applies the critical tools of genealogy to Saussurean linguistics and he analyzes concepts as symptoms of the dominant powers and forces. For Baudrillard, Saussurean linguistics presents us with a theory of language and it describes the consumer "morality" of late modernity (Baudrillard 1998, 79). Baudrillard thereby argues that neither structural linguistics nor our current morality of consumption is inevitable or universal.

Baudrillard seeks to show that structural linguistics ignores that it is a historically-based semiological structure, not a universal truth about language. The sign, separated from the referent and understandable only at the level of signifier relations, is a reduction of what Baudrillard calls the symbolic. Baudrillard argues that so-called "primitive societies" engage in symbolic communications: the signifier, signified and referent are all united in the act of communication. In symbolic communication, "signs include[...] words that [are] attached to referents and [are] uttered in a context that held open their possible reversal by others" (Poster 1988, 4).[11]

Unlike capitalist political economy, which isolates objects from their cultural meaning and subjects them to a specific (and therefore non-ambiguous) code of signs, symbolic exchange is ambivalent. Signs are detached from lived relations, and this makes possible their endless combination and recombination in a limitless process of integration. Signs even replace lived relation; they present a coded version of lived (symbolic) relation, one that is controlled and less threatening.

---

[11] With her emphasis on 'forgiveness', Hannah Arendt holds out the possibility of constructing a symbolic world in which the consequences of our actions can be reversed. See Hannah Arendt, *The Human Condition* (Chicago: University Press 1958, 237-8). It would be important to pursue the connection between Arendt and Baudrillard on this point.

The consumption of sign-value is based on a meaningful "totality" which is unreachable (Baudrillard 2005, 224). Sign value always defers satisfaction by referring the process of consumption to another object/sign in the system. Like Christian morality, I claim that for Baudrillard, consumer society exposes man to a "*piercing* sensation of his nothingness" (Nietzsche 2007, 115).

Nietzsche's *On the Genealogy of Morals* 'foretells' the general outline of Baudrillard's critique of the morality of consumption, but Baudrillard also transforms certain Nietzschean positions, processes, practices and figures. In chapter 2, I show how the Nietzschean figure of the ascetic priest becomes the modern advertiser in Baudrillard's works on consumer society.

In chapter 3, one of the central questions I will tackle is whether the sign-object sold by the advertiser to the consumer is otherworldly and non-sensuous – or in some way close to or identical with the features that pertain to the world of being in Plato. The ascetic ideal propagated by the priest is something that does not bear the features of the sensuous world, like truth; as a result, it can only reject this world.

I discuss to what extent consumption as it is outlined by Baudrillard represents an "*impoverishment of life*" (Nietzsche 2007, 114; italics in the text). In the final section of chapter 3, I focus on how consumer society is run by pseudo-objects and pseudo-events. Consumer society is beyond the true and the false and this will allow me to introduce the concept of simulation to which I dedicate the next chapter 4.

It was already in his short text "On Truth and Lie in a Non-Moral Sense" that Nietzsche (1999, 143) saw the "pure drive towards truth" as an effect of deception. I start chapter 4 (section 1) with a background discussion to Nietzsche's reversal of Platonism by scrutinizing Nietzsche's early text "On Truth and Lie in the Non-Moral Sense" as well as his later text *Twilight of the Idols*.

Nietzsche calls into question (a) the moral interpretation of the difference between truth and error (that truth is something good and error something evil), (b) the metaphysical interpretation of the difference between truth and error (that truth represents a world of unchanging facts, and error, a world of becoming), (c) the logical interpretation of the bivalence between truth and error (truth is not opposed to error). In this scepticism, 'error' becomes the metaphor for a world without vertical antitheses and oppositions between good and evil, being and becoming, beauty and ugly.

According to Deleuze (2004, 300), living after Nietzsche's reversal of Platonism means living in a world where "simulacra" at last prevail over immutable Platonic Ideas. Nietzsche's reversal of Platonism thus sets the scene for my comparison between Deleuze's view of the simulacrum and Baudrillard's (chapter 4, sections 2 and 3). I regard Deleuze's view as close to Baudrillard, as they both stress the undecidability between appearance and reality in simulacra. For Deleuze (2004, 295), the simulacrum produces an "effect of resemblance" that simulates the real. Resemblance for Deleuze here continues only as an external effect of the internal differential dynamic of the simulacrum. For Baudrillard, there now only exists an "empty space of representation", which produces "effects of the real" (Baudrillard 1993, 70). Baudrillard calls this situation "the hyperreal", to which I dedicate chapter 5 (Baudrillard 1993, 70). In chapter 5, I take a closer look at Baudrillard's problematization of the true and false in hyperreal simulation.

In chapter 6, I tackle Baudrillard's problematization of the separation between life and death and how this recalls Heidegger's analysis of human existence as constituted by its relation to death. Nick Hanlon's (2004: 518) article entitled "Death, Subjectivity, Temporality in Baudrillard and Heidegger"[12] shows how Baudrillard's analysis of Heidegger raises the problem of subjectivity, a problem crucially connected with death. Baudrillard critiques the economization and compartmentalization of death by investigating the social role and place of death

---

[12] This is the only in-depth study that scrutinizes the relation between Heidegger and Baudrillard's view on death.

away from a certain "tour subjectif", which he identifies in Heidegger's conception of death (Baudrillard 1976, 228-29). [13]

In Hanlon's view, Baudrillard's analysis of Heidegger as subject-centred leads him away from the situatedness (*Befindlichkeit*) entailed in the *Jemeinigkeit* of death. For Hanlon (2004, 524), Baudrillard places all the emphasis on the contingent and the aleatory and regards "his theorising as somehow outside any structural conception of temporality and history – in a sense ahistorical". Hanlon (2004, 513) claims that Baudrillard takes on an approach that revolves around "pure critique" rather than the proposition of "alternative structures" which can be critiqued. Hanlon uses Heidegger to claim that this leaves us with a conception of subjectivity that does not take account of our "situatedness" in a temporal framework. According to Hanlon,

> "[t]he aporia concerning 'situatedness' in Baudrillard is clearly an aporia concerning Baudrillard's approach to history, historicity and temporality. It may be understood as a weakness in Baudrillard's theorizing in as much as if he is employing a Heraclitean ontology of flux, implying a conception of temporality along the lines of Nietzschean *Werden* and with his concept of reversibility being explicitly related to Nietzsche's notion of 'eternal recurrence', then there must be an acceptance that identity implies difference, that the eternal recurrence of the same also implies the absolute particularity of a moment and vice versa" (Hanlon 2004, 524).

In my view, and contra Hanlon, Baudrillard's reversible temporality is not "ahistorical" and it does very well permit us to consider our immersion ("situatedness") in a historical context. Genealogy as practiced by Baudrillard (in the footsteps of Nietzsche) chal-

---

[13] In chapter 6, I focus on Heidegger's early work *Sein und Zeit* published in 1927. During the 1920s, as Rafael Winkler (2018, xv) explains, Heidegger "leans towards transcendental idealism ..., identifying the intelligibility of entities (their being) with Dasein's understanding of being. During the 1930s and 1940s, Heidegger thinks of the relation of being and Dasein as a relation of reciprocal implication or mutual dependency (*belonging* and *need* are his two key terms, the first for Dasein's relation to being, the second for being's relation to Dasein), which means that he does not collapse one into the other. Being, the intelligibility of entities, unfolds as a play of differences and contrasts (*Auseinander-setzung*), whereas Dasein shelters that play in beings (at least as long as it exists authentically)" (Winkler 2018, xv).

lenges assumptions based upon linear and progressive orders of descent that would enable one to derive notions and practices from a natural single and stable origin. But I also think that Baudrillard (following Nietzsche) does want to show how the past inheres in the present.[14]

Nietzsche and Baudrillard's genealogies are interested in constructing fictionalized hypothetical primal scenes through for instance so-called noble morality (in the case of Nietzsche) and primitive symbolic exchange (in the case of Baudrillard). These "alternative structures" are hypothetical and serve as a contrast to current self-understandings.

In *On the Genealogy of Morals,* Nietzsche uses the story of masters and slaves to narrate the origin of our most basic moral values and to suggest a difference between the values "good and bad" and "good and evil". Nietzsche thereby claims that there cannot be an original or true designation of value since the master and the slave always evaluate the world in different ways.

Like Nietzsche, Baudrillard does not claim to discover an ideal society of symbolic exchange in 'non-Western' cultures. Symbolic exchange is presented as a form or principle, rather than as the specific 'content' of cultural practices. Baudrillard's discourse on symbolic exchange (like Nietzsche's noble morality) has no representational content or truth value. Baudrillard's notion of symbolic exchange is a figure of speech or metaphor[15] that serves

---

[14] Michel Foucault's reading of genealogy places undue emphasis on the role Nietzsche accords to contingency and discontinuity within history. See Michel Foucault, "Nietzsche, Genealogy, and History" (1971), in *The Essential Works of Foucault*, Volume II: 1954–84, ed. James Faubion, trans. Robert Hurley and others (London: Penguin Books, 2000), pp. 369–93.

[15] It must be borne in mind that in the final chapter of *Symbolic Exchange and Death*, in the section 'An Anti-Materialist Theory of Language', Baudrillard (1993, 235) differentiates the "symbolic operation" from "a positive economy of metaphor: the idea of a reconciliation between the 'thing' and the word given back its materiality."
For Baudrillard (1993, 236) "[t]here is no materialist reference in the symbolic operation, not even an 'unconscious one; rather there is the operation of an 'anti-matter.'"
Quoting Julia Kristeva (from *Poésie et Négativité*), Baudrillard (1993, 220) claims that metaphor is simply the transfer of value from one field to another

to enable us to make sense of what we do and what we believe. Baudrillard's genealogical narrative seeks to integrate multiple genealogical perspectives into our conception of moral values.

In the words of Rafael Winkler, I intend to show that Baudrillard and Nietzsche are thinkers "of the limit of metaphysics" (Winkler 2018, 88). According to Winkler (2018, 87) Nietzsche does not aim to "neutralise metaphysical characterisations of the world whether as reality or appearance, being or becoming". Winkler claims that Nietzsche proposes a "new practice of self-discipline", whose aim is

> "to incorporate the insight that the totality of propositions that has defined Western humanity's self-understanding since Plato rests on simplifications, errors or fictions. The principal question here is not *Is that insight true*? but, rather, *What would that insight do to me, how would it transform me, if it were true?* and *Am I able to overcome resistances to it?* In Nietzsche's eyes, what remains at the end of metaphysics, once the distinction between the supersensuous and the sensuous worlds have collapsed in the general insight of our most cherished and prized truths rests on illusions, is a practice that uses the so-called truths as a means and tests of self-overcoming. Nietzsche is, like Heidegger, a thinker of the limit of metaphysics." (Winkler 2018, 88)

In my study, I show that genealogy is mobilized by Baudrillard as such a practice at the limit of metaphysics. For Baudrillard (1993, 159) "[t]he subject needs a myth of its end, as of its origin, to form its identity". Science demands an end to mythological thought. Nietzsche, Heidegger and Baudrillard criticize the attempt of science to regard subjects, objects and practices as examples of scientific laws; as unilateral irreversible facts; as universal and interchangeable.

This book shows that Baudrillard seeks to expose the myths surrounding consumer society (e.g., surrounding 'needs' and 'per-

---

to the point of the 'absorption of a multiplicity of texts (meanings) in the message.'" Against this multiplicity of meaning and value, Baudrillard (1993, 220) advocates "radical ambivalence … non-valence".

In the above, I use metaphor merely to emphasize that 'symbolic exchange' is not to be taken literally (i.e., it does not refer to specific practices in 'primitive societies'). The symbolic does not refer to anything directly, nor does it seek to represent or express a repressed dimension (emanating for instance from an 'unconscious'). I use 'metaphor' in the non-technical, non-psycho-analytic sense of the term.

sonalisation'), hyperreality and biological, natural, impersonal death. In the process, Baudrillard proposes alternative myths (in the form of symbolic exchange). Baudrillard, in my view, like Nietzsche provides a theory of the historical variables that give rise to subjectivity. Genealogy, as practised by Nietzsche and Baudrillard, is a critically motivated art of drastic presentation, which should help us overcome our current perspectives of the world and ourselves. But before this transformation can take place their work seeks to enable us to make sense of what we do and what we believe in.

1. The Morality of Consumption: Reading Baudrillard's *Consumer Society* with Nietzsche's *On the Genealogy of Morals*

Introduction

In this chapter, I investigate to what extent Nietzsche's *On the Genealogy of Morals* anticipates the general outline of Baudrillard's critique of the morality of consumption, which he develops in his first two published works, *The System of Objects* (1968; 2005) and *Consumer Society* (1970; 1998). As already mentioned in my Introduction, not many scholars have paid sustained and in-depth attention to Baudrillard's relation to Nietzsche and to my knowledge, no scholar has tried to reconstruct the links between Nietzsche's *On the Genealogy of Morals* and Baudrillard's *Consumer Society*.

In my view, both Nietzsche and Baudrillard are interested in analyzing the power structures upholding moral systems. In *Consumer Society*, Baudrillard defines the role of consumption in Western society as an element structuring social relations and he claims that he is describing "a new form of hyper-civilisation" (Baudrillard 2005, 202). The world of consumption is treated like a discourse. Consumption is a way in which people communicate with each other. It is an order of significations, which requires knowledge of an organized system of established codes of signs. Consumers desire objects in a competitive relationship with other consumers, as mediated by the social signs of prestige and status. Baudrillard's central point is that objects have become signs whose value is determined by a disciplinary cultural code. In this code, the idea of the relation (between signs) is consumed. The differential relationship between signs is what structures social meaning. It is what is ultimately desired and consumed.

Baudrillard's *Consumer Society* is a culturally and institutionally critical text, just as Nietzsche's *On the Genealogy of Morals* is a radical critique of morality. Nietzsche's *On the Genealogy of Morals* looks at the power configurations that have driven the development of our moral valuations, and the language that underlies these valuations.

Nietzsche's polemic disputes the assumption that there is a linear order of descent that can be traced to a common ancestor, and that would enable one to derive moral notions and legal practices from a natural, single and stable origin. Nietzsche does not simply reject the search for origins. Nietzsche uses the story of masters and slaves to narrate the origin of our most basic moral values and to suggest a difference between the values "good and bad" and "good and evil". The story shows that the master and the slave always perceive and judge the world in different ways. As a result, there cannot be an original or true designation of value. A search for origins must involve the discovery of a difference and a struggle at the origin, namely an origin that challenges us.

Nietzsche and Baudrillard do not attempt to offer a foundational account of morality, but, rather, they both aim to treat it as a contingent historical creation whose value can be taken as an object of critical reflection. Nietzsche and Baudrillard scrutinize the struggles and differential relations that are responsible for the creation of values. Genealogy, as practiced by Nietzsche and Baudrillard, reminds readers that their perspectives are contextual and proposes different perspectives. It motivates readers to compare the value of their perspectives in relation to other perspectives.

In section 1, I will provide a short review of the fragmented and scattered secondary literature available on the relation between Baudrillard and Nietzsche. I will then move on to show how Baudrillard's views on consumer society revisit and update Nietzsche's mode of genealogy.

In section 2, I provide an exposition of how Baudrillard is interested in understanding the structures of consumer society. Baudrillard applies the critical tools of genealogy to Saussurean linguistics and he analyzes concepts as signs of the powers and forces that have become dominant.

In section 3, I will move on to an account of perspectivism and how it underlies Baudrillard's genealogy of consumption in

Consumer Society and Nietzsche's *On the Genealogy of Morals*. By presenting us with different perspectives, such as noble morality, Nietzsche motivates us to re-evaluate our values. I suggest that Nietzsche's noble morality, and his views on excess may be at work in Baudrillard's texts through his notion of symbolic exchange. I argue that Nietzsche and Baudrillard's fictional accounts of noble and symbolic societies aim to problematize and undermine a morality that people share and find binding.

1.1 Baudrillard Reading Nietzsche

First of all, in this section, I give a brief overview of Baudrillard's relation to Nietzsche, and I look at the literature surrounding this relationship. This will set the scene for my argument that Baudrillard's work on consumer society subtly follows and adapts Nietzsche's mode of genealogy to a modern context.

The influence of Nietzsche on contemporary French thought has been dealt with extensively and has been heavily criticized.[16] Deleuze's (2006) study *Nietzsche et la philosophie,* first published in French in 1962, played an important role in developing French interest in Nietzsche's philosophy during the early 1960s and 1970s. Some of Nietzsche's French readers came to his texts directly; others came via Heidegger[17] and others through Bataille.[18]

---

[16] For a critique of New French Theory and its German ideological roots, see Jürgen Habermas, *The Philosophical Discourse of Modernity* (Cambridge, Mass.: MIT Press, 1987). On Nietzsche and poststructuralism, see *The New Nietzsche*, ed. David Allison (New York: Dell, 1977). Baudrillard is often ignored within the "post-structuralist" body of thought: Belsey's (2003) overview does not include him, nor does Schrift's (1995).

[17] On Heidegger's engagement with Nietzsche and values see Catherine F. Botha's (2014) study on *Heidegger, Nietzsche and the Question of Values* (http://hdl.handle.net/2066/129844).

[18] On the relation between Bataille and Baudrillard see Pefanis (1991); Pawlett (2007). See also Leslie Anne Bolt- Irons, "Bataille and Baudrillard - From a General Economy to the transparency of Evil" in *Angelaki*. Vol 6. No. 2 (2001).

In *Nietzsche's French Legacy: A Genealogy of Poststructuralism*[19] Alan D. Schrift (1995) traces the affiliations of certain contemporary French thinkers to Nietzsche, but he does not engage with Baudrillard in his book.[20] Schrift identifies two approaches of French thought to Nietzsche; first, the one in which Nietzsche's philosophy appears as the "object" of interpretation and the second one, in which Nietzsche is "used" as a platform for philosophers to develop their own projects. Schrift explains, for instance, how the trajectory of Deleuze's thought on Nietzsche moved from a philosophical interpretation of Nietzsche, in *Nietzsche and Philosophy* (2006), to a self-conscious utilization of Nietzsche for purposes other than the philosophical explication de texte (Schrift 1995, 60).

Unlike Deleuze, Baudrillard does not in any of his works systematically use Nietzsche. Explicit references to Nietzsche are rare and in a book of interviews collected as *D'un fragment l'autre* with François L'Yvonnet, Baudrillard (2001, 10) said "Nietzsche n'a jamais été à proprement parler une référence, seulement une mémoire infuse". In an interview with Paul Hegarty, Baudrillard also admits: "I read Nietzsche in German when I was very young – all of it, and since then I haven't opened a book of his…it's better than a reference, as it's hidden away, part of the fabric, in the threads" (Hegarty 2004, 149).

Baudrillard, in Nietzsche's footsteps, practices an "interpretative violence" and it is in *On the Genealogy of Morals* that Nietzsche suggests (as I already mentioned earlier) that interpretation is always a matter of "forcing, adjusting, shortening, omitting, filling-out, inventing, falsifying and everything else essential to interpretation" (Nietzsche 2007, 112; italics in the text). The stylis-

---

[19] As Pawlett points out "Baudrillard is somewhat of an oddity even within poststructuralism. While poststructuralism has become a recognized strand of theory in the humanities and social sciences, a respectable body deftly summarised by Belsey (2003), Baudrillard remains marginal or unacceptable. Belsey's (2003) overview makes no mention of Baudrillard" (Pawlett, 2007:3).

[20] Schrift (1995, 41; note 23) only refers to Baudrillard in a footnote, with regards to Baudrillard's attack on Foucault in Baudrillard's book *Forget Foucault* (first published in French in 1976).

tic resonances of Nietzsche with Baudrillard are to be found in the latter's use of aphorisms, especially in Baudrillard's (1990) *Cool Memories*. Throughout his career, Baudrillard steadily leaves the conventions of academic writing behind and attempts to critique all systematic thought. Paul Hegarty (2004, 1) explains that Baudrillard's texts become increasingly speculative, and often free of argument as such. "Instead, there is a wall of assertions, claims, twists of logic, fictions, spews of metaphors losing their representative value..." (Hegarty 2004, 1).

In this chapter, I focus on Baudrillard's first two books, *The System of Objects* (1968; 2005) and *Consumer Society* (1970; 1998). The latter book proceeds, according to George Ritzer, largely according to a "scholarly format [...]. Intellectual predecessors and antagonists are clear and, as a result, so are the roots of many of Baudrillard's ideas" (Ritzer 1998, 1).[21] In *Consumer Society*, Baudrillard (1998, 75) elaborates a "genealogy of consumption", and although Baudrillard does indeed allude to scholarship and refer to past events, his use of the past could belong more to a historical novel than to a scholarly treatise.

Following Nietzsche's *On the Genealogy of Morals*, Baudrillard uses a complex and conditional philosophical and stylistic presentation form that contains three central elements. He puts forward a certain historical point of view of the subject and thereby puts forward a thesis about the variability of the subject. He also hypothesizes on the constitutive relation between subjectivity and structures of power (section 1.2). These theses are presented in a certain narrative rhetorical form. The most important stylistic component of such a genealogy is its exaggerated, polemical and fictional character. This style serves to ensure an urgency to the hypothesis regarding the (violent) invention of subjects.

This style also connects with Baudrillard's and Nietzsche's engagement with the concept of truth as perspectival (section 1.3). The fundamental task of Baudrillard's *Consumer Society*, like Nietzsche's *On the Genealogy of Morals*, the one upon which the suc-

---

[21] *On the Genealogy of Morals* is also according to Deleuze (2006, 81) "Nietzsche's most systematic book".

cess of their texts rest, is to effect a change in perspective or ethical orientation of their audience. The genealogical text achieves this effect due to its mode of presentation and not only due to its contents which includes hypotheses and speculations about origins.

1.2 Baudrillard's critical semiology

In the previous section, we established that Baudrillard's references to Nietzsche are rare and indirect. I now set the scene for my argument that Baudrillard's work on consumer society re-contextualizes and transposes Nietzsche's genealogy into a modern setting. This requires first an exposition of Baudrillard's interest in understanding the structures of consumer society and how there is nothing inevitable or natural about them.

According to George Ritzer (1998, 7) Baudrillard's *Consumer Society* is influenced by a range of structuralist ideas, which is made evident by the book's subtitle, *Myths and Structures* and the content of the book. Baudrillard treats the world of consumption like a mode of communication and makes use of the tools of Saussurean linguistics including sign, signifier, signified, code. Although Baudrillard's early work on consumer society operates within a semiological/structuralist paradigm, Mark Poster rightly argues that Baudrillard is reluctant to accept Saussurean linguistics in its dominant forms.[22]

In Saussure's theory of the sign, a word is a sign, and a sign consists of a signifier and a signified; the signifier is the sound pattern of the word, and the signified is the meaning of the word, which Saussure describes as a "mental image". The referent is the thing, which is simply left out of his structuralist account.

Saussure's contribution to the study of language is to show that the meaning of a word, the signified, is not determined by the referent but rather by its place in the system of signs and its relation to other signifieds: the meaning of a word is determined differentially or negatively, i.e., by its relation to other meanings.

---

[22] See Mark Poster's (1981) article, 'Technology and Culture in Habermas and Baudrillard: From Marx to Baudrillard'.

Saussure sees a relation of arbitrariness between signifiers, and between signifiers and their signified. The signification of words and phrases is neither based on verifiable facts or observations, so signification can only be expressed with a set of words or concepts that belong to a shared language system.[23]

For Baudrillard, in Saussure's model of linguistic signification, there is no significance outside the system (of significance) to act as its (external, transcendent) assurance of significance – or, of its truth, because meaning is determined within the language. Saussurean linguistics, as applied by Lévi-Strauss, divides an object into its binary oppositions thereby revealing a play of rules and patterns, without the help of a concept of subjectivity. According to structural linguistics, phenomena are to be analyzed 'objectively', irrespective of time and normative evaluations. According to Poster, the "formalism of linguistics, when carried over into social science, implies a de-historicization and a weakening of critical powers" (Poster 1981, 468). Baudrillard, however, revises the a-historicity of semiology and "was probably the first thinker in France to employ semiology both historically and critically" (Poster 1981, 468).

As we shall see below, for Baudrillard, Saussurean linguistics does not merely present us with a theory of language. It describes the consumer morality of late modernity. Baudrillard argues that neither structural linguistics nor our current morality of consumption is universal or natural.

From a Saussurean perspective, consumption is an order of signs. Objects are defined by what they signify and what they signify is defined by their relationship to the entire system of signs.

---

[23] According to Saussure (1966, 120): "in language there are only differences *without positive terms*. Whether we take the signified or the signifier, language has neither ideas nor sounds that existed before the linguistic system, but only conceptual and phonic differences that have issued from the system. The idea or phonic substance that a sign contains is of less importance than the other signs that surround it. Proof of this is that the value of a term may be modified without either its meaning or its sound being affected, solely because a neighbouring term has been modified".

Like the elements of language, no object has a meaning in itself but acquires meaning only in its relationship with other objects. *The System of Objects,* Baudrillard's first book, looks at everyday objects in family and social structures. Objects are elements in a code or "system of signification" (Baudrillard 1968, 9-19; 2005, 2) in an abstract system of emblematic meanings, signs.

Individual things can only be adequately described within the overarching system, because their cultural meaning lies only in the context and the frame of the "global system" (Baudrillard 1968, 86; 2005, 70). What Baudrillard means by global system is society and its cultural system of signification, which encompasses the whole of life. This cultural system of meanings is the actual theme of Baudrillard's investigations. The analysis does not focus on objects themselves but rather on the system of objects. It is not a question of a system of actual objects but more "the system of signification of these objects" (Baudrillard 1968, 10; 2005, 2).

Baudrillard's system of objects is a secondary semiological system. Above and beyond the world of objects, which is a technical world, there is a second level, which gives things a secondary meaning. "Each of our practical objects is related to one or more structural elements but at the same time they are in perpetual flight from technical structure towards their structural meanings, from the technological system towards a cultural system" (Baudrillard 1968, 15; 2005, 6).

Marx (2018, 49) already indicates this move to secondary signification in his first volume of *Capital.* There, he describes how exchange value takes over use value. Use value refers to the concrete use of a thing for the person who is using it, whereas exchange value involves the turning of a thing into a commodity (Marx 2018, 49-50). As a commodity, an object can be exchanged for a certain price for another commodity. Use value obeys a logic of human needs, whereas exchange value follows an economic logic of equivalence.[24]

---

[24] Baudrillard later will criticize use of value as the "alibi" of exchange value (Baudrillard 1981, 130-142).

In Marx, the moment of abstraction plays an important role. The capitalist production process reduces not only the producer or labourer to abstract social labour (Marx 2018, 53) but reduces also the produced thing itself to the abstract carrier of exchange value, where the entire material, sensual world has been abolished. The secondary signification inscribes the object and consumer into the abstract system of exchange value (the capitalist market). The object is turned in one go from a useful thing geared to satisfying concrete needs into an exchangeable object, equivalent to other objects, a substitute, a sign.

Baudrillard radicalizes this thought by claiming that what the capitalist economy does with people and things, namely transforming them into abstract elements within a system, is what the system of consumption also does. The thing becomes a sign not only within the economic system, but also within the cultural one. In the *System of Objects*, Baudrillard speaks of sign function, which is determined by its being purely cultural, separated from the material level of nature and technique.

> "The coherence of the functional system of objects depends on the fact that these objects – along with their various properties such as colour, form and so on – no longer have any value of their own, but merely universal value as signs. The order of Nature (primary functions, instinctual drives, symbolic relationships) is everywhere present in the system, but present only as signs. The materiality of objects no longer directly confronts the materiality of needs, these two inconsistent primary and antagonistic systems having been suppressed by the insertion between them, in a word, of functionality" (Baudrillard 2005, 68).

The role of the word "functionality" in this quote and in *The System of Objects* as a whole is important. The technical implication of this concept is misleading, and Baudrillard's approach shows the irrelevance of the technical function within the cultural system of meaning. Functionality is a "myth" (Baudrillard, 2005:60). It is a cultural construct and an "alibi" for function (Baudrillard 1968, 86). Functionality is not a technical category, just like technicity in contrast to technique is not a technical category but rather a mode in a cultural system, which the suffix "ity" indicates. Functionality refers finally to the system of objects itself (Baudrillard 2005, 68).

Baudrillard seeks to emphasize in *System of Objects* that 'function' and 'use' are only effects of the sign and rhetorical values within the system of objects. Function must have the "exchangeability of the sign or it is no function at all...everything becomes a sign of a sign, an allegory of the system itself" (Butler 1999, 33). Functionality is emphasized more than ever, yet objects do not have one function but are variable, multi-purpose and adaptable.

> "The *social logic* of consumption ... is by no means that of the individual appropriation of the *use-value* of goods and services ... It is not a logic of satisfaction, but of the production and manipulation of social signifiers" (Baudrillard 1998, 61).

This quote stems from *Consumer Society*, Baudrillard's second book, and in it Baudrillard critiques the notion of the sovereign individual consumer who functions to maximize pleasures in relation to a finite but uncoordinated set of needs. Needs (like "functionality" discussed above) are for Baudrillard produced as a "system elements", and they are not a direct "relationship of an individual to an object" which might in principle satisfy a desire (Baudrillard 1998, 75). Consumption is a structure of exchange and differentiation, situated between a logic of production and one of significations. From the point of view of the "social logic" of consumption, Baudrillard's (1998, 61) analysis can be understood on at least two levels:

- that of signification and communication (consumption is a system of exchange but also a language (albeit without a syntax)
- that of classification and social differentiation (differences can be ordered in a hierarchy of statutory values).

What is sought in consumption is social meaning. Far from consuming concrete objects for vital needs, "it is the *idea of relationship* that is signified in these objects, that is 'consumed' in them and hence abolished as anything to be directly experienced"

(Baudrillard 2005, 221; italics in the text).[25] That relationship between signs is what structures social meaning and it drives our desire for consuming objects. The value of any sign is determined by a disciplinary cultural code. The code that drives consumer society cannot finally be a language in the true sense because it lacks a "living ... syntax" and functions with a repertoire rather than a diction. It is an "order of classification" – in other words, a taxonomy (Baudrillard 2005, 212).

> "The object-cum-advertising system constitutes less a language, whose living syntax it lacks, than a set of significations. Impoverished yet efficient, it is basically a code. It does not structure the personality, but designates and classifies it" (Baudrillard 2005, 212).

What is peculiar to consumer society for Baudrillard is the construction of individual 'difference' through the object system. This construction is only possible because "*there is no one there – no person.* This 'person'...is absent, dead, swept out of our functional universe" [26] (Baudrillard 1998, 88; italics in the text). Consumers construct a "personality", "a synthetic individuality" through the manipulation of "marginal differences", which constitute the sign system (Baudrillard 1998, 88).

Differences are systematically produced in tune with an order, which absorbs and combines them all as identifying signs. Signs are substitutable one for another so there is no more tension between them. As a result, the whole culture becomes a combinatorial machine (Baudrillard 1970, 155; 1998, 104). Consumers must choose from a range of objects, questions and credit companies.

The subject for Baudrillard becomes a 'person' through the process of 'personalisation', the terms of which are set by the sign-

---

[25] Charles Levin (1996, 46) sees here the "ironic vulgarisation of the Idea" [i.e. the Platonic super-sensuous Idea]. The *System of Objects* is for Levin "a parodic inversion of Platonism – a social simulacrum – just as Deleuze had proposed in the same year (1968) for philosophy". I will turn to the Nietzschean "reversal of Platonism" in chapter 4 and connect it to Deleuze and Baudrillard's views on the rise of simulacra.

[26] "c'est précisément *qu'il n' y a personne*" (Baudrillard 1970, 125). Lost in translation is the ambiguity Baudrillard plays with here in French between *'une personne'* (a person) and *'personne'* (nobody).

object system. Individual choices are made in terms of objects, signs or images. As Baudrillard explains in *Consumer Society*:

> "The real differences which characterised persons made them *contradictory* beings. Differences of the 'personalising' type no longer set individuals one against another; these differences are all arrayed hierarchically on an indefinite scale and converge in models, on the basis of which they are subtly produced and reproduced" (Baudrillard 1998, 89; italics in the text).

For Baudrillard, advertising maintains the whole system of 'imposed differentiation', the choice of coded differentials by which individuals are integrated into the system. William Pawlett rightly emphasizes that the process of "personalisation" is "a site of contestation and active investment not a *fait accompli* determined from above the system" (Pawlett 2007, 9). The available variety of choice makes 'personalisation' possible so that individuals define themselves in opposition to other individuals (Pawlett 2007, 16).

The consumer system is grounded on the idea that the consumer has a choice and the freedom to choose.[27] Advertising seeks to represent the explosion of this freedom as we are "given" advertising, so it is "the most democratic of products, the only one that is 'free' – and 'free' to all" (Baudrillard 2005, 187). Consumers

---

[27] As Saussure puts it: "[i]f, with respect to the idea it represents, the signifier appears to be freely chosen, then, on the contrary, with respect to the linguistic community which uses it, it is not free, it is imposed. The social mass is not consulted, and the signifier chosen by the language could not be replaced by another. This fact, which seems to envelop a contradiction, could be called familiarly the 'forced card'. One says to the language 'Choose!' but adds: 'it'll be this sign and no other.' Not only would an individual be incapable, if he wanted to, of modifying in any way whatsoever the choice which has been made, but the mass itself cannot exercise its sovereignty over a single word; it is bound to the language just as it is" (Saussure 1983, 104). According to Joseph (2000, 127): "Change in language for Saussure always occurs unconsciously, never as result of a willful decision, either by an individual or by the language community" (Joseph 2000, 127). In Saussure, the arbitrariness of linguistic signs takes a central place within Western language theory. Saussure, at the same, puts forward the complete systematicity of languages as sign systems. For Saussure, only the level of *parole* (speech, the use of language) is voluntary for the individual. "Language is impervious to individual will (the social and the unconscious is a connection that remains only implicit however-er)" (Joseph 2000, 127).

"personalise" themselves according to their choice of brands (Hegarty 2004, 16).

Through his notion of symbolic exchange, Baudrillard seeks to show that structural linguistics ignores that it is a historically-based semiological structure, not a universal truth about language. The sign separated from the referent and understandable only at the level of signifier relations, is a reduction of the symbolic. Baudrillard argues that so-called "primitive societies" engage in symbolic communications: the signifier, signified and referent are all part of the communicative act. In symbolic communication, "signs include [...] words that [are] attached to referents and [are] uttered in a context that held open their possible reversal by others" (Poster 1988, 4).

It is important to bear in mind that the relationship between signs and symbols is complex and there is an ongoing tension between the two notions. As William Pawlett (1999, 14) explains both "the symbolic order and modern semiotic system are forms of social discipline. There is little ... freedom in either of them (though it is not an either/or situation because they are always found together)."

The main difference is that the symbolic order does not claim to offer freedom. The tensions and constraints involved in symbolic communication are clear and the meanings created are highly charged. This is because symbolic values provoke opposed emotional attitudes within the same person, such as love and hate, fear and desire, attraction and repulsion. For Baudrillard, the emotional-symbolic bonds of human relations are not straight-forward or unproblematic. Whereas, Mark Poster (1988, 4) sees Baudrillard's notion of symbolic communication as "somewhat nostalgic", William Pawlett (2007, 14) on the other hand rightly stresses that symbolic relations are not "lost" or "repressed" by the sign-system. "Baudrillard privileges ambivalence" and its "emotional intensities, not specific norms or structures of a symbolic society" (Pawlett 2007, 14).

Before going further into the details of 'symbolic exchange' and that it does not represent a lost or separate, ideal realm, I first need to rehearse some elements of Nietzschean genealogy. This will help me clarify the Nietzschean roots of Baudrillard's critical semiology and show that Baudrillard's notion of symbolic exchange is not nostalgic.

1.3 Aristocratic and Slave Narratives

Secondary critics on Baudrillard, such as Mark Poster, stress that Baudrillard's early work is an exercise in critical semiology. But they have not focused on the Nietzschean genealogical element of Baudrillard's critique. In section 1.2, I show how Baudrillard gives an exposition of the Saussurean linguistic dynamics that constitute the consumer morality of late modernity.

In my view, a vital dimension of Baudrillard's critique of structuralist semiology is that he applies the critical tools of genealogy to it in order to show that neither structural linguistics nor our current morality of consumption is atemporal, universal or natural. Let us now dig deeper into what Nietzsche's genealogical work (and its French post-structuralist reception) has revealed for the study of language systems.

According to Foucault, Nietzsche was the "first to connect the philosophical task with a radical reflection upon language" (Foucault 1973, 305) and it is in his *Nietzsche and Philosophy*, that Deleuze (2006, 3) inaugurates the 'linguistic turn' in French Nietzsche reception:

"We will never find the sense of something ...if we do not know the force which appropriates a thing, which exploits it, which takes possession of it or is expressed in it. A phenomenon is not an appearance or even an apparition, but a sign, a symptom which finds its meaning in an existing force. The whole of philosophy is a symptomatology, and a semeiology."

A radical reflection upon language drives much of the First Essay of *On the Genealogy of Morals* and in the First Essay's closing note in section 17, Nietzsche poses the following rhetorical question to advance the "historical studies of morality": "What signposts does linguistics, especially the study of etymology, give to the history of the evolution of moral concepts?" (Nietzsche 2007, 34). Nietzsche's "etymological point of view" seeks to highlight the trajectory of moral concepts (Nietzsche 2007, 13). Nietzsche traces the genealogy of moral concepts (Nietzsche 2007, 7).

In the First Essay of *On the Genealogy of Morals,* Nietzsche writes that it is

> "only the seduction of language (and the fundamental errors of reason petrified within it), which construes and misconstrues all actions as conditional upon an agency, a 'subject,' […]. But there is no such substratum; there is no 'being' behind the deed, its effect and what becomes of it; 'the doer' is invented as an after-thought, - the doing is everything" (Nietzsche 2007, 26).

In the above quote and elsewhere in *On the Genealogy of Morals,* Nietzsche emphasizes that language seduces us into accepting all kinds of metaphysical presuppositions, such as the division between subject and object, cause and effects and he asks us to scrutinize our grammatical habits.

This does not mean that Nietzsche's genealogical etymology aims to uncover the true and accurate meaning behind the "hieroglyphic script" (Nietzsche 2007, 7). A search for origins must involve the discovery of a "difference" at the origin, namely an origin that unsettles and challenges us to think differently. In the Preface to *On the Genealogy of Morals,* Nietzsche makes it clear that he is dealing with morality as a "problem" (Nietzsche 2007, viii).

> "In reality, I had set my heart on something much more important than the nature of the theories of myself or others concerning the origin of morality (or, more precisely, the real function from my view of these theories was to point to an end to which they were one among many means). The issue for me was the value of morality" (Nietzsche 2007, vi).

In this quote, Nietzsche claims that the question regarding the value of morality is his actual goal. Nietzsche's historico-genealogical investigation of morality is functional – one tool among many for the serious question regarding the non-self-evident value of morality or in other words for the problematization of morality.

For Nietzsche, historical research must recognize that the origin of the development of any word or thing and its ultimate meaning or usefulness are altogether separate. This is because what exists is "continually interpreted anew ... transformed and redirected to a new purpose" by a superior power (Nietzsche 2007, 50). Nietzsche goes against the assumption that the apparent purpose of a thing ("its utility, form and shape") is the reason for its existence, for instance in the case of the eye that it was always made to see, or the hand to grasp. He argues against the view that we can consider "the 'development of a thing'" in terms of a "*progressus* towards a goal, still less is it a logical *progressus*, taking the shortest route with least expenditure of energy and cost" (Nietzsche 2007, 51).

The teleological conception of development naively ignores the accidental and contingent aspects within the development of a thing, tradition or an organ:

> "every purpose and use is just a *sign* that **the will to power** has achieved mastery over something less powerful, and has impressed upon it its own idea [*Sinn*] of a use function; and the whole history of a "thing", an organ, a tradition can to this extent be a continuous chain of signs, continually revealing new interpretations and adaptations" (Nietzsche 2007, 51; italics and bold in the text)

The will to power unfolds in multiple ways and there is no single conclusive account because there are multiple perspectives that may be genealogically related but are never alike. Nietzsche challenges the assumption that there is a line of descent that can be continuously traced from a common ancestor, and that would enable one to derive moral notions and legal practices from a natural single and stable origin. Nietzsche emphasizes the changes, accidents, psychological innovations and moral inventions that arise within specific material and cultural contexts. Nietzsche does not simply oppose himself to the search for origins. He does want to show how the past continues in the present. Paul J. M. van Tongeren (2000, 204) explains genealogy as

> "the method which describes phenomena as the products of a history of different and conflicting ways in which they are interpreted without there being a firm basis on which one could decide about the right interpretation. The genealogical basis is not an original truth behind all interpretations but it nevertheless is presupposed of those interpretations in a certain

way. Genealogy points to struggle as the origin of everything: *polemos patèr pantón"*.

Genealogy "presupposes" a power struggle and Nietzsche focusses on the conditions under which a morality developed. The values of a particular moral system reside neither in a stable origin or end. Such a view prevents us from looking at the struggles for power that led to the emergence and establishment of a morality. As Deleuze also puts it:

> "What directs us to the origin is the fact that every force is related to another, whether in order to command or to obey. The origin is the difference at the origin, difference in the origin is *hierarchy*, that is to say the relation of a dominant to a dominated force, of an obeyed to an obeying will" (Deleuze 2006, 7; italics in the text).

Nietzsche seeks to discover multiple origins and to classify and rank them (Kofman 1993, 87). Genealogy establishes distinctions "between epochs, peoples, grades of rank between individuals" (Nietzsche 2007, 5).

In the First Essay of *On the Genealogy of Morals*, Nietzsche uses the story of masters and slaves to narrate the origin of our most basic moral values and he suggests a difference between the values "good and bad" and "good and evil". Nietzsche thereby claims that there cannot be an original or true designation of value since the master and the slave always evaluate the world in different ways (White 1988, 684).

The masters' use the term "good" to refer approvingly of their life and of themselves as people who are powerful enough to lead. The noble masters healthily celebrate their instinctual powers, expend their force without concern for utility or even the preservation of their life. According to the evaluative frame of reference by which the masters live, the term "bad" refers to those people – for instance, the "slaves" who cannot live a life of self-affirming physical dynamism.

"Good" and "bad" are two terms that constitute the basic code of "master" morality. In paragraph 10 of the First Essay, Nietzsche outlines the slave revolt against the masters' form of valuation. Being physically inferior, the slaves take imaginary revenge on the masters against whom they are not strong enough to compete. This revenge involves the creation of an associated new form of valuation: "evil". "Evil" now refers to the life the masters lead (which the masters themselves call "good"). In a "slave" morality, this negative term "evil" is central. Slaves define themselves by observing that they are "not like" the "evil" masters. For the slaves, "good" refers now not to a life of vitality and exuberance, but to one that is "not-evil", i.e., not in any way like the life that the masters live.

Nietzsche (2007, 20; italics in the text) says

> "Whereas all noble morality grows out of a triumphant saying "yes" to itself, slave morality says "no" on principle to everything that is "outside," "other", "non-self": and *this* "no" is its creative deed. This reversal of the evaluating glance – this *essential* orientation to the outside instead of back onto itself – is a feature of *ressentiment:* in order to come about, slave morality first has to have an opposing, external world, it needs, physiologically speaking, external stimuli in order to act at all – its action is basically a reaction."

Slave morality is a "reaction" to the *ressentiment* and discomfort the slaves feel towards their enemies, the aristocrats. Nobles have a different attitude towards their enemies. They regard their enemies as opportunities for new perspectives that can trigger self-overcoming; they respect their enemies as a chance for productive engagement. Nietzsche (2007, 21) observes "[h]ow much respect a noble man has for his enemies! – and a respect of that sort is a bridge to love" (Nietzsche 2007, 21). To embrace one's enemies illustrates the noble capacity to take distance from immediate stimuli; the incapacity to resist a stimulus is reactive.

The noble "pathos of distance" generates the "good/bad" valuation, whereas the "good/evil" value antithesis springs from slavish reactive *ressentiment* (Nietzsche 2007, 11-12). In the "good/evil" opposition, good is only the after-effect of a description that labels someone evil, which is primary. Nietzsche shows that unlike the active masters, the weak slaves can create their meanings "only by reaction, by inverting, disfiguring, and displacing the meaning attributed by the strong" (Kofman 1993, 87).

In slave morality, the denigration of the other (the master) is the basis for the elevation of the self.

On the other hand, in "good/bad" noble morality, calling something good emerges affirmatively and independently. Genealogy reveals the dominance of a group of spontaneous and strong-willed forces such as the nobles, which are capable of generating new interpretations and new meanings. The distinction "good/bad" overcomes the oppositional morality of slaves ("good/evil") because nobles affirm their own value as a source of self-overcoming.

It is important to emphasize however that the attitude of the masters towards the slaves is described by Nietzsche in an ambivalent fashion. The aristocratic attitude towards the slave is one of contempt (Nietzsche 2007, 20) but also "cheerfulness" (Nietzsche 2007, 20). The "bad" slaves are not directly criticized by the nobles, rather they are pitied (Nietzsche 2007, 20) and masterful "birds of prey" even (cynically perhaps) "love" little lambs (Nietzsche 2007, 26). Nietzsche adds that the word "bad" when applied by the masters to the slaves, possesses "kindly nuances" that one should not overlook (Nietzsche 2007, 20).

Nietzsche does not elevate the master as a straightforward ideal (Nietzsche 2007, 21). Nietzsche refers to the "activity" of the master as opposed to the "reactivity" of the slave, but Nietzsche also points to the cruel aspects of the master as a "blonde brute" and "beast of prey" (Nietzsche 2007, 15). Nietzsche does not seek to lament a lost origin and according to Richard White: "the terms Master and Slave refer to basic modalities, and in this respect, they are "types" which still concern us all" (White 1988, 683). It is difficult to be certain that Nietzsche effectively 'praises' the masters; his description might perhaps be value-neutral instead, in spite of the language he uses which apparently praises the masters and condemns the slaves.

Nietzsche makes it clear that without the slave, humanity would have remained an unreflective beast and would not have attained the height of culture that derives from controlling spontaneous instincts, which is why the aim of his 'contempt' might be rhetorical rather than substantive, i.e., independent of the content – the type of life – that is being described.

The point, I think, is that Nietzsche is contrasting different types of life. The way Nietzsche decides to assess 'values' is according to whether they have empowered or weakened the will to life. Nietzsche scrutinizes to what extent prevalent values promote or restrict life. The active creation of values associated with noble morality is life-affirming. On the other hand, the slaves are not only physically weak and oppressed, they are due to their weakness unable to spontaneously see themselves and their lives in an affirming fashion (Ansell-Pearson 2007, xxi).

Nietzsche is concerned with the evaluative modes that encompass human existence as certain presentations of the human "will to power", which for Nietzsche is "the essence of life" (Nietzsche 2007, 52). As Martin Saar (2009b, 464) puts it: "Metaphysically, Nietzsche is a monist: power is everywhere. But as far as the *forms* of power go, Nietzsche is a pluralist: the various expressions of the will to power are its autonomous and independent articulations" (Saar 2009b, 464). The will to power unfolds in a variety of different ways and there are a multitude of perspectives – or ways of knowing.

In *On the Genealogy of Morals,* Nietzsche stresses the importance of exploring different perspectives, drives, affects or passions. Nietzsche rejects the idea that there can be one account of truth that corresponds with the way things are in themselves, "independently of the mediation of perspectives by relations of willing" (Allsobrook 2009, 703). When claiming in the Third and Final Essay of *On the Genealogy of Morals* that philosophy must for the first time confront the question of the "value of truth", Nietzsche (2007, 113) decides to analyze 'truth' within a complex social and political system.

Nietzsche (2007, 87) attacks an unconditional will to truth that claims to be free of conflicting interests that inform perspectives. It is in terms of the metaphor of "perspectival seeing" that Nietzsche offers his definition of objectivity, "*having in our power* the ability to engage and disengage our "pros" and "cons": we can use the *difference* in perspectives and affective interpretations for knowledge" (Nietzsche 2007, 87; *italics in the text*).

Nietzsche refuses a final position transcending ongoing conflicts of perspectives and according to Allsobrook this serves to empower our sense of agency[28] (Allsobrook 2009, 710). Nietzsche provides fictionalized hypothetical primal scenes that seek above all to problematise current habits, moral traditions and legitimation stories. Nietzsche encourages a re-evaluation of values, by presenting us with different perspectives, such as aristocratic morality.

According to Pawlett, Baudrillard follows Nietzsche with regards to the importance placed on the human self's perspective, its self-identification through images and objects. It is our capacity to represent that produces the illusion of the real world, that is, a world as seen from God's point of view, *sub specie aeternitatis*[29] (Pawlett 2007, 58-59).

In my view, Baudrillard's notion of "primitive" "symbolic exchange" like Nietzsche's "noble morality" is precisely a fictionalized hypothetical primal scene that enables us to make sense of what we do and what we believe. Both notions are not meant to be representational or strictly true. Let me explain below.

In contrasting the exchange systems of primitive societies with capitalism, Baudrillard draws on the anthropological works of Marcel Mauss and Marshall Sahlins on the gift. Baudrillard contrasts the gift economy against capitalism because in the gift economy, exchanges are always symbolic. Baudrillard argues there is

---

[28] Douglas Kellner (1989, 120) claims that "whereas Nietzsche celebrated the sovereignty of the superior individual as the mode of transition to a higher stage of being, Baudrillard comes to attack the subject as such" (Kellner 1989, 120). On my reading, Baudrillard does not reject the subject, he accounts for its genesis.

[29] Under the aspect or species (or 'from the point of view') of eternity. This Latin expression refers to Benedict de Spinoza. See 'Ethics' trans. Edwin Curley (London: Penguin, 1996) II/126 Cor. 2.60. According to this 'view', the epistemic subject is thought to have access to knowledge that is universally true since it occupies a universal perspective outside the world that goes beyond contingencies and variations that are associated with any position in this world.

no such thing as an economy of use, need or necessity – there is always surplus, the extent and nature of which result from socio-political arrangements. In addition, "the symbolism of exchange means that it always represents the individual and his relations" (King 1998, 91). The secondary critic on Baudrillard's work, Douglas Kellner (1989, 120) claims that

> "Baudrillard attacks the bourgeoisie, capital political economy from the point of view which valorises "aristocratic" expenditure and sumptuary aesthetic symbolic values" (Kellner 1989, 43).

Kellner rightly identifies that Baudrillard provides a version of Nietzsche's "aristocratic", "master morality," in which value articulates an excess, an overflow and intensification of life energies (Kellner 1989, 45).

However, for Kellner, the notion of symbolic exchange also reveals "something of an essentialist anthropology" because Baudrillard's "celebration of symbolic exchange...emerges as a distinctive and privileged form of human activity" (Kellner 1989, 45). In the same vein, in his book *Libidinal Economy*, published in 1974, Lyotard (1993, 103 – 127) critiques Baudrillard's apparent nostalgia for symbolic exchange. According to Lyotard, Baudrillard attempts to ground the idea of symbolic exchange in anthropological societies of primitive societies and is utopian.

It must be emphasized, against Kellner and Lyotard, that Baudrillard does not idealise[30] symbolic society. Baudrillard uses symbolic society to multiply genealogical perspectives into our conception of moral values.

Douglas Kellner (1989, 120) claims that "whereas Nietzsche celebrated the sovereignty of the superior individual as the mode of transition to a higher stage of being, Baudrillard comes to attack the subject as such" (Kellner 1989, 120). Regarding Baudrillard's views on the subject in consumer society specifically, Kellner states that by "presenting the concepts of needs and use values as

---

[30] As Charles Levin (1996, 88) puts it: "[w]hile apparently joining Rousseau to denounce historical civilisation as a perversion, however, Baudrillard has demonstrated no particular faith in the innate 'goodness' of human nature. In this respect, he is Nietzschean (and Freudian) to the core"

solely the product of capitalism and political economy, Baudrillard is unable to articulate standpoints from which to criticize capitalist society or present oppositional consumer practises or politics, since in his view all consumption serves simply to integrate individuals into the system of needs and objects" (Kellner 1989, 36-37). In addition, Kellner claims that Baudrillard's perspectives on needs and consumption are "one-sided and incomplete. For he is theorizing use-values and needs strictly from the standpoint of how they are perceived by capital and how capitalists might fantasise that they are actually producing use-values and needs" (Kellner 1989, 37).

Against Kellner, I think that Baudrillard does not deny the phenomenon of subjectivity. Baudrillard, like Nietzsche, is interested in dramatizing the genesis of the subject. Baudrillard's genealogy of consumptive practices 'recounts', as does Nietzsche's genealogy, in a hyperbolic[31] and highly speculative way, a history of the self in the form of a history of power. Both Nietzsche and Baudrillard provide a practical conception of subjectivity, that is to say, a theory of historical variables, practices and procedures that give rise to subjectivity. Both Baudrillard and Nietzsche thematize the subject according to complex everyday practices, upon which self-understandings are built. Language, knowledge, power, art and bodily and consumptive practices are, from this perspective, not realms in which "ready-made" subjects act, but rather arenas that build the self.

In the next chapter, I will further develop the genesis of the subject as outlined in Nietzsche's *On the Genealogy of Morals*. Nietzsche's genealogy of the subject demonstrates the oppressive uses made of the idea of subjectivity as a basis for domination that invents the concept of responsibility and freedom to hold individuals accountable and judge them guilty. I will show how Nietzsche challenges the subject's privileged status by looking at its life-

---

[31] Nehamas argues that "hyperbole, the trope of excess or exaggeration has been largely ignored" because it is not philosophical enough to fit into previous conceptions of what constitutes philosophy or a properly philosophical text (Nehamas 1985, 22-23).

negating uses. It will become clear that it is precisely Nietzsche's account of the subject that leads Baudrillard to link the modern form of power with subjects and subjection to objects.

Conclusion

In this chapter, I tried to show that genealogy, as practiced by Nietzsche and Baudrillard, offers different perspectives but it also appeals to our own perspective, putting it into question. Genealogy opens up possibilities within the perspective being addressed without directly rejecting it. Genealogy, as a critically motivated art of drastic presentation, should help readers see themselves differently.

The constructed and fictionalized hypothetical primal scenes of subjectivity that genealogies use against the current self-understandings, are not strictly factual because they are less concerned with the past and more concerned with the not-yet historical present. Our own development is not an external object of disinterested and neutral observation and we therefore need to "distance" ourselves from our past, which according to genealogical hypothesis, is always a history of power.

In the next chapter, I will look at the technological invention of the subject through economies of debt, guilt and obligation as sketched out by Nietzsche in the Second Essay of *On the Genealogy of Morals*. I will move to the specific ways in which Baudrillard draws upon Nietzsche's genealogical account of church practices as he analyzes consumer society. In the process, I bring together Nietzsche's figure of the ascetic priest and that of the advertiser in Baudrillard. For Nietzsche, priestly power achieves a kind of cultural, interpretative hegemony, by giving a meaning to man's suffering. Like Nietzsche's ascetic priests, advertisers create for themselves a mask of "health" that has the power to seduce the healthy by infecting and poisoning their conscience.

2. Processes of Subjection and the Figure of the Ascetic Priest

Introduction

In the previous chapter, I showed the importance of perspectival truth in Nietzsche and Baudrillard, and how it permits Nietzsche and Baudrillard to include multiple genealogical perspectives into our conception of moral values. I discussed how Baudrillard's critique of the morality of consumption arises from the importance of symbolic exchange in so-called primitive societies and I brought forward Nietzschean resonances, in the form of noble morality. Noble morality and symbolic exchange, I argued, are metaphors that refer to experiences or processes. Nietzsche and Baudrillard both read philosophical truth claims not according to their alleged accurate reflection of reality as it is 'in-itself', but as symptoms of a certain form of life.[32]

In this regard, we saw how for Baudrillard consumers consume social signs whose value is determined by a disciplinary cultural code. In consumer society, we see the construction of individual 'difference' through the sign-object system. The sign-objects that make up the consumer system are lifted out of lived, symbolic relations, and this makes possible their endless combination and recombination in a limitless process of integration. By consuming signs, consumers gain a personality (become "personalised") and are subsequently also "integrated" into the system.

In this chapter, I seek to show how Baudrillard's exploration of the construction of subjects in consumer society resonates with Nietzsche's own view in *On the Genealogy of Morals*. Nietzsche's *Bildungsroman* narrates man's cruel moral past and reveals the high price the human animal pays to become disciplined by civili-

---

[32] For an analysis of Nietzschean symptomatology see van Tongeren (2000: 7,9,140-141)

sation and Christian moralization (Ansell-Pearson 2007, xiii).[33] For Nietzsche, the human being only exists as such through the distinction between those who subject others and those who are subjected.

In section 1, I explore how, in addition to class distinctions, Nietzsche is interested in "psychological" processes such as *ressentiment,* bad conscience and guilt. These processes mark out the different origins of the subject. The subject has multiple origins and it is internally divided, i.e., divided at the origin, and cannot properly serve the purpose of unification or identification.

In section 2, I look at how debt and obligation (as outlined by Nietzsche in the Second Essay of *On the Genealogy of Morals* and by Baudrillard in *The System of Objects* as well as *Consumer Society* (are integral technological tools towards the invention of subjects.

In section 3, I discuss Nietzsche's genealogical hypotheses about the origin of our moral values and how they are connected to speculations about the functioning of power in processes, such as bad conscience and guilt. I bring together the specific ways in which Baudrillard can be regarded as drawing upon Nietzsche's genealogical account of church practices as he analyzes consumer society. I explore Nietzsche's priestly power, which is generated mainly through the creation of meaning and a set of self-understandings. I connect Nietzsche's figure of the ascetic priest and the advertiser in Baudrillard.

2.1 The Genesis of the Subject

In the previous Chapter (section 2), I discussed Baudrillard's process of 'personalisation' to show how the available variety of choice (of object-signs) offers the possibility of individuals to define themselves in opposition to other individuals. Baudrillard emphasizes that in the general 'code' of the structure of consumption, needs and pleasures do not explain consumption, but are

---

[33] Nietzsche's stereotypical, 'perspectival' attack on Christianity has been dealt with extensively by Stephen N. William, The Shadow of the Antichrist: Nietzsche's Critique of Christianity (Grand Rapids, MI: Baker, 2006).

only effects of the communication system, integrated in the 'language' of consumption. In what follows, I show in more detail how it is specifically Nietzsche's account of the subject that leads Baudrillard to link the modern form of power with subjects and subjection to object-signs.

In section 3 of Chapter 3, I introduced the Nietzschean notions of noble and slave morality. Both moralities, I emphasized, have a violent act of "subjection" as their "genealogical *basis*" (Van Tongeren 2000, 203; italics in the text). This initial violent subjection is the origin of the distinction between the noble and the slave as two types of human beings. The victors are thereby transformed into those out of whom a powerful type of human being can develop. On the other hand, the subordinated are turned into those in which *ressentiment* and bad conscience (as I shall explain in more detail below) grow (Van Tongeren 2000, 203).

The First Essay of *On the Genealogy of Morals* is an on-going account of noble and slave moralities and their approaches towards struggle, difference and distance. On the one hand, there is the "pathos of distance" of the strong and noble which generates the "good/bad" valuation (Nietzsche 2007, 11-12). In describing the origin of noble morality, Nietzsche appeals to "the continuing and predominant feeling of complete and fundamental superiority of a higher ruling kind in relation to a lower kind, to those 'below'" (Nietzsche 2007, 12). Class difference plays an important role in Nietzsche's view of the origin of the morality, but Nietzsche also sees the terms master and slave in "the *psychological* sense as well: i.e., as denoting certain distinctive psychological and moral attitudes such that a member of the ruling class in a social-economic sense may nonetheless be 'slavish' in his morality" (Leiter 2002, 201).

As we shall see in section 3, the noble was initially the type 'warrior-priest'; these functions become separated after the internal struggle between the status of knightly and priestly evaluations (Nietzsche 2007, 15-17). The priest is a noble, that is, someone who sees himself as a creator of values and who regards his manners as embodying the good. Yet, the priest also displays certain slavish traits (such as *ressentiment*, to which I will turn shortly).

As Simon May righty puts it, "'slave' and 'master' are intended to apply as *manners* of thought and being, exemplified across a broad range of human activities, rather than simply to historical individuals" (May 1995, 51). In this sense, the manner of being "good", according to noble morality, is to act spontaneously according to one's nature. From the perspective of noble morality, an action is valued according to who performs the action. From a noble's point of view, a slavish action is expressive of just what the slave is. One cannot expect the slave not to be weak (Elgat 2017, 92).

Ressentiment is the most important 'slavish' characteristic or "mode of orientation towards the world" (Leiter 2002, 202). *Ressentiment* is essentially a negative evaluative reaction to a situation that one cannot change by means of direct physical action. The physically weak slaves are unable to take physical action against the source of their misery (the masters). "The beginning of the slaves' revolt in morality," writes Nietzsche, occurs when "*ressentiment* itself turns creative and gives birth to values: the *ressentiment* of those beings who, being denied the proper response of action, compensate for it only with imaginary revenge" (Nietzsche 2007, 20). Slaves are driven by hatred of the masters to create new values – "good and evil" – which are based on the devaluation and inversion of the masters' form of valuation. Slavish values are "projections of …powerful reactive emotions" (Leiter 2002, 203).

Ressentiment appears throughout *On the Genealogy of Morals* (not just the First Essay). It also arises in relation to the origin of the ascetic ideal in the Third Essay, to which I return in section 3 of this chapter, when I shall have occasion to discuss priestly modes of power. Although *ressentiment* is largely a negative affect because it is triggered by an unpleasant feeling of powerlessness, Nietzsche paints *ressentiment* in an ambivalent light. It is thanks to *ressentiment* that "the human soul became deep" (Nietzsche 2007, 16). Nietzsche even attributes this accomplishment to the ascetic priests, the rogue section of the noble caste. Priests are themselves consumed by *ressentiment* because they "are turned away from action and are partly brooding and emotionally explosive" (Nietzsche 2007, 16). Priests plot revenge and create new evaluations. Rather than directly act against the physically more powerful warriors, they think and reflect, as a result "man first became an interesting animal" (Nietzsche 2007, 16). Nietzsche makes it clear that

> "...the history of mankind would be far too stupid a thing if it had not had the intellect of the powerless injected into it" (Nietzsche 2007, 17).

As already mentioned, I will consider the role of the ascetic priest in section 3 when I bring this figure together with Baudrillard's advertiser. For now, I wish to focus on how slavish "cleverness" (Nietzsche 2007, 21) transforms weakness into strength through conceptual inventions such as "free will" and "the subject". The slaves turn their own weakness into the result of a choice for which they can claim moral credit (Nietzsche 2007, 13).

Slave morality achieves this by introducing a division between one's actions and one's self, the "subject" (Nietzsche 2007, 26). Actions of this subject are not merely continuous expressions and outward manifestations of this subject, but they are separated from the subject, because the subject is '*free*' to act one way rather than another (Elgat 2017, 93). The subject is to be conceived as a neutral "substratum" (Nietzsche 2007, 26) who is *free* to act in this way or that way. It is this subject that should be identified with one's real self or "the *soul*" (Nietzsche 2007, 27). The belief in the subject is thus exploited by vengefulness and hatred to convince the strong that they can freely choose to be weak, that is 'good' and therefore are to be held accountable for their failure to be weak, that is, "good".

In addition, the subject is conceived not only as neutral and free but also equal. In slave morality, it is now "possible to condemn *everyone* for performing actions of a certain type (those that are evil)" (Elgat 2017, 92). Slave morality claims that all humans are equal. Those who know this are better than those who deny it. Instead of entering the fight with others, as the nobles do, the slaves declare their triumph according to a criterion which they claim is universal. "Slave morality denies its own ranking through fixing it" (Van Tongeren 2000, 196). Everyone is equally subjected to the same values. The self or the soul now becomes the focus of moral criticism, and it opens a dimension of depth of moral responsibility.

Closely linked to the concept of the subject is the notion of internalisation, which involves the channelling and controlling of instincts. Instincts towards hostility, cruelty and destruction are prevented from being discharged (Nietzsche 2007, 16). In the Second Essay, Nietzsche explains that the transition to a peaceful, sedentary society with its limited space leads to a devaluation of the instincts: instincts are no longer outwardly discharged, but turn inwards, and Nietzsche insists that this is the origin of "bad conscience". Nietzsche writes of the "basic instinct of freedom – the will to power – being forced back and repressed" (Nietzsche 2007, 59). For Nietzsche, the "prospect of an animal soul turning against itself" is a "puzzling, contradictory and momentous [*Zukunftvolles*]" event (Nietzsche 2007, 57) and he also sees bad conscience in an ambivalent light.

On the one hand, bad conscience is conceived as a "serious illness" and a "terrible heaviness" (Nietzsche 2007, 56) and as man's sickness of himself. Yet, Nietzsche also speaks of the "active bad conscience" (Nietzsche 2007, 58), which can be regarded as the "true womb of ideal and imaginative events"; it is responsible for creating "novel, disconcerting beauty and affirmation" (Nietzsche 2007, 60).

In Essay Two paragraph 16, Nietzsche explains that in its 'raw' or 'animal' form, bad conscience involves controlling the cruel instincts (Nietzsche 2007, 104). In this primitive state, it has no ethical or moral significance whatsoever. There is a feeling that "'something has gone unexpectedly wrong here', *not* 'I *ought* not to have done that'" (Nietzsche 2007, 56; italics in the text). At this level, one submits to punishment with a "fatalism that still gives Russians, for example, an advantage over Westerners in the way they handle life" (Nietzsche 2007, 56).

Bad conscience is transformed into guilt when the subject feels she was free to have acted differently and she begins to perceive herself as justifiably punishable for transgressing the norms of the community. Unlike bad conscience, guilt is a "distinctively moral emotion, the feeling produced by a perceived moral transgression of some kind" (Leiter 2002, 229). In Essay Two paragraph 4, Nietzsche suggests a connection between guilt and the notion of free will. With the introduction of the free will, the subject must take responsibility for his or her (mis)deed. The free subject according to Nietzsche arises with Christianity – but guilt is not limited to Christianity (Elgat 2017, 102).

The double meaning of *Schuld* (debt/guilt) in German is at work in Nietzsche's genealogy of the origin of punishment, which arises from the inability to pay back the debt. *Schuld* (debt/guilt) is part of the logic of compensation that seeks to establish equivalences between creditors and debtors: the debtors have to offer something they possess: their body, their honour, freedom, or even their life (Schrift 1995, 75). The moral concept of 'guilt' (*Schuld*) conceived as a debt (*Schuld*) that is essentially unredeemable has its origin in the economic legal notion of debt as essentially redeemable.

For Nietzsche, moral values arise from a basic social process of economic exchange, as an unintentional consequence: there is no morality prior to exchange and the establishment of reciprocal obligations. As van Tongeren (2000, 212) rightly puts it, all the moral phenomena that Nietzsche describes contain a relation between wills to power: between the strong and the weak, the powerful and the submitted, between "buyer and seller, creditor and debtor" (Nietzsche 2007, 45).

As society evolved, the basic creditor/debtor relation took the form of a relation between the present generation and its ancestors. By obeying customs, debts to ancestors are paid back. Debts to ancestors increase to the extent that the power of the community increases. Ancestors are transformed into gods and in the successive generations, this unpaid debt to ancestors is inherited with interest. In Christianity, Nietzsche sees a "stroke of genius" with the moralization of debt/guilt and duty, as the Christian God, "the maximum God attained so far," is accompanied by ultimate indebtedness (Nietzsche 2007, 62).

In Christianity, God sacrifices himself for (the guilt of) humanity. By sacrificing himself for the debtor, the creditor (the Christian

God) both removed the debt and made the debt eternal and ultimately unredeemable.

The origin of the Christian God is this (irrational) will to guilt and punishment that is incapable of becoming equal to the debt. Punishment is the consequence of God's judgment. It is no longer seen as the result of the human desire or instinct for cruelty and mastery. The moral function of punishment is to generate the feeling of guilt and it is supposed to function as a tool to breed ever more bad conscience (Schrift 1995, 76). When infinite debt is combined with bad conscience, the result is endless self-torture (Nietzsche 2007, 64) in the hopeless attempt to redeem one's sinfulness. One now tortures one's self for being a worthless creature, and not only for one's misdeeds (Elgat 2017, 102).

I have discussed how *ressentiment,* bad conscience, responsibility, internalization, guilt mark out different origins of the concept of subject. Nietzsche's genealogy of the subject exposes the oppressive uses made of the idea of subjectivity as a basis for domination that invents the concept of responsibility and freedom to hold individuals accountable and judge them guilty.

In the next section, I look further at the themes of guilt, debt and obligation as sketched out by Nietzsche in the Second Essay of the *Genealogy of Morals* and by Baudrillard in *The System of Objects* as well as *Consumer Society*. I discuss the connection between debt and *mnemotechnics* in Baudrillard's credit-driven consumer society.

2.2 Economies of Debt and Exchange in Nietzsche and Baudrillard

In the previous section, I discussed the multiple origins of the subject through processes such as *ressentiment* and bad conscience. When the instinct for cruelty cannot be discharged externally, the instinctual energy needs to find an internal alternative: this it does in bad conscience. I concluded the section with the transformation of bad conscience (internalisation of the instinct towards cruelty back against oneself) into the moral concept of guilt.

Nietzsche emphasizes that debt (*Schuld*) has a major role in forming the modern mind (Nietzsche 2007, 45). As mentioned at the end of section 1, Nietzsche explains that incurring debts is one of the earliest and most fundamental customs. The contractual relation between debtor and creditor, as a relation between the individual and society, was the primitive means to forge and construct a memory, a social and individual memory. The debtor must come to look upon his debt as binding him to act in some way in the future. The debtor has to remember and feel obligated to pay back when the time comes.

Rafael Winkler (2007, 92) emphasizes that:

> "What has often escaped commentators is that there is no slave-master relation, no consciousness of guilt, no ascetic ideal, prior to (both in the temporal and logical sense) this 'bad conscience', this consciousness of debt, the morality of custom, which is to say, man's prehistoric labour upon himself. It is here that the threshold to the human is crossed, that drives must stave off their direct satisfaction and be internalised, drives whose discharge must be controlled and channelled through artificially contrived means with the help of a memory, with a memory of the will" (Winkler 2007, 92).

In the above paragraph, Winkler rightly brings attention to the link between consciousness of debt and memory. Prehistoric humans, like all animals, lived in the grips of "forgetfulness": an active force by means of which all lived experience is thoroughly digested and processed by the psyche of the animal organism (Nietzsche 2007, 35). To counter this force, prehistoric human beings devised a *system of mnemonics* that operated on the principle of pain: "A thing must be burnt in so that it stays in the memory: only something that continues *to hurt* stays in the memory" (Nietzsche 2007, 38). Through this technique of mnemonics, human beings became reliable and could be depended on to follow social rules. Memory is:

> "[A]n active desire not to let go, a desire to keep on desiring what has been, on some occasion, desired, really it is the will's memory: so that a world of strange new things, circumstances and even acts of will may be placed quite safely in between the original "I will", I shall do and the actual discharge of the will, its act, without breaking the long chain of the will. In order to have that degree of control over the future as the present and

> anticipate it, to grasp with certainty what is end and what is means, in all to be able to calculate, compute – and before he can do this, man himself will really have to become reliable, regular necessary even in his own self-image, so that he, as someone making a promise is, is answerable for his own future!" (Nietzsche 2007, 36; italics in the text).

In the creditor-debtor relation, the will to repay institutes a time frame between an original "I will," "I shall do this" and the actual discharge of the will, its act. Something like a "future perfect" is inaugurated by the proclamation and preservation of a promise towards its projected execution.

In the *System of Objects*, Baudrillard (2005, 170; 1968, 220) puts it in the following way: "An object bought on credit will be mine when I have paid for it: it is conjugated, as it were, in the future perfect" (*"L'objet à crédit sera à moi quand il 'aura été payé': c'est quelque chose comme un futur antérieur"*).

According to George Ritzer "Baudrillard's foresight as far as consumption is concerned is exemplified by the fact, among others, that he dealt with the issue of credit at this early stage in the development of the modern credit, especially credit card, system" (Ritzer 1998, 3).

Credit is a critical aspect of consumer society and Baudrillard sees it, like Nietzsche does, as part of its disciplinary process (Baudrillard 1998, 82). Baudrillard refers to an article by Marc Alexandre (1969) "Sur la société de consommation" regarding the "*mental* training of the masses through credit (with the discipline and budgetary constraints it imposes) in economic foresight, investment and 'basic' capitalist behaviour" (Baudrillard 1998, 82; italics in the text). This "mental training" closely follows Nietzsche's own description regarding the "breeding [of] an animal with the prerogative to promise" (Nietzsche 2007, 36).

When Baudrillard was writing in the late 1960s, the credit industry was just starting to gain momentum and it radically began to change society only after *Consumer Society* was published in French in 1970. Baudrillard was ahead of his time in recognizing the importance of this issue within consumer society (Ritzer 1998, 3). Baudrillard (2005, 167-177) dedicates a section to credit in his first book on the *System of Objects*, originally published in French in 1968. In the sub-section entitled "The Precedence of Consumption: A New Ethic", Baudrillard (2005, 172) claims that the traditional movement from production to consumption has been reversed. Before, people imposed their own rhythm on objects (which they perpetuated from one generation to another thanks to a system of inheritance). Today, however, objects are bought before being actually paid for, before the necessary sum has been accumulated for the purchase.

Credit is a means of guaranteeing there is always more demand than the goods available to satisfy it. It induces the consumer to acquire more objects and take on ever more credit because, when the money is finally paid and when the object becomes ours, it is already late in comparison to new models appearing in the meantime on the market. In addition, it is always possible that the object will be "used up before it is paid up" ("que l'objet soit déchu avant d'être échu") (Baudrillard 2005, 170; 1968, 220). Objects organize themselves into a system that imposes a rhythm that is more and more constraining on everyday life. We are always late in relation to our objects, a situation, that leads to the "precedence of consumption" (and later Baudrillard will theorise the "precession of simulacra" over the real – which I discuss in chapters 4 and 5). According to Baudrillard,

> "What the buyer consumes and appropriates thanks to credit along with the object prematurely acquired is the myth of magical functionality ... naturally he will very soon come face to face with the socio-economic reality, just as the mythomaniac either collapses or takes refuge in another telltale" (Baudrillard 2005, 175).

In chapter 1.2, I discussed the important role of the word "functionality" in Baudrillard's *System of Objects*. "Functionality" is a cultural construct and an "alibi" for function (Baudrillard 1968, 86). It refers to the system of objects itself (Baudrillard 2005, 68). Advertising encapsulates what Baudrillard has in mind with the "myth of magical functionality". Advertising is a discourse on objects for selling objects, yet it is also an object itself, and it is as meaningless and useless discourse that it becomes consumable as cultural evidence. Even if the object advertised disappoints the consumer, the consumer still consumes the discourse of advertising as such.

The individual turns into a kind of enterprise constantly seeking opportunities for investment or as Baudrillard (1998, 81; italics in the text) says in *Consumer Society*:

> "[T]he consumerist man *(l'homme consommateur)* regards *enjoyment* as an obligation; he sees himself as *an enjoyment and satisfaction business*. He sees it as his duty to be happy, loving, adulating/adulated, charming/charmed, participative, euphoric and dynamic. This is the principle of maximising existence by multiplying contacts and relationship, by intense use of signs and objects, by systematic exploitation of all potentialities of enjoyment".

Baudrillard shows the ways in which consumer "liberation" promised by credit requires that it imprison desire within the obligation to acquire objects (Baudrillard 2005, 173).

> "The illusionism is truly remarkable: society appears to extend credit to you in exchange for formal freedom, but in reality it is you who are giving credit to society, alienating your future in the process. Of course, the system of production still depends fundamentally on the exploitation of labour-power, but today it is strongly reinforced by the circular consensus or collusion whereby subjection itself is experienced as freedom, and is thus transformed into an independent and durable system" (Baudrillard 2005, 174).

Here we see again the close connection between "formal freedom" offered by the system (via "credit", and "choice") and subsequent collusion with the consumer system via a process of "subjectification". Consumers follow the movement of Nietzsche's bad conscience (consciousness of debt) – projected onto objects while turning back against themselves.[34] In the following paragraph from *System of Objects*, Baudrillard links the modern form of power with a guilt-ridden and endless "subjection" to objects:

> "[i]ndividuals are gradually conditioned by their ceaseless consumption – at once gratifying and frustrating, glorious and guilt-inducing – of the social body in its totality" (Baudrillard 2005, 185).

---

[34] "In this respect the credit system is the acme of man's irresponsibility towards himself: the buyer alienates the payer, and even though they are in fact the same person, the system ensures, by separating them in time, that they never become aware of the fact" (Baudrillard 2005, 175).

In the next section 3, I show how Nietzsche and Baudrillard analyze the social consequences of these values and processes (bad conscience, guilt/debt). This involves considering the role of the ascetic priest in Nietzsche and the advertiser in Baudrillard and how they exercise power.

2.3 The "Liturgy of Solicitude"

In the previous section, I discussed the role of credit and advertising as a means of integration into the system (that generates an endless desire towards consumer spending). In addition to credit (as a vector of integration and discipline), in this section, I will outline how the advertiser in Baudrillard's work can be seen in conjunction with Nietzsche's ascetic priest, who is a variant and outgrowth of the "noble" that is, someone who understands himself as a creator of values.

First let me remind the reader that in chapter 1 (section 2), I already showed how Nietzsche's *On the Genealogy of Morals* exposes the real and felt power of the nobles over the slaves. It is this power which is recounted by Nietzsche as the origin of moral values, including the imaginary change from the opposition 'good/bad' to the dichotomy 'good/evil'. This power is based on the master's ability to exert physical strength on the slaves. It is a matter of struggle, victory and survival. In the Second Essay, the main type of power that is described is the ascetic priest's power over the slave and even over the (other warrior) nobles. This process will become clear below.

The noble was initially the type 'warrior-priest', but these functions become separated (Nietzsche 2007, 15-17) after the struggle between the status of knightly and priestly evaluations. The priestly aristocratic and warrior caste "confront one another in jealousy and cannot agree on the prize of war" (Nietzsche 2007, 17).

The priest is a noble, that is, someone who regards his manners as embodying good values. Yet, the priest is also subject to bad conscience, characterized by the will to mistreat his animal self. In the First Essay, Nietzsche introduces the priest as a type that distinguishes itself from other masters by an extreme concern for purity. As a result, the kind of values that the priest approves of, unlike other warrior-nobles, are those that deny the spontaneous or violent desires of humankind, in favour of, for example, "poverty, humility, chastity" (Nietzsche 2007, 78).

Physically, the priestly nobles are powerless against the chivalric-aristocracy. As a result, priestly *ressentiment* devalues the "powerful physicality" of the warrior nobles and there is an affinity between the priestly valuations and the valuations to which the "slave revolt in morality" give rise (Nietzsche 2007, 78).

As mentioned in section 1, Nietzsche explains that the priest, like the slave, is characterized by *ressentiment* towards knightly, warrior aristocracy due to their relative lack of physical power (Nietzsche 2007, 17). Unlike the slave, the priest gives expression to his desire for revenge and secures a maximal feeling of power. He does so by means of the construction of the ascetic ideal. "The ascetic priest not only rests his faith in that ideal, but his will, his power, his interest as well. His *right* to exist stands and falls with this ideal" (Nietzsche 2007, 85; italics in the text).

The ascetic ideal solves two problems. Confronted by the physical dominance of the knightly mode of evaluation, the ascetic ideal expresses the priest's triumph over warrior's mode of evaluation through the devaluation of the physical realm.

The priest regards the ascetic ideal as a necessary condition for his own contemplative mode of life and values ascetic procedures such as self-discipline. Additionally, and crucially, the priest "construes and uses ascetic procedures as a model for living *tout court* – as a means for mastering life" (Owen 2007, 115). The ascetic ideal goes beyond ascetic procedures that are directed at mastering specific instincts and desires. The ascetic ideal treats existence itself as an ascetic procedure and the larger goal is to transcend existence.

This ideal offers a closed system of will, goal and interpretation:

> "The ascetic has a goal, – this being so general that all the interests of human existence appear petty and narrow when measured against it; it inex-

orably interprets epochs, peoples, man, all with reference to this one goal, it permits no other interpretation, no other goal, and rejects, denies, affirms, confirms only with reference to its interpretation (– and was there ever a system of interpretation more fully thought through?)" (Nietzsche 2007, 109).

Nietzsche clarifies the sense in which this ideal is an expression of *ressentiment* by noting that it expresses "an unfulfilled instinct and power-will that wants to be master, not over something in life, but over life itself and its deepest, strongest, most profound conditions" (Nietzsche 2007, 86). To secure their power, priests propagate eternal, fixed or otherworldly values. The priest's mode of evaluation is legitimized by locating the source of values in a transcendent realm. The extent to which other "knightly" aristocrats accept this ideal also secures the power of the priests in "this world" (Owen 2007, 117).

The priest addresses another problem that faces the entire aristocratic class. The problem the elite faces is that a populace consumed with unresolved *ressentiment* is a potential danger. The question is how to "detonate this explosive material [*ressentiment*] without blowing up either the herd or the shepherd" (Nietzsche 2007, 93). The priest is a creative force because he wants to give a direction to man's suffering.[35] Nietzsche sees the priest as a "direction-changer" of the course of *ressentiment* thanks to the ascetic ideal (Nietzsche 2007, 93). As mentioned in section 1 of this chapter, prior to the priest's arrival on the scene, the slave directs his *ressentiment* outwards, to the noble master.

Nietzsche assumes that this is because the slave, like everyone who suffers, cries out for someone to blame for his suffering. Whatever the cause of suffering, Nietzsche thinks that it always calls forth the feeling of *ressentiment*, this desire for revenge – im-

---

[35] In his book *Seduction (De la Séduction)*, Baudrillard makes a (paradoxical) attempt to outline the theory, principle and effects of 'seduction' in all its forms. It was first published in France in 1979 (translated in 1990) and in it Baudrillard emphasizes the etymological derivation of the word 'seduction' – from Latin *se-ducere* – to take aside, to divert from one's path (Baudrillard 1990 S, 22). Nietzsche's priests can be regarded as Baudrillardian 'seducers'. In this chapter, I will limit myself however to Baudrillard's early work, on consumer society.

aginary or real – this desire "for a *guilty* culprit...upon whom [the sufferer] can release his emotions" (Nietzsche 2007, 93). Here, the assumption is that the discharging of strong emotions reduces suffering or that pain is anaesthetised through emotion. All powerful emotions, such as "anger, fear, voluptuousness, revenge, hope, triumph, despair, cruelty" – "throw the human soul out of joint...to such an extent that it rids itself of all small and petty forms of lethargy, apathy, depression, as though hit by lightning" (Nietzsche 2007, 103). The problem is that "[e]very such excess of emotion has to be *paid* for afterwards, it goes without saying – it makes the sick person even sicker" (Nietzsche 2007, 104).

The ascetic priest identifies an alternative outlet for discharging powerful emotions, someone to blame, a culprit: the sufferer himself. The sufferer himself is to be the object of his own *ressentiment*. The sufferer is taught that he himself is the cause of his suffering. He discharges his emotions against himself (instead of against another i.e., the noble). Although this causes more pain and suffering, this suffering is now given a meaning. At the start of the Third Essay, Nietzsche says that there is nothing worse than enduring meaningless suffering and feeling that one suffers for no reason. In cases of meaningless suffering "*ressentiment*...piles up" (Nietzsche 2007, 93).

The priest explains the 'meaning' of the slave's unhappy suffering (when the latter is just due to the impotence of the slave and his basic physiological depression), and his 'ministry' is to make suffering more bearable. Priests become experts in dealing with all forms of suffering:

> "The priest brings ointments and balms with him, of course; but first he has to wound so that he can be the doctor; and while he soothes the pain caused by the wound, he poisons the wound at the same time" (Nietzsche 2007, 93).

Nietzsche delineates the way in which ascetic priests (as the founders of Christianity) construct an interpretation of the modern world in which they are made to appear essential. Thanks to the introduction of the ascetic ideal, the priest renders suffering meaningful. The ascetic ideal gives the will a goal to overcome meaningless and such an ideal valorises for instance the denial of rapacious sexual desires. Yet humans are doomed to always fall short of the ascetic ideal because all "basic instincts and inclinations are fundamentally anti-ascetic" (Leiter 2002, 261). The ascetic priest exploits this contradiction and explains that humans suffer as punishment because they fail to live up to ascetic ideal. By creating an unattainable ideal, the priest reinterprets human suffering as "feelings of guilt, fear, punishment" (Nietzsche 2007, 105). Priests claim that we suffer because we are guilty for transgressing the ascetic requirements of the ideal, we suffer for betraying god and being sinners.

The ascetic priest takes bad conscience in its raw state (discussed above, as the internalisation of instincts for cruelty) and gives it a "priestly reinterpretation" and turns it to guilt and sin (Nietzsche 2007, 105). The reinterpretation involves attaching the internalised cruelty (i.e., bad conscience before it was fully moralized) to an ascetic ideal, so that it is transformed into guilt. The ascetic ideal brings all suffering within the perspective of guilt and this renders it meaningful. Priestly concepts such as guilt, sin, "make the sick *harmless* to a certain degree" by giving their "*ressentiment*" a backwards direction [towards themselves] ...and in this way ...*exploit*[s] the bad instincts of all sufferers [to find a culprit] for the purpose of self-discipline, self-surveillance and self-overcoming" (Nietzsche 2007, 94).

In Essay Three paragraph 13, Nietzsche provides his most nuanced analysis of the ascetic ideal. Even though the ascetic ideal may be life-negating (this is its metaphysical vision) Nietzsche claims that it also arises

> "*from the protective and healing instincts of a degenerating life*, which uses every means to maintain itself and struggles for its existence; it indicates a partial physiological inhibition and exhaustion against which its deepest instincts of life, which have remained intact, continually struggle with new methods and inventions" (Nietzsche 2007, 88; italics in the text).

The ascetic priest creates fictional explanations for human suffering:[36] we suffer because we violate the ascetic ideal. Suffering is rendered meaningful. Meaningless suffering leads to "suicidal nihilism" and the piling up of ressentiment (Nietzsche 2007, 12). When this ressentiment is discharged against the agent himself in the form of guilt, the pain associated with the original suffering is anaesthetized.

By generating guilt, the priest's story about the ascetic ideal brings "new suffering with it, deeper, more internal, more poisonous suffering that gnawed away more intensely at life" (Nietzsche 2007, 120) "But in spite of that," Nietzsche adds, "man was saved, he had a *meaning*" (Nietzsche 2007, 120; italics in the text) and thus "from now on he could will something...*the will itself was saved*" (Nietzsche 2007, 120; italics in the text) i.e., it was possible for the human to will to do things in life, since their suffering at last had meaning (Leiter 2002, 263).

Against life-negation (in favour of another world) or life-preservation (survival), Nietzsche proposes life-affirmation. "Great health" is needed to succeed "in redeeming humanity from the will to nothingness, ... which, for Nietzsche, is the real nihilism" (Zeitlin 1994, 94). In the Third Essay, Nietzsche shows that asceticism is inextricably linked to that same will to nothingness (God) that has produced the life negating processes such as guilt and bad conscience (Zeitlin 1994, 94).

At the end of *On the Genealogy of Morals*, Nietzsche comments on the state of contemporary scholarship, to argue that in modern times yet another version of the ascetic ideal dominates: one that is manifest by the scholar's dedication to the 'truth'. Nietzsche speaks of the "industry of our best scholars, their unreflective diligence" and he comments, "how often does all that mean trying to conceal something from themselves? Science as a means of self-anaesthetic: do you know that?" (Nietzsche 2007, 110). The ascetic ideal has infiltrated non-religious domains like science.

---

[36] Nietzsche does not distinguish between the genuinely existential causes of suffering – e.g., desire, physiological malady, bad conscience – and the contingent causes.

At the close of paragraph 24 of the Third Essay, Nietzsche (2007, 113) summarizes the problem:

> "the ascetic ideal has so far been master over all philosophy, because truth was set as being, as God, as the highest authority itself, because truth was not *allowed* to be a problem."

The problem that Nietzsche claims has been suppressed revolves around the idea of truth as the binary opposite of 'error'. It is the absolute, unquestioning value of truth that Nietzsche targets, the ascetic impulse to eradicate disturbance to a presumed truth, in whatever form a conviction may take, even an anti-metaphysical conviction. A genuine alternative to the ascetic ideal "tentatively" puts the value of truth "into question" (Nietzsche 2007, 113). Nietzsche concludes the Third Essay by claiming that science is not the self-evident opponent of the ascetic ideal because regarding "truth", it also rejects unstable forces, in favour of control (Hatab 2008, 114).

As Rafael Winkler rightly explains: "Nietzsche dispels the illusion that modern science constitutes an antidote to the ascetic ideal. Science exposes man to a 'penetrating sense of his nothingness'" (Winkler 2018, 103). For Nietzsche, scientists are metaphysicians, because they still believe in truth. Science rests on the unnegotiable, absolute value of truth, but for Nietzsche there is no such thing as a science that is presupposition-free. Science is as a result only a vehicle for the ascetic ideal and it presuppose certain values which give it direction (Zeitlin 1994, 97).

In the next section, I return to Baudrillard, who identifies another version of the ascetic ideal in modern consumer society, propagated by advertisers.

2.4 Ascetic ideals and consumer society

In the previous section, we saw how from the perspective of genealogy, meaning is a tool of social conflict. The ascetic priest uses meaning, in the form of the ascetic ideal to gain power. Nietzsche's genealogical narration of the "slave revolt in morality"

(Nietzsche 2007, 20) shows that a refined form of power emerges out of a complex intellectual and affective strategy.

In Baudrillard's work there is a similar genealogical conception of power in which lies a complex thesis about how power is constituted and exercised. In *Consumer Society*, we can see Baudrillard's 'advertiser' as the most recent figure of the priest. Baudrillard claims advertisers (along with architects, town planners, designers) "see themselves as demiurges or rather as *thaumaturges* of social relations and the environment" (Baudrillard 1998, 168; italics in the text). Advertisers belong to "apparatuses of solicitude" (Baudrillard, 1998, 168). In a dramatically entitled subsection "Ambiguity and Terrorism of Solicitude", Baudrillard looks at the "liturgy of solicitude" and the "double meaning of the verb to 'solicit'" (Baudrillard 1998, 168).

On the one hand, "to solicit" has a "'caring', 'favouring', 'mothering' sense. The **gift**" (Baudrillard 1998, 168; bold in the text). It also contains the opposite meaning of "'requesting'… 'demanding' or even 'commandeering' … What is involved here is a diverting, a seizing of something; turning it to one's own ends" (Baudrillard 1998, 168). For Baudrillard, the mechanism of control, at the deepest level, lies in the fact that advertising is a "gift" (Baudrillard 1998, 164). It reassures us that society is thinking of ways to solve our problems and assuage our anxieties.[37]

Baudrillard develops the ways in which consumer "liberation" promised by advertisers requires that it trap desire within the confines of a network and choice of objects (network of signs in a code which I explained in more detail in the previous chapter in section 3). In addition, the mythic language of advertising forges a pact between advertiser and shopper.

> "Consumption is a myth. That is to say, it is *a statement of contemporary society about itself*, the way our society speaks to itself. And, in a sense, the only

---

[37] William Pawlett explains that in "Baudrillard's thought there is a strong sense of 'determination by social structure': a level of causality that is quite real, although it is largely hidden or unconscious" (Pawlett 2007, 20). By scrutinizing consumer myths (for instance 'needs' and 'uses') Baudrillard (1998, 60) seeks to provide "a genuine analysis of the social logic of consumption".

> objective reality of consumption is the idea of consumption; it is this reflexive, discursive configuration, endlessly repeated in everyday speech, which has acquired the force of *common sense*" (Baudrillard 1998, 194; italics in the text).

Consumption is a way of communicating with one another. Consumers 'read' the system of consumption to know what to consume. Baudrillard argues for the study of signs, structural relations and an overall unconscious social system in which conflicts and struggles for meaning are supressed. In the world of advertising, the "conflicted" world is neutralized into an abstract, ordered one, a world of consumable signs where "the signifier becomes its own signified ... we see the abolition of the signified and the tautology of the signifier ... the substitution of the code for the referential dimension defines mass media consumption" (Baudrillard 1998, 125). This prevents the reciprocal exchange of meaning, and allows only pre-fabricated, simulated responses, responses drawn from a predefined range or code.

Baudrillard makes it clear that

> "[i]t is not, therefore, that advertising 'alienates' or 'mystifies' us with its claims, words or images; rather we are swayed by the fact that 'they' are sufficiently concerned to want to address us, to show us things, to take an interest in us" (Baudrillard 2005, 185).

Like a caring and protective mother, advertisers are attentive and have solutions for problems. Advertising suggests who one can become:

> "The abundance of products puts an end to *scarcity*; the abundance of advertising puts an end to *insecurity*. The worst thing possible is to be obliged to invent one's own motives for acting, for preferring, for buying. The individual in such circumstances is brought face to face with his own misapprehensions, his own lack of existence, his own bad faith and anxiety" (Baudrillard 2005, 186).

Advertisers (like Nietzsche's ascetic priests) have thus created for themselves a mask of "health" that has the power to tyrannize the healthy by poisoning their conscience. When Nietzsche notes the irony of the Christian God sacrificing himself for humanity "out of love" (Nietzsche 2007, 63), Baudrillard ironically chronicles the various expressions of concern of advertisers for their crippled consumers and how they are "committed to the idea of happiness – to YOUR happiness" (Baudrillard 2005, 184). The ultimate results of these ironic spirals also parallel one another: where Christianity's self-sacrificing God makes infinite its adherents' guilt and debt, advertising creates its own infinite debt in the form of interminable buying of objects. The consumer can never be satisfied, and the consumption of objects/signs is a *process without end*, exactly as Christian redemption, which is interminable. Consumption is the continuation of an economy of guilt by other means than Christian redemption and the asking for forgiveness.

Baudrillard views advertiser's interpretative practices as no less reductive than the interpretations of Nietzsche's ascetic priest. Just as Nietzsche's priests reduce all events to a moment of divine reward and punishment, Baudrillard's advertisers reduce all desire to a fixation for objects on offer. Baudrillard explains this consumptive cycle: "The aim is to allow drives hitherto inhibited by psychic agencies (taboos, superego, guilt) to crystalize upon objects, which themselves thus become capable of negating the explosive force of desire" (Baudrillard 2005, 203).

Consumer society in its entirety, through its ideology, seems to be transformed into a therapeutic society in which fragile, tired and disorientated citizen-consumers are cared for, advised and cured. The consumer is a virtual sick man situated at the interior of a social body that is itself sick (Baudrillard 1998, 182). To Nietzsche's bad conscience (which is based upon the internalisation of man and the suspension of the human instincts), Baudrillard adds man's "personalisation" within the consumer system of objects (Baudrillard 1998, 87–91). The consumer repeats the split movement of Nietzsche's bad conscience – projected onto objects while turning back against oneself.

Conclusion

This chapter culminated in the fusion of Nietzsche's figure of the ascetic priest with that of the advertiser in Baudrillard. For Nietzsche, priestly power is based upon giving suffering a meaning through fictional explanations. Priests influence experiences and perceptions through a network of meanings and significations that are unconscious to the subjects themselves. Social struggles over meaning are concealed and one set of values thus become 'internalised' as acceptable (Saar, 2009b). Instincts towards cruelty are redirected inwards and the sufferer is made to believe he is responsible for his own misfortune for failing to live up to the ascetic ideal, which is propagated by priests. By creating an unattainable ideal, the priest reinterprets human suffering as "feelings of guilt, fear, punishment" (Nietzsche 2007, 105). Priests claim that we suffer because we are guilty for betraying the ascetic ideal. We suffer because we are sinners. By providing subjects with a set of self-understandings, ascetic priests establish one specific and dominant world-view.

I have shown how Baudrillard in his turn ironically narrates the 'concern' of advertisers for their sick consumers and their commitment to consumer happiness. Just as Christianity's self-sacrificing God makes infinite its adherents' guilt and debt, advertising creates its own infinite debt in the form of the endless acquisition of (signs)objects.

In what follows, I will draw on Rafael Winkler's (2007) comparative study "I Owe You: Nietzsche, Mauss" (2007) in order to show how several themes in Nietzsche, Mauss and Bataille play a central role in Baudrillard's critique of consumer society and how Baudrillard's critique arises from a sense of the importance of gift-exchange, as it exists, in part, in 'primitive society' and "more generally in an abstract model of such an exchange process" (Ritzer 1998, 10).

In the process, I unpack further the impoverished and indefinitely exasperated desire that characterizes consumer society. For Baudrillard, poverty is not reducible to the quantity of goods a group possesses, but instead it concerns the quality of its human relationship. In the case of primitive hunter-gathers there are reciprocal human relationships. There is no accumulation or monopolisation of technologies, or products that would interrupt free exchange. The source of their wealth is symbolic exchange and, since the latter is endless, wealth is unlimited.

The point lies in social relationships, so the problem will not be solved by increasing production or by innovating productive forces. A social relationship based on the wealth of symbolic exchange is required, rather than one based on "luxurious and spectacular penury" (Baudrillard 1998, 68). Consumer society hollows out individual experiences and relationships – this I argue, is an extension of Nietzsche's analysis of the ascetic ideal.[38]

---

[38] Nietzsche is often seen as a philosopher who focuses on the individual. In my view, it matters to read Baudrillard with Nietzsche because it shows, on the one hand, that Baudrillard does not deny the phenomenon of subjectivity as Douglas Kellner (1989, 19) claims and that Nietzsche in his turn is not a philosopher who is "obsessed with romantic existential fantasies about self-creation or self-transcendence and whose ideal type is nearly thoroughly unsuited for social life and unable to achieve the bonds of meaningful community" (Acampora 2006, 158). I am in agreement with Christa Davis Acampora (2006), who, in her article "On Sovereignty and Overhumanity: Why it Matters How We Read Nietzsche's Genealogy 11:2", emphasizes that inattentive translation of Nietzsche's texts has permitted a (mis)reading of Nietzsche that focuses on his individualism.

3. The End of Transcendence in *Consumer Society*

Introduction

In the previous chapter 2.3, we saw how the ascetic priest mobilizes his power with intellectual strategies by inventing fictional explanations for why we suffer, in the form of the ascetic ideal.

One of the central questions I will tackle in this chapter is whether the sign-object sold by the advertiser to the consumer is extra-mundane, otherworldly, non-sensuous – or in some way close to or identical with the features that pertain to the world of being in Plato. The ascetic ideal propagated by the priest is transcendent: it is something that does not bear any resemblance to the physical or empirical world, like truth; as a result, it can only depreciate this world. Is that also true of what the advertiser sells?

In *The System of Objects,* Baudrillard claims that consumption is "a totally idealist practice" (Baudrillard 2005, 223). The consumption of sign-value is based on a meaningful "totality" which is out of reach (Baudrillard 2005, 224). Sign-value always defers satisfaction by referring the process of consumption to another object/sign in the system. Rather than the intensity of symbolic engagement, modern consumption involves the external manipulation of abstract signs (Baudrillard 1998, 94). Consumer society is characterized by differentiation and competition which contributes to the sense that there is never enough. Like Christian morality, I claim that for Baudrillard, consumer society exposes man to a "*piercing* sensation of his nothingness" (Nietzsche 2007, 115).

In section 1, drawing on Rafael Winkler's (2007) article "I Owe You: Nietzsche, Mauss", I will show how several themes in Nietzsche, but also Mauss and Bataille, play a central role in how Baudrillard's critique of consumer society arises from a sense of the importance of gift-exchange, as it exists, in part, in 'primitive society' and "more generally in an abstract model of such an exchange process" (Ritzer 1998, 10). Importantly, Nietzsche's views on debt, excess and the will to power are clearly at work in Baudrillard's (re)view of the true function of waste and excess.

In section 2, I discuss to what extent consumption as it is outlined by Baudrillard rests on the same basis of the ascetic ideal which Nietzsche sees as an *"impoverishment of life"* (Nietzsche 2007, 114; italics in the text). A social relationship (and a social logic) based on the affluence of symbolic exchange is required, rather than one based on "luxurious and spectacular penury" (Baudrillard 1998, 68).

In section 3, I focus on how consumer society is run by pseudo-objects and pseudo-events. Consumption is beyond the true and the false (and this will allow me to introduce the concept of simulation to which I will dedicate the next chapter 4). Baudrillard's discussion of the short novel *Les Choses* by Georges Perec is given a crucial place in the *System of Objects* for dramatic effect to show how consumer society impoverishes life.

3.1 Wasteful Expenditure

In the previous chapter 2.1, I looked at the processes that mark out the different origins of the subject for Nietzsche. I outlined the forms and processes of subjection (such as bad conscience and guilt) as well as Nietzsche's technological invention of the human through economies of guilt, debt and obligation. In chapter 2.2, I established a link between the socially constraining character of the creditor-debtor relation in Nietzsche, the production of a social memory, and the equally socially constraining character of credit and consumption in Baudrillard. In the Second Essay of *On the Genealogy of Morals,* Nietzsche distinguishes between an economy based on the endless imputation of guilt (i.e., the ascetic ideal of Christianity) and another one based on the reciprocal exchange of debts. According to Nietzsche, Christianity's self-sacrificing God makes infinite its adherents' guilt and debt. In similar fashion, in consumer society, advertising creates its own infinite debt in the form of the interminable buying of sign-objects.

In his article "I Owe You: Nietzsche, Mauss", Rafael Winkler (2007) brings to light how Nietzsche's discourse resonates with

Marcel Mauss's study on *The Gift*, Georges Bataille's *Accursed Share* and Jacques Derrida's *Given Time*. In what follows, I draw on Winkler's comparative study in order to show how several themes in Nietzsche, Mauss and Bataille also play a central role in Baudrillard's critique of consumer society. Using Mauss, Bataille and Nietzsche, Baudrillard contrasts different economies of debt, (gift) exchange and expenditure (section 1). By outlining this "total social logic" at play in consumer society, I hope to show how the ascetic ideal lives on in it (section 2).

Mauss's 1924 book *The Gift: The Form and Reason for Exchange in Archaic Societies* is an investigation into the inner workings of the gift, especially regarding the obligation to reciprocate. Using Malinowski's ground-breaking work in ethnology, Mauss analyzes case studies of groups such as the eastern Melanesians (who exchange necklaces and armbands), the Kwakiutl (and their practice of potlatch[39]), and the New Zealand Maoris (with their complex philosophy of how the essence of a person is carried in their gifts) (Wilk and Cliggett 2009, 159).

Mauss draws upon the system of exchange, known as the Kula ring, in the eastern Melanesian Islands, in order to emphasize how exchange solidifies power and status, even though no material profit is made. In understanding this exchange, Mauss identifies three interrelated moments: the obligation to give a gift, the obligation to receive a gift and the obligation to reciprocate. The aim is to build social relationships, which in turn builds societies. The obligation to reciprocate is at the heart of all these systems.

---

[39] See William Pawlett (2007, 51) for more on the term 'potlatch' and its relation to Baudrillard's thought. Mauss uses the word in a general way in his study *The Gift* and Baudrillard uses it even more generally. Potlatch ceremonies have been studied by social anthropologists and ethnologists. There are indigenous accounts available, as well as philosophical and deconstructive readings of different kinds. Mauss himself did not physically go to the region and relied on second-hand accounts by Franz Boas, Maurice Leenhardt, Bronislaw Malinowski and others. The kula is another example of gift-exchange, practised traditionally in the Pacific Islands which Mauss argues are similar in form and function to the potlatch (Pawlett 2007, 51).

Mauss's exploration into the dynamic towards reciprocation results in his elaboration of the concept of *hau*, a Maori term for the force of the identity of the owner of an object, which cannot be detached from the object. When an object is given, part of the owner's *hau* goes with it. The gift carries within it a moral force, it carries the "soul" of the giver (Mauss 1990, 10-13, 43-44): "to make a gift of something to someone is to make a present of some part of oneself ... to accept something from someone is to accept some part of his spiritual essence, his soul" (Mauss 1990, 12). Gifts entail the identity of the giver and they are not anonymous or neutral mediums of equivalence, because as Mauss puts it "persons and things merge" (Mauss 1990, 48). In addition, gift-exchange is not a rudimentary system of money or barter. Mauss argues that such gift-cultures show that the notion of credit precedes the emergence of barter and money (Pawlett 2007, 53).

Mauss recognizes the imprecision of the terms 'gift' and 'potlatch'; he therefore puts forward his own term: "total services and counter-services" (*prestations et contre-prestation totales*; Mauss 1950, 187). This term describes systems of exchange including presents, but also loans or services in the widest sense.

For Mauss (2002, 45-7), "the gift necessarily entails the notion of credit". There is an obligatory time-frame for repayment in which the performance of counter-services must be made.[40] The circulation of wealth in archaic societies is driven by the desire to reciprocate gifts with interest in order to build relations, challenge rivals and gain power. The network of gift-exchange prevents "the accretion of destabilising concentrations of power and wealth" (Moore 2011, 3). Mauss shows that debts can always be balanced in the cycle of giving and returning gifts.

Mauss regards the potlatch as a "total service of an antagonistic kind", with a "very acute rivalry and the destruction of

---

[40] Winkler (2007, 94) sees in Mauss's study on *The Gift* a revival of Nietzsche's *mnemotechnics* – a memory is crucial for the relationship between creditor and debtor to work. In addition, the exchange of gifts as any other form of exchange builds a "a social unconscious. Values get registered and chronicled, compiling into an unconscious, in acts of cruelty" (Winkler 2007, 95).

wealth"; such ceremonies are "rare but highly developed" (Mauss 1990, 7). In the potlatch ceremony, there is honour in destruction:

> "[C]onsumption and destruction of goods really go beyond all bounds. In certain kinds of potlatch one must expend all that one has, keeping nothing back. It is a competition to see who is richest and also the most madly extravagant. Everything is based upon the principles of antagonism and rivalry" (Mauss 1990, 37).

To receive gifts amounts to accepting a challenge, and to fail to "out-bid" one's rival or not reciprocate with interest entails losing one's status and rank.

Rafael Winkler (2007, 105) identifies in the potlatch a power struggle with a "Nietzschean element of play and simulation". Through a display of unconditional power to the point of the sacrifice of all one has, the potlatch seeks to unravel the debtor and creditor structure with an action that destabilizes the recipient by making it impossible for him to reciprocate.[41] Nothing specific has been given however beyond a *display* of pure expenditure and loss. The donor in the potlatch sacrifices all that he has without reserve; and in exchange for this sacrifice, he acquires power. The debtor, when unable to repay his debt, substitutes something else for it: his honour or his rank. In this way, debts always get equalized and there is no such thing as a unilateral gift. The debtor makes a "present" of his status in order to compensate for his ina-

---

[41] How do we respond to the symbolic challenge of death and the dead, the challenge they pose to our conscious experience? This is for Baudrillard the question of September 11 2001. For Baudrillard, the event known as '9/11' is a "pure event" (Baudrillard 2002, 4). The event of '9/11' for Baudrillard is "the act that restores an irreducible singularity to the heart of a system of generalised exchange" (2002, 9). We have seen how the symbolic dimension in Baudrillard seems to be that which questions the total commutability and exchangeability of semiology (chapter 1.2). There is an "internal fragility" to the West, a kind of suicidal self-destruction that is triggered by too much power (Baudrillard 2002, 8). For Baudrillard, Western global capitalism has achieved ultimate power and pervasiveness but so has the will to destroy it from within. The suicide of the terrorists is a metaphor. If political economy is the most rigorous attempt to put an end to death (the system's unilateral gift of life) it is clear for Baudrillard that only death (suicide terrorism) can put an end to political economy. I will deal with Baudrillard's views on "symbolic exchange and death" in relation to Heidegger in chapter 6.

bility to reciprocate the gift. The aim is to temporarily stabilize the rivalry between chiefs into a hierarchy.

Bataille found in the description of Mauss's potlatch a challenge to the necessity and role of rational capitalist economies. Bataille formulated a theory of exchange that was based on destruction and loss (*dépense*) instead of acquisition, calculation and accumulation. For Bataille, the primitive relation to the object was *consummation*, which is a social process that cannot be reduced to reason. *Consummation* is related to Bataille's idea that meaning arises from non-meaning, or from un/de-codified social material.[42] Meaning for Bataille arises from and through excess, which is beyond 'rational' and result- driven production (Levin 1996, 70).

According to Winkler, "… for Bataille the movement of the gift economy pursues, to a certain extent, the general movement of life, that of the expenditure of useless energy … just as in Nietzsche the human animal follows the drift of life by reconstructing its will to power, its body, symbolically, in terms of an economy of debt" (Winkler 2007, 102). Nietzsche and Bataille claim that an organism receives more energy than is required for maintaining life. It is therefore necessary that the excess energy also be spent uselessly, luxuriously or violently. Nietzsche and Bataille both oppose utilitarian or classical economists, for whom exchanges take place for the "useful" acquisition of goods to satisfy needs or self-interest.

Nietzsche and Bataille's attempts to connect the gift to an overall framework (beyond a mere utilitarian view) are also in evidence in Baudrillard's work. Julian Pefanis in his *Heterology and the Postmodern: Bataille, Baudrillard and Lyotard,* writes: "We could say that Baudrillard's critique of the systems and modes of productivist thought are filiated, via the agency of the situationists and the critique of the spectacle, to Bataille's analysis of modes of *dépense*" (Pefanis 1991, 50). Baudrillard is interested in expenditure (*dépense*) as it is opposed to the rationale behind the capitalist

---

[42] See Jacques Derrida 'From Restricted to General Economy: a Hegelianism without Reserve', in *Writing and Difference,* trans. and intro. Alan Bass. (Chicago: University of Chicago Press, 1978), pp 251-77.

economy, which is accumulative and where spending is seen as a function of utility, growth and production, and is connected with the expectation of return, return on the investment.

Relying on Mauss's study *The Gift*, Baudrillard compares the restrictive frame of reference of wasteful expenditure offered by economists with a more general "total social logic", which means that all aspects of the society (e.g., the public and the private, the economic to the aesthetic) are engaged at once. The gift-exchange ceremonies are "total social phenomena" because economic, religious, juridical and moral institutions are given expression at one and the same time (Pawlett 2007, 63).

Baudrillard contrasts the gift economy against capitalism (and he refers to to the anthropological works of both Mauss and Sahlins in this regard) because in the gift economy, exchanges are always symbolic. Baudrillard argues that an economy of use, need or necessity is a myth. There is always surplus, the extent and nature of which result from socio-political arrangements.

In the sub-section entitled "Waste" in *Consumer Society*, Baudrillard calls for a "review" of that "whole moral vision of waste as dysfunction ... from the perspective of a sociological analysis which would bring out its true functions" (Baudrillard 1998, 43). Baudrillard does not see wasteful expenditure as immoral and socially dysfunctional:

> "All societies have wasted, squandered, expended and consumed beyond what is strictly necessary for the simple reason that it is in the consumption of a surplus, of a superfluity that the individual – and society – feel not merely that they exist, but that they are alive" (Baudrillard 1998, 43).

Baudrillard discusses the functionality of idols of consumption (`great wastrels') such as movie stars and sports heroes, who fulfil the function of "symbolic", useless and excessive expenditure (Baudrillard 1998, 46). He also points out that (expensive) cars are wasteful expenditures that have symbolic, extra-economic value because as soon as they are bought, they decrease in market price (antique cars belong to the category of the "collection" which Baudrillard (2005) describes in *The System of Objects*. Such collectors' objects do not undergo "market-based" depreciation).

Referring to the Maussean potlatch and Nietzschean aristocratic classes, Baudrillard re-evaluates waste:

> "waste, far from being an irrational residue, takes on a positive function, taking over where rational utility leaves off to play its part in a higher social functionality – a social logic in which waste even appears ultimately as the essential function, the extra degree of expenditure, superfluity, the ritual uselessness of 'expenditure for nothing' becoming the site of production of values, differences and meanings on both individual and the social level" (Baudrillard 1998, 43).

Human society revolves around the generation of 'meaning'. Baudrillard rejects notions of 'primitive' and 'advanced' societies as being founded on survival (and the idea of a progress from survival to 'higher' things). In the sub-section "Waste" Baudrillard quotes Nietzsche's *Will to Power* (and he mentions Bataille's agreement to Nietzsche's position):

> "Physiologists should think again before positing the 'instinct of preservation' as the cardinal drive in an organic creature. A living thing wants above all to discharge its force: 'preservation' is only a consequence of this. Beware of superfluous teleological principles! The entire concept 'instinct of preservation' is one of them ... The 'struggle for existence' – this formula refers to an exceptional situation; the rule is much rather the struggle for power, the ambition to have 'more' and 'better' and 'quicker' and 'more often'" (Nietzsche, The Will to Power [Fragment 650] quoted in Baudrillard 1998, 45).

Baudrillard follows the Nietzschean rejection of instincts of preservation (Baudrillard 1998, 44). From the perspective of Nietzsche's will to power, preservation is a mere side-effect. As we saw in chapter 2. 3, though the ascetic ideal may be life-negating (which is its metaphysical vision) Nietzsche claims that it also arises *"from the protective and healing instincts of a degenerating life, which uses every means to maintain itself and struggles for its existence; it indicates a partial physiological inhibition and exhaustion against which its deepest instincts of life, which have remained intact, continually struggle with new methods and inventions"* (Nietzsche 2007, 88; italics in the text).

For Nietzsche, the ascetic ideal is a creation that is projected onto the world to render it meaningful, but the source of meaning is located outside the world. Ascetic ideals are a tool to ward off "suicidal nihilism" but they do so by preserving a sick impoverished life that is incapable of fully affirming life (Nietzsche 2007, 120).

As mentioned already in the previous chapter 2, section 3, at the end of *On the Genealogy of Morals*, Nietzsche argues the ascetic ideal has infiltrated non-religious domains like science. The scholar's categorical, unconditional dedication to the 'truth' is a continuation of the ascetic ideal. For Nietzsche, the practices and epistemological assumptions in science show a similar opposition toward instinctual, affective and tension-ridden drives and Nietzsche shows "how certain results in the modern scientific worldview [has] reinforced or reconstituted a central feature of the ascetic ideal – that natural life on its own terms exhibits no intrinsic meaning" (Hatab 2008, 114).

In my view, in consumer society, Baudrillard finds a further extension of the ascetic ideal. Nietzsche sees the ascetic ideal as an "*impoverishment of life* – the emotions cooled, the tempo slackened, dialectics in place of instinct, *solemnity* stamped on faces and gestures" (Nietzsche, 2007, 114; italics in the text). In the next section, I will discuss to what extent consumption as outlined by Baudrillard can be seen to rest on an ascetic ideal.

3.2 Ascetic consumption

In section 3.1, I started by discussing how Mauss elaborates a theory of group behaviour and the total social fact (first developed by his uncle Émile Durkheim). For Mauss, society is not an aggregate of self-interested, utility maximizing individuals, organized around separate public and private spheres, the market *(agora)* and the home *(oikos)* (Moore 2011, 3). Mauss regards the "individual" as only meaningful within wider kinship networks, as a "channel" along which gifts circulate, as a ritual agent (Pawlett 2007, 52). This was an important influence on Baudrillard's notion of individuality and agency. For both Mauss and Baudrillard, the idea of man existing in a state of nature for immediate survival – is a fictional construct of economic theory. [43]

From this "total social" perspective, we saw the positive function that Baudrillard attributes to waste. It produces social values of prestige, rank and status.[44] Following Mauss's work on the potlatch, Bataille's notion of *dépense* but also "the something more" in Nietzsche's 'will to power', Baudrillard claims that it is not some basic level of biological existence that underlies what can be wasted but what can be wasted that drives this basic 'biological' level.

> "This law of symbolic value, which states that the essential element always lies beyond what is indispensable, is best illustrated in expenditure, in loss" (Baudrillard 1998, 45).

Baudrillard here also follows Bataille's version of consummation (*la consumation*) whereby objects are consumed in sacrificial gift and/or destruction (i.e., forms of the Maussean type of potlatch). Such consumption completely 'uses up' the object.[45] According to

---

[43] The obligatory nature of reciprocation and the power of "counter-prestations" theorized by Mauss (or what Baudrillard prefers to call the *contre-don* or counter-gift) to challenge existing power relations is also crucial for Baudrillard.

[44] Towards the end of *The System of Objects* Baudrillard (2005, 178) says "Advertising in its entirety constitutes a useless and unnecessary universe" and in the section *of Consumer Society* entitled "Advertising and the Ideology of the Gift" Baudrillard emphasizes that:
"The social function of advertising is to be understood in the same extra-economic perspective as the ideology of the gift, of free offers and service. For advertising is not merely sales promotion or the use of suggestions for economic ends. It is perhaps not even these things first and foremost (its economic effectiveness is increasingly being questioned): the specific message of 'language of advertising' is the denial of the economic rationality of commodity exchange under the auspices of a general exemption of payment" (Baudrillard 1998, 164).

[45] "There is a profound tendency within consumption for it to surpass itself, to transfigure itself in destruction. It is in destruction that it acquires its meaning. Most of the time in daily life today, it remains subordinate - as a managed consumptivity - to the order of productivity. This is why, most of the time, objects are present *by their absence*, and why their very abundance paradoxically signifies penury. Stock is the excessive expression of lack and a mark of anxiety. Only in destruction are objects there *in excess* and only then, in their disappearance, do they attest to wealth" (Baudrillard 1998, 49).

the productivist point of view, according to which societies are defined by their mode of production, sacrifice comes from objects that are surplus to a subsistence level.

> "[W]e have to distinguish individual or collective waste as a symbolic act of expenditure, as a festive, ritual and an exalted form of socialisation, from its gloomy, bureaucratic caricature in our societies, where wasteful consumption has become a daily obligation, a forced and often unconscious institution like indirect taxation, a cool participation in the constraints of the economic order" (Baudrillard 1998, 47).

In consumer society, the individual is disciplined by a new ideological obligation to enter consumption by "trying out" the latest gadget. An obsessive new "universal curiosity" develops into the fear of missing the latest fashion, something new (Baudrillard 1998, 81). This structure cannot be recognized by individualist assumptions of the nature of the consumer, for it is a "social fact" in the primordial sense yet the social fact is realised in an individual manner so the consuming mass does not have a collective existence.[46] Consumers are fragmented and unorganized.[47]

Against this vision of an anonymous and unorganized consuming mass, Baudrillard discusses the anthropologist Marshall Sahlins's ideas on reciprocity in hunter-gathering societies. Sahlins' book *Stone Age Economics* identifies particular kinds of social structures. What Sahlins (1972, 194-195) calls "generalised reciprocity" takes place in tight-knit social relationships and families, where exchange occurs so frequently that controlling the val-

---

[46] Baudrillard focuses his attention on collective phenomena on "Durkheimian social facts", according to Ritzer (1998, 4). Baudrillard describes consumption in very Durkheimian terms as "collective behaviour" something "enforced, a morality an institution" and a whole system of values" (Baudrillard, 1998: 79).

[47] "Just as 'the People' is glorified by Democracy provided that it remains the people (and does not intervene on the political and social stage), so consumers are recognized as enjoying sovereignty (Katona speaks of the 'powerful consumer') so long as they do not attempt to exercise it on the social stage. The People are the workers, provided they are unorganized. The Public and Public Opinion are the consumers, provided they content themselves with consuming" (Baudrillard 1998, 87). Originally in English from George Katona, The Mass Consumption Society (New York: McGraw-Hill, 1964). The translator cannot identify the page of this citation.

ue and the amount is nearly impossible. Food distribution among the Kung!/San Bushmen in the Kalahari are cited by Sahlins as examples of "generalised reciprocity" (Wilk and Cliggett 2009, 163).

In the recent past, the Kung!/San lived in flexible kin groups and practised hunter-gatherer livelihood. Food storage techniques were largely unavailable and mobility required minimal possessions. After a hunt, dividing all the meat among the whole group of kin was the most efficient way to use the food (Wilk and Cliggett 2009, 163).

Baudrillard argues, following Sahlins, that primitive societies are affluent while "industrial and productivist" societies are "dominated by scarcity" (Baudrillard 1998, 67). Primitive nomad tribes of the Kalahari like the Kung!/San do not calculate economically and everything is shared between the members of the group, as there is a "trust in the wealth of natural resources" (Baudrillard 1998, 67). In contrast, consumer society worries about scarcity and insufficiency:

> "Where, in primitive exchange, every relationship adds to the social wealth, in our differential societies every social relationship adds to individual lack, since everything possessed is relativized in relation to others (in primitive exchange, it is valorised by the very relationship with others)" (Baudrillard 1998, 60).

To Baudrillard, poverty does not revolve around the number of goods a group possesses, but it is based upon the character of its human relationship. Primitive hunter-gathers engage in reciprocal human relationships. Here technologies are not monopolized and there is no one-sided accumulation that would restrict free exchange. Their wealth is based on an irreducible symbolic exchange.

Primitive societies are characterized by a "wealth" of the "dialectic of human relations"; modern societies are built upon a sense of unlimited need and a "dialectic of penury" (Baudrillard 1970, 92; 1998, 68). In modern society, differentiation and competition (*concurrence*) is central. The point lies in social relationship (or in the social logic), so poverty will not be addressed by increases in production, technological innovations or more resources. A social relationship (and a social logic) based on symbolic exchange is required, rather than one based on "luxurious and spectacular penury" (Baudrillard 1998, 68).

The notion "luxurious and spectacular penury" is important for my overall question as to whether consumer society is related to Nietzsche's ascetic ideal. The consumption of sign value is namely based on a meaningful, yet unreachable "totality" (Baudrillard 2005, 224). As Baudrillard puts it:

> "The systematic and limitless process of consumption arises from the disappointed demand for totality that underlies the project of life. In their ideality sign-objects are all equivalent and may multiply indefinitely; indeed they *must multiply* in order at every moment to make up for a reality that is absent. Consumption is irrepressible, in the last reckoning, because it is founded on *lack*" (Baudrillard 2005, 224).

Sign value, like the ascetic ideal, always delays satisfaction by referring the process of consumption to another object/sign in the system. Charles Levin also rightly brings attention to the "attenuation of the affective dimension of social life [...] this functional stripping of the object world also erodes the subject's capacity to 'mean'. The semantic dimension no longer emerges from the body because everything in relation to which it might emerge is already a plenitude: a 'construction', a 'production', an 'effect'" (Levin 1996, 179).

According to Ashley Woodward (2008), Baudrillard's analysis of consumer society parallels Nietzsche's analysis of religious nihilism. 'Religious' nihilism in Nietzsche's work has its double origin in Platonic and Christian interpretations of the world. Both the Platonic and Christian interpretations rely on a transcendent source of value which gives life "aim, unity and truth" (Nietzsche 1968, 13),[48] all of which are thought to be missing in the phenomenal world of sensuous becoming (Woodward 2009, 33-4).

---

[48] Friedrich Nietzsche, *The Will to Power*, trans. Walter Kaufmann and R. J. Hollingdale (New York: Vintsage, 1968). [Unpublished in Nietzsche's lifetime]. These are a collection of posthumously published notes containing Nietzsche's views upon nihilism and his theory of the will to power as the foun-

The Christian moral interpretation of the world is nihilistic according to Nietzsche in the sense that the highest values it sets up are beyond and against life. The categories of "aim, unity and truth" negate life itself as it is experienced in the merely apparent world. According to the Christian moral interpretation, this world lacks inherent meaning. It is therefore in need of purpose and redemption. This interpretation involves a devaluation of life and it finds expression in the ascetic's denial of world existence (and the forms of gratification that can be found in life, in the name of the higher ideals).

The consumer system that Baudrillard describes cannot be deemed 'other-worldly', religious or transcendent in relation to the sensuous world of becoming. It must be emphasized that the consumer system "does not unfold in the manner of a Platonic realm of pure, immutable Forms" (Levin 1996, 46-47). Baudrillard does not use the terms "system" or "code" as "rational abstractions" or "universal structures existing independently of material social reality" (Levin 1996, 46-47). The discourse of sign value is one of "unity in variety: the unique, the universal and the uniform all at once" (Levin 1996, 47). The system is part of the universe of particular things or signifiers. "The object and the sign are bound within this self-regulating cultural system" (Levin 1996, 48).

For Baudrillard, with the advent of consumer society, we have reached "the end of transcendence" (Baudrillard 1998, 191). Baudrillard dedicates a separate section to the "End of Transcendence", which is a phrase Baudrillard borrows from Marcuse.[49] The consumer is "immanent in the signs he arranges" (Baudrillard, 1998: 192). According to Baudrillard:

---

dation of life. It must be kept in mind that Nietzsche never saw these notes through the press and the integrity of these notes remains a matter of scholarly dispute.

[49] For more on alienation and the influence of Marcuse on Baudrillard see Douglas Kellner, 'Critical Theory, Commoditise and the Consumer Society,' Theory, Culture and Society, 1, 3 (1983), pp. 66-83, and Douglas Kellner, *Herbert Marcuse and the crisis of Marxism* (London and Berkley: Macmillan and University of California Press, 1984).

> "in the generalised process of consumption, there is no longer any soul, no shadow, no double, and no image in the specular sense. There is no longer any contradiction within being, or any problematic of being and appearance. There is no longer anything but the transmission and reception of signs, and the individual being vanishes in this combinatory and calculus of signs" (Baudrillard 1998, 191).

In consumer society, advertising for instance, "absorbs and regurgitates the seemingly radical forms of the avant-garde: thus a piece of art that attempts to challenge the whole system of aesthetics can be used to advertise some ... haircare product" (Lane 2009, 128). The avant-garde is neutralized as style, fashion or trend in advance which means there is no point in even trying to (artistically) challenge any system (Lane 2009, 128). According to Baudrillard:

> "counter-discourse ...establishes no *real* distance…just as medieval society was balanced on God **and** the Devil, so ours is balanced on consumption **and** its denunciation…Our magic is white…it is the prophylactic whiteness of a saturated society, a society with no history and no dizzying heights, a society with no other myth than itself" (Baudrillard, 1998: 196; italics and bold in the text).

Rather than being a form of "religious nihilism", in my view, Baudrillard's consumer society resonates with Deleuze's (2006, 148) description of reactive nihilism. Reactive nihilism is a rejection of the higher values, for example the denial of God or a religious system. "[With reactive nihilism] essence is denied but appearance is retained: everything is merely appearance" (Deleuze 2006, 148). Deleuze contrasts reactive nihilism with negative nihilism: "[with negative nihilism] essence was opposed to appearance, life was turned into appearance" (Deleuze 2006, 148). With negative nihilism, the 'essence' of human beings, such as the soul or spirit is seen as real, while the appearances or how the world appears into being are regarded as false and dishonored. On the other hand, with reactive nihilism 'the essences' and higher-values are denied, for instance God or the holy spirit in man and there is only appearance or perspective. Meaning in the reactively nihilistic world is a human product of this world, not the product of some super-sensuous being who precedes or transcends humanity (Lane 2009, 128).

For Baudrillard, consumer society is about the play of abstract signs and manipulated appearances (and the destruction of ambivalently charged, symbolic meaning). We are involved in the empty play of advertising signs (play as in chance and play as in the pre-recorded piece of information, music, movies). In the next section, I argue that consumer society is an extension of the ascetic ideal in so far as it offers only a systematically unfulfilling and limitless play of pre-coded signs and pre-fabricated network of appearances.

3.3 Pseudo-Events in Consumer Society

In the previous section 2, the "attenuation of the affective dimension of social life" (Levin 1996, 179) of consumer society was contrasted with the total engagement and intensity of human relations in symbolic society. In *Consumer Society,* Baudrillard refers to "*simulation-models*" and "vast *processes of simulation*" as part of a "*neo-reality*" to avoid using notions of the false and the artificial (Baudrillard 1998, 126; italics in the text). The simulation process has steadily been generalized by the mass media to the extent that people are exposed to simulations which involve the endless recombination of different signs and images of the code.

Like symbolic exchange, Baudrillard's notion of simulation becomes a central concern and the title of a book. In chapters 4 and 5, I will discuss Baudrillard's notion of simulation in detail (Baudrillard 1983; 1994) and relate it to Nietzsche's *Twilight of the Idols* and 'Truth and Lie in the Extra Moral Sense'. For now, let us consider the early manifestations of "simulation" in Baudrillard's book *Consumer Society* (1970; 1998) in light of Baudrillard's notion of symbolic exchange and how it could be related to Nietzsche's ascetic ideal.

Baudrillard's concept of simulation appears in *Consumer Society* largely under the attribute "pseudo" and it refers to the entire societal realm, which includes the media, events and culture. Influenced by Marshall McLuhan (see Genosko, 1999; Huyssen,

1989) and the American sociologist Daniel Boorstin (see Merrin, 2005, 54-56; Zapf, 2010, 118-121), Baudrillard argues that the media are a central mode of social control and integration in consumer society.

Baudrillard (1998: 102) borrows the term "pseudo" from Boorstin's study *The Image: A Guide to Pseudo-Events in America* (first published in 1962) [50] and he uses the term to develop his theory of simulation. Merrin (2005, 54-56) emphasizes the important role Boorstin plays in Baudrillard's early discussion of simulation (Merrin 2005, 54) and he claims that Baudrillard's affinities to Boorstin surpass those with McLuhan. In *Consumer Society*, Baudrillard indeed draws heavily on Boorstin's book *The Image*, and although Boorstin had no structuralist or semiological background, Baudrillard does read him in this way (Baudrillard 1998, 126).

Boorstin's book *The Image* is concerned with the mid- to late-nineteenth century's "Graphic Revolution...and how it has produced new categories of experiences" that "are no longer simply classifiable by the old common-sense tests of true and false" (Boorstin 1992, 211). Fundamental to the processes of the Graphic Revolution are what Boorstin calls (media generated) "pseudo-events" (Boorstin 1992, 7-44) which he sees as experiences of our own contriving. Pseudo-events do not happen in a spontaneous way, and Boorstin, for instance opposes a pseudo-event such as an "interview" to a "train wreck and earthquake" (Boorstin 1992, 11). Pseudo-events are arranged and as such they must conform to the conditions of the reporting. Pseudo-events are "planned, planted or incited...for the immediate purpose of being reported or reproduced" (Boorstin 1992, 11). This definition of pseudo-events also parallels Baudrillard's later definition of simulation in *Symbolic Exchange and Death* as a "...reversal of origin and end, since all

---

[50] McLuhan (1962, 90) claims Boorstin has a "tendency to substitute moral disapproval for insight and to look at the oncoming electronic culture from a fixed point of the receding mechanical culture". Yet in his foreword Boorstin does insist that the book was written from an "affection for America and an amazement at America" (Boorstin 1992, ix).

forms...are conceived according to their very reproducibility" (Baudrillard 1993, 56).

Boorstin discusses advertising as a prototype for "made-news" and how it is responsible for "reshaping our very concept of truth" (Boorstin 1992, 211). An advertisement is designed not only to suggest something has happened but it also conjures up an image to persuade people that something is "good" and "worth buying" (Boorstin 1992, 211). Advertising combines "the pseudo-event with a pseudo-ideal" (Boorstin 1992, 211).

For Boorstin, advertising reduces complex experience to reassuringly intelligible and simplified images (Boorstin 1992, 185-94) which are "more vivid, more attractive and more persuasive than reality itself" (Boorstin 1992, 36). Boorstin argues that our consciousness has become flooded with illusions; for we "are living in an age of tautological experience" (Boorstin 1992, 115). The artificial is preferred over the authentic, the remote over the direct. In addition, Boorstin observes: "[t]oday the master of truth is not the master of facts but the practitioner of the arts of the self-fulfilling prophecy" (Boorstin 1992, 212).

Boorstin's (1992, 181-238) book dedicates a major section to the self-fulfilling prophecy entitled "From Ideal to Image: The Search for Self-Fulfilling Prophecies" which parallels Baudrillard's discussion in *Consumer Society* of how cultural models seem to circulate as "self-fulfilling prophecies" (Baudrillard 1998, 128). Baudrillard regards advertising as "the reign of the pseudo-event *par excellence*. It turns the object into an event. In fact, it constructs it by eliminating its objective characteristics. It constructs it as a model, as a spectacular news item" (Baudrillard 1998, 126).

Baudrillard (1998, 127) does distance himself however from Boorstin's discourse on the 'pseudo', in a world that has gone "beyond the true and the false". Boorstin repeatedly calls for an individual liberation from media "illusions": "each of us must disenchant ourselves (Boorstin 1992, 260) and "disillusion ourselves" (Boorstin 1992, 6).[51] Baudrillard for his part emphasizes the

---

[51] Boorstin's book claims to know what reality is not: Boorstin concedes from the outset "Because I cannot describe 'reality' I know I risk making myself a sit-

power of "persuasive statements which are neither true nor false. For the good reason that there is no longer either any original or any real referential dimension and, like all myths and magic formulas, advertising is based on another kind of *verification*, that of the self-fulfilling prophecy [...]. The consumer, by his purchase, will merely ratify *the coming to pass of the myth*" (Baudrillard 1998, 128; italics in the text). Even if Boorstin and Baudrillard disagree regarding the importance of illusions,[52] both emphasize that a preconceived model takes the place of an original experience or perception. What is significant is not that a certain form of deception occurs but that this deception adheres to certain modular prescriptions, which must be reproduced.

Baudrillard uses "kitsch" in *Consumer Society* as a major example of "pseudo-objects" and it is linked to the development of a mass-production market and a fast-paced mobile society (Baudrillard 1998, 111). Kitsch, as "the equivalent of the 'cliché' in speech", is a "cultural category" and "should not to be confused with any particular *real* objects" (Baudrillard 1998, 110; italics in the text). Kitsch offers objects that have a "superabundance of

---

ting duck for my more profound philosopher-colleagues. But I remain convinced that what dominates American experience today is not reality. If I can only dispel some of the mists, the reader may then better discover his own real perplexity" (Boorstin 1992, x).

[52] Like Nietzsche, Baudrillard does not believe that *truth remains truth when the veil has been lifted*. Baudrillard does not attack the illusion behind advertising. As we shall see in the next chapter on simulation, the problem for Baudrillard is different: "The realising of the world through science and technology is precisely what simulation is – the exorcism of the terror of illusion by the most sophisticated means of the realisation of the world" (Baudrillard 1993 BL, 184). According to some commentators Baudrillard also retains a lingering faith in the 'real' with his concept of symbolic exchange that he raises against simulation (see for instance Merrin 2005, 55). For Rex Butler (1999, 23-25) if there is a real in Baudrillard's work it is not an external one since every system creates its own real (simulation) it is the real as a problem that is central to Baudrillard. I will discuss this further in the next chapter with a discussion of Nietzsche's 'How the 'Real World' Finally became a Fable' in *Twilight of the Idols*. For Nietzsche, science like religion is based on the orderly distinction between real and illusion. 'Enlightened' from superstition, science cannot grasp the 'real' world because the 'real' has become a fable; 'reality' was part of the enchantment.

signs" but lack "real signification" (Baudrillard 1998, 110). They reproduce and repeat: "kitsch is never innovative: it is defined by its derived and weak value" (Baudrillard 1998, 112).

Baudrillard also sees the "gadget" as another example of a pseudo-object (Baudrillard 1998, 111). The gadget is a "technical parody" and is "defined by the way we act with it, which is not utilitarian or symbolic in character but **ludic**" (Baudrillard 1998, 111; 113; bold in the text). The gadget is a useless, impoverished object that "simulates" a function without having any practical referent (Baudrillard 1998, 112). The gadget is part of a broader process (growing number of useless, simulated objects) affecting consumer society as a whole.

Baudrillard characterizes consumer society as being ruled by "pseudo-events" and "pseudo-objects" (Baudrillard 1998, 110) but also by pseudo or simulated relationships. Boorstin and Baudrillard share "the belief that something is lost in the social and technical advance of the contemporary media, and that the latter do not merely transform experience but *kill* it" (Merrin 2005, 55; italics in the text). As Boorstin sees it: "[w]e fill our lives with images of experiences" (Boorstin 1992, 252).

For both Baudrillard and Boorstin, technological advances blur rather than sharpen our vision. In addition, they have severe repercussions on social relations and lived experiences. We already saw above how Baudrillard characterizes advertisers (and journalists) as "mythic operators" (Baudrillard 1998, 127) and how they parallel Nietzsche's figure of the ascetic priest (in chapter 2.3). Advertisers try to establish a "simulated" intimacy with potential customers, as well as between the latter and the products being advertised. Baudrillard sees this as an overall game of human relations, which lacks the reciprocity of primitive symbolic exchange. In consumer society, a (simulation) model of reciprocal human relations is established in the form of bureaucratized solicitation.

As mentioned earlier, in relation to Nietzsche's ascetic priest (chapter 2.3), the solicitude of advertising serves to pacify and constrain consumers within the consumptive cycle (Baudrillard 1998, 94). Communication through the mass media, for instance is "technical, aseptic" and "is no longer achieved through a symbolic medium"; it lacks "real symbolic or didactic processes" (Baudrillard 1998, 104).

Baudrillard's concept of 'pseudo' and 'simulation' are not to be reduced to mass mediated images, there is a reality behind the TV screen but this reality is also 'simulated', for instance the environment (ambiance) of a shopping mall is a pseudo-environment with its "eternal springtime" (Baudrillard 1998, 29). This commercial environment, open seven days a week, becomes a whole community, where there is the total organization of everyday life with fountains, artificial vegetation, shops, swimming pools, clubhouses and housing developments. Nature and real life seem sublimated into endless shopping. These "new means of consumption"[53] are not only important as places within which people consume mythical signs on offer, but also important in their own right as structures that lead people to endless consumption (Baudrillard 1998, 29).

Baudrillard describes a world of obligatory consumption but also obligatory free time. The consumption of time and especially free time is at the heart of consumer society. The cyclical time that characterized primitive society has turned into the time of production, dominated by the motto that "time is money" (Baudrillard 1998, 153). Time is itself an object of consumption, the demand for time being, according to Baudrillard equivalent to the demand for all other goods. Time can be exchanged with other goods within the system of production: it is an exchange value but also a public or private property (the time of work can be bought and sold).

Baudrillard calls such time a "functional mechanism" (Baudrillard 1998, 154). It is not a rhythm at all (a succession of natural moments of a cycle). Time as a functional mechanism is a single systematic process, which is split into working time and leisure time. Free time, as a factor of cultural distinction, is governed by the idea of doing nothing useful. Baudrillard sees this

---

[53] According to Ritzer (1998, 17) Baudrillard was ahead of his time in recognizing the importance of shopping malls as "means of consumption". Baudrillard uses the phrase to mean structures that serve to make consumption possible.

apparent division into working time and leisure time as a "myth", because the "laws of the (production) system do not take holidays" (Baudrillard 1998, 154).

Baudrillard claims "holidays perpetuate the same eager moral and idealistic pursuit of accomplishment as in the sphere of work, the same ethics of pressured performance. No more than consumption, to which it belongs entirely, is leisure a praxis of satisfaction. Or, at least, we may say that it is so only in appearance" (Baudrillard 1998, 156). Holidays are based on the obligation to be happy, on a "fun morality" (Baudrillard 1998, 156). If free time is defined as the "consumption of unproductive time" from the economic point of view, then it too must be interpreted from the point of view of production – free time is in fact the production of value. Free time contains the fundamental demand to consume time or the "freedom to lose one's time and possibly even to 'kill' it, to expend it as pure loss" (Baudrillard 1998, 154).

Here Baudrillard makes reference to the 'potlatch':

> "The *consummation* of empty time is, therefore, a kind of *potlatch*, in which free time serves as a material of signification and sign-exchange (in parallel with all the activities subsidiary and internal to leisure). As in Bataille's *The Accursed Share*, it assumes value in its very destruction, in being sacrificed. And leisure is the site of this "symbolic" operation" (Baudrillard 1998, 158; italics in original).

The power of the gift as shown in section 1, lies in loss, and leisure time as lost time (free time) is therefore a site of a symbolic operation. Yet Baudrillard claims that the goal of the operation today is merely individual. On the other hand, in "the archaic festival, time is never expended 'for oneself': it is the time of collective prodigality" (Baudrillard 1998, 158).

For Baudrillard, in primitive society, there is no time; it is therefore meaningless to ask whether or not one has time. Time here is the rhythm of collective activities, especially the rituals of work and feasting. Time cannot be dissociated from such activities. It cannot be divided, abstracted or manipulated. It cannot be "consumed" because it is neither economically constrained nor "free" as sign function. Time in primitive societies is integral to symbolic exchange. Baudrillard's overall position regarding the rupture from primitive to modern society is that the fundamental characteristic of the latter is the loss of spontaneous, reciprocal and symbolic human relations.

So far, we discussed the important role of pseudo-objects, pseudo- events and simulated experiences and relations in consumer society. We already set the scene for the next chapters 4 and 5 dealing with simulacra and simulation by discussing the dynamics involved in the production of truth in consumer society. Chapter 1.3 concluded with the central role of fiction and dramatization in Baudrillard's work and how this is a central link to Nietzsche's *On the Genealogy of Morals* and the construction of fictional narratives.

In what follows, I will shortly discuss Baudrillard's use of Georges Perec's[54] novel *Les choses: une histoire des années soixante (Things: A Story of the Sixties)*.[55] The novel serves to bring attention to how consumer society is an extension and encapsulation of Nietzsche's ascetic ideal. Baudrillard gives his discussion of the novel an important place – the 'final word' is given to Perec's novel in his book *The System of Objects*.

Baudrillard concludes his book by claiming that he wishes to use the novel to "get a sense of how a system of sign-objects […] functions" (Baudrillard 2005, 221). Baudrillard discusses Perec's work in terms of the semiotics of consumer culture and he regards Perec's characters as representatives for an entire consumer sys-

---

[54] Georges Perec was born in Paris in 1936, the son of Jewish immigrants from Poland: his father died in 1940, fighting in the French Army, his mother in 1943, after being deported. There was enough of family money for him to complete his secondary education at a boarding school, thirty miles south of Paris, and for him to go on to the Sorbonne, where he spent two years studying history and sociology, but did not take a degree. Georges Perec's career as a writer began in 1965: when he received the *Prix Renaudot* for *Les Choses*. Perceived as a critique of consumer society, the book was raised to a whole new level, a few years later, in May 1968.

[55] Georges Perec, *Les choses* (Paris; Rene Juillard, 1965); trans. David Bellos as *Things* (Boston: Godine, 1990).

tem.[56] Perec's novel anticipates Baudrillard's analysis of the hegemony of consumerism (to be fully developed in his next book *Consumer Society*) and how its parasitic code takes over that of all other discourses (Petruso 1985, 55).

Perec's book *Les choses* is a meticulous and austere "descriptive critique"[57] of how "things" take over the lives of a young Parisian couple, Jérôme and Sylvie. Jérôme and Sylvie find themselves, as Baudrillard would say, in a "a world of *generalized hysteria*" (Baudrillard 1998, 77; italics in the text). Trying to understand the world of needs will lead into the trap of trying to "cure" the symptom only to find another one appearing somewhere else.[58] The couple is caught up in a succession of objects of desire, all of which remain undifferentiated – objects only have sign value which point to a lack (i.e., for the reader; for the character, the sign functions as a defensive mask).

Jérôme and Sylvie try to find satisfaction but the pursuit of mere signs can never eliminate the emptiness of their lives, of

---

[56] In the *Nouvel Observateur* (16 December 1965) Perec remarks: "A whole field of American and French sociology has begun to discuss the problems of solitary man in a world of production...but that has never previously been a literary theme. So far, there has not been a novel, or a story, which presents people living at the heart of that society, subject to the pressures of the market economy. That is the essence of my book" (quoted in: Schwarz 1988, 6).

[57] Georges Perec warns his reader: "People who think I have denounced consumer society have understood nothing of my book" (Georges Perec, "Georges Perec Owns Up: An Interview with Marcel Benabou and Bruno Marcenac," (*The Review of Contemporary Fiction* 13.1, (Spring 1993): 17

[58] "Objects and needs are here substitutable, within reason, like the symptoms of hysterical or psychosomatic conversion. They obey the same logic of slippage, transference, limitless and arbitrary convertibility. When an illness is *organic*, there is a necessary relation between the symptom and the organ (similarly, when taken as an appliance or tool, there is a necessary relation between the object and its function). In hysterical or psychosomatic conversion, the symptom is, like the sign, (relatively) arbitrary: there is a chain of somatic signifiers – migraine, bowel disorder, lumbago, throat infection, general fatigue – along which the symptom 'wanders', just as there is a long sequence of signs/objects or symbols/objects over which wanders not needs (which are always linked to the rational finality of the object), but desire and a further determination which is that of the unconscious social logic" (Baudrillard 1998, 77).

which their relationship to objects is symptomatic. In this world, there is a hierarchy of signification, but things and events become homogenized; difference can only be quantitative. In the couple's worldview everything is put on equal footing and measured.[59] All objects are unfulfilling since the object is not really the target of their desire; the couple simply seeks to be 'other' than they are. This wanting- to-be- other however is characterized by a frenetic impatience that takes little account of the actual historical situation or the necessary steps which would be required to realize desire. Perec's characters are unable to both possess the object of their desire and to desire the object of their possession.

Jérôme and Sylvie's fascination for objects and the language used to describe them, drives the plot of the book forward but it also reduces Jérôme and Sylvie to a *status quo* and inertia. In Chapter IX, after four pages of scenario planning to attain instant wealth, the couple ends up doing nothing; they do not even purchase a lottery ticket (Perec 1990, 86).

Perec gives his characters no psychology and no existence as such. No personal details are provided and there is no exchange of dialogue in the novel. Jérôme and Sylvie are not given any sexual being whatsoever, they remain indistinguishable (except by name) as to gender. They are therefore also examples of Baudrillard's idea (developed later in *Seduction*) that in the modern world there is no sex, only its parody, seduction, which leads to nothing. What Baudrillard (1990 S: 35) says of pornography in *Seduction* applies to consumer society: "Pornography says: there must be good sex somewhere, for I am its caricature. In its obscenity, it attempts to save sex's truth and provide the faltering sexual model with some credibility". Jérôme and Sylvie are caricatures of the consumption model: they have no identity outside the system of objects and its code (Petruso 1985, 48).

According to Baudrillard:

---

[59] Jérôme and Sylvie criticize the weekly magazine-digest *L'Express* yet read it fanatically, because it "offered them all the signs of well-being". The magazine offers 'digest' and a mix of in-depth analysis, portraits, gossip, fashion, recipes all rolled into one.

> "Jérôme and Sylvie do not exist as a couple: their sole reality is as 'Jérôme - and-Sylvie' – as a pure complicity surfacing within the system of objects that signifies it. Nor can it be said that objects are an automatic substitute for the relationship that is lacking, that they serve to fill a void: on the contrary they describe this void, the locus of the relationship, pursuant to a process which is a way of not living the relationship while at the same time (save in the cases of complete regression) exposing it to the light of the possibility of its being lived. Thus, the relationship is ...articulated with those objects as with so many solid points in a chain of signifiers – except that here the signifying configuration of objects is usually impoverished, schematic and closed, and deals only with the idea of relationship that is signified in these objects, that is 'consumed' in them and hence abolished as anything to be directly experienced (Baudrillard 2005, 221; italics in the original).

The object system reduces Jérôme and Sylvie to abstract partners in consumption. Jérôme and Sylvie can be regarded as a peculiar doubling of an individual desire. They "purchase one another ... on the basis of a community of desire" (Petruso 1985, 53). As a 'unit' their desire is all-consuming and self-defeating.

In his implicitly sociological book, Perec seeks to recreate the flat reality of consumer society by means of an objective phenomenological description of things and of the external behavior of people. The reader voyeuristically follows "not actions but the projected worlds imagined by the milieu" (Oniki 1995, 116). Perec communicates the overall 1960s ambience and this young middle-class couple's immersion in "things". The accumulation of things is on a purely quantitative level since the valorized objects and the characters only rarely come into contact. The novel could be regarded as a consumer-culture *Bildungsroman*, even though there is little development or "sentimental education" that takes place for these characters.[60]

Yuji Oniki (1995, 116) in his article "Perec, Marx and *Les Choses*" points out that Perec published his story on the sixties when the decade had not even been completed (the book ap-

---

[60] According to Petruso (1985, 47) "just as Flaubert called his *L'Education sentimentale* a "roman des moeurs moderne" and "l'histoire morale d'une génération" these descriptions apply equally to what Perec has subtitled "Histoire des années soixante". For more on the relation between Flaubert and Perec see Petruso (1985)

peared in 1965). Perec's use of the conditional tense and his avoidance of the present tense could perhaps be a condition for his evocation of the sixties as a decade that has not happened yet, a decade full of delayed meanings, aspirations and projects whether they be against or a part of consumer culture.[61]

I have taken the liberty of discussing Perec's novel in detail, as I think it plays a significant role in Baudrillard's concern regarding the impoverished state of human relations in consumer society. Baudrillard's discussion of the novel also supports my claim (chapter 1) that Baudrillard, like Nietzsche mobilizes the power of fiction to undermine a morality that people share and find binding. Genealogy, as practised by Baudrillard, in the footsteps of Nietzsche makes use of fiction and a drastic style of presentation to help readers see themselves in a different way.

Conclusion

In this chapter, I investigated the extent to which the ascetic ideal as outlined by Nietzsche persists in Baudrillard's consumer society. We can conclude that consumer society offers an "impoverished life", but not in the sense that consumers suffer from a restriction in the quantity of available objects or signs. For Nietzsche, the ascetic ideal is an invention projected onto the world in order to give it value, but it places the source of value outside the

---

[61] Baudrillard quotes extensively from the novel, notably the first opening paragraph, that begins with: "L'oeil, d'abord, glisserait sur la moquette grise d'un long corridor, haut et étroit". The first substantive 'eye' establishes a distance, an impersonality, which continues throughout the novel; the third word 'would slip' is in in the conditional tense to show how objects belong to a nonmaterial, atemporal world. It is also unclear where exactly one is to place this introduction within the rest of the diagetic space of *Les choses*. In this sense, we do not know when this story of the sixties begins. It is unclear whether this is a real or an imaginary beginning, in the future or the past, or both. The apartment described at the beginning of the novel "remains a conjecture, an anticipation of a future happy life that offers the possibility of turning into the present, while escaping it at the same time. The conditional tense allows objects to be constantly renewable and utterly banal, a repetitive loop of things never taking place" (Oniki 1995, 102).

immediate physical world and displaces it to a transcendent realm.

In consumer society, we have reached "the end of transcendence" (Baudrillard 1998, 193), but this does not make meaning any more accessible or less abstract. The consumption of sign-value is based on a "disappointed demand for totality… Consumption is irrepressible, in the last reckoning, because it is founded on *lack*" (Baudrillard 2005, 224). Consumption is a sign-system based on a strategy of endlessly deferred value. What people desire in consumption is not a particular object but a sign that signifies social meaning.

In consumer society, collective rituals with the object are transformed by the sign-object into an overall idea of a social relation (e.g., status, power, prestige) which is consumed merely privately as 'sign-value'. To Baudrillard, poverty is a matter of the quality of the human relationship within a group. We have seen how Baudrillard contrasts the systematic penury of social relations in consumer society with so-called primitive society to make his point. In the case of primitive hunter-gathers, there are rich and rewarding reciprocal human relationships.

In the chapter, I discussed how Charles Levin brings attention to an "attenuation of the affective dimension of social life" in consumer society and how Ashley Woodward links consumer society to Nietzschean "religious nihilism" (Woodward, 2008). Yet the limits of the term "religious nihilism" must be borne in mind, and I propose Deleuze's Nietzschean inspired "reactive nihilism", which refers to the rejection of higher, transcendent values in favor of only a coded network of appearances. Consumer society revolves around the empty play of advertising signs and offers a limitless play of pre-coded signs and pre-fabricated network of abstract signs.

To understand the full significance of this culmination of the ascetic ideal into a limitless play of pre-coded signs and appearances, in the next chapter, I start by looking at how Nietzsche subjects the history of truth formation to genealogical scrutiny and how he overturns the belief that truths are fixed or that they represent an unchanging reality (as supra-sensuous Platonic Forms).

As we shall see below, Deleuze (2004, 291) claims that Nietzsche's philosophical mission is to "reverse Platonism" and I will explore Deleuze's contention that living after Nietzsche means living in a world where simulacra[62] have at last prevailed over immutable Platonic Forms and Ideas. I will bring Deleuze's reading of the simulacrum together with Baudrillard's view of simulation.

For Baudrillard and Deleuze, simulation is creation, not deception in relation to reality or to truth. They both accentuate the new non-mimetic mode of simulation as well as the self referentiality of simulacrum (the undecidability between simulacra and reality). Despite their similarities on the simulacrum, Baudrillard and Deleuze develop unique styles of reading that give rise to different philosophical consequences and considerations, as the next chapter will show.

---

[62] The noun "simulacrum" (simulacra is the plural form) refers to a concrete object, whereas "simulation" refers to a process, an action, a relation. A simulacrum (which has undergone the process of simulation) from the Latin, means "image", "semblance" or "likeness". The Oxford English Dictionary emphasizes the material nature of the simulacrum, the image as thing, as produced and constructed.

4. The Reversal of Platonism

Introduction

In chapter 1, I showed how Nietzsche and Baudrillard scrutinize the differential relations that are responsible for the creation of values.

In chapter 2, I brought Baudrillard's figure of the advertiser together with Nietzsche's figure of the ascetic priest. The ascetic ideal is propagated by the priest and it is an invention projected onto the world to give it a super-sensuous, transcendent meaning.

In chapter 3, I discussed the extent to which consumption, as it is outlined by Baudrillard, rests on the same basis as the ascetic ideal. In consumer society, the source of value and meaning remains endlessly deferred. I introduced Baudrillard's concept of simulation by showing how consumer society is run by pseudo-objects and pseudo-events. Baudrillard discusses how cultural models seem to circulate as "self-fulfilling prophecies" (Baudrillard 1998, 128). No distinction between fact and fiction is possible because consumer society no longer produces an external, transcendent myth, "it is itself its own myth" (Baudrillard 1998, 193). Consumer society is a self-legitimizing system that sets the standards for its own evaluation.

Baudrillard is concerned with a constructed conceptual system that results in a world where the real ("defined in ego-psychological terms as something that is external and beyond personal control"[63]) is not represented (which requires a distance between fact and fiction, copy and model) but rather 'simulated'. The simulation process has steadily been enhanced and generalized by the mass media to the extent that people are exposed to simulations involving the constant recombination of various signs, of elements of the code.

In his book *Simulacra and Simulation*, which will be dealt with in section 3 of this chapter, Baudrillard accentuates the non-

---

[63] Levin 1996, 200

mimetic mode of simulation and refers to simulation as the "divine irreference of images" (Baudrillard 1994, 3). Images and signs are their own models; they precede reality due to the "precession of simulacra".[64] The logical and temporal relation between the image and the real has been reversed. For Baudrillard, 'the precession of simulation', means that social and geopolitical events repeat themselves in an endless cycle. Before examining Baudrillard's notions of simulation and simulacra, this chapter will first look at their connections to Nietzsche's reversal of Platonism and Deleuze's simulacrum.

The subtitle of Nietzsche's *Twilight of the Idols* is "How to Philosophize with a Hammer" and the first target of Nietzsche's hammer is Plato's belief in super-sensuous Forms. For Deleuze, Nietzsche inaugurates a philosophy of the future for an era of simulacra.[65] Deleuze publishes (starting from the 1960s) essays on the simulacrum and, although Deleuze's analysis of the simulacrum proceeds in less historical fashion than Baudrillard (Section 2), Deleuze is close to Baudrillard in the sense that they both stress the inseparability of appearance and reality in simulacra.

In this chapter, I show how Baudrillard and Deleuze analyze simulacra in the spirit of Nietzsche's demand, as a cultural physician, to "philosophize with a hammer" in order to "sound out" all the hollow "idols" (such as Plato's super-sensuous Forms) through a process of "auscult(ur)ation".[66] Conflating the musical and the medical, Nietzsche emphasizes that it is *"eternal* idols,

---

[64] The word 'precession' stems from the Latin verb praecedere, meaning to 'happen before'. A precession of simulacra is not a procession of simulacra, because that would reduce simulacra to an order of time as movement, a sequential or linear notion of time. A procession is an orderly process, but in simulation, time does not flow in an orderly manner. For Baudrillard, time does not flow from past to future, so simulacra form a precession that undoes a linear sequence. Baudrillard also theorises the 'precession of consumption' (as we saw in chapter 2 which is the essential for his later theory of simulation).

[65] Simulacrum is the Latin term for "statue" or "idol," and translates the Greek phantasma. The plural form is simulacra.

[66] Duncan Large, 'Introduction,' *Twilight of the Idols*, Friedrich Nietzsche, trans. Duncan Large (New York: Oxford University Press, 1998).

…[that] will be touched here with a hammer as with a tuning fork" (Nietzsche 2005, 155).

What Nietzsche considers as 'idols' are those unexamined prejudices that claim to be truths and are worshiped as such. Nietzsche's method involves enfeebling the highest values and pushing them off their pedestals, reversing established hierarchies as preparation for their revaluation.

I start this chapter with an outline of Nietzsche's "reversal of Platonism." In "On Truth and Lying in the Non-Moral Sense," Nietzsche regards the "pure drive towards truth" as an "effect" of deception and he exposes the production of truth as an illusionary process (Nietzsche 1999, 143), I then move to Deleuze's view of Nietzsche's reversal of Platonism (section 2) and Deleuze's affirmation of the simulacrum's disruptive power. For Deleuze, the simulacrum produces an "effect of resemblance" that simulates the real (Deleuze 2004, 295). Similarly, Baudrillard's work sketches the rise of the "hyperreal," which itself produces "effects of the real" in an "empty space of representation" (Baudrillard 1993, 70).

Unlike Deleuze, Baudrillard is much more ambivalent about the simulacrum. But before examining Baudrillard's problematization of simulation[67] and simulacra, I first set the scene with an outline of Nietzsche's challenge to Platonism.

4.1 The Reversal of Platonism

Nietzsche argues that Western epistemology has attempted to create a timeless foundation to guarantee knowledge and truth. The Judeo-Christian tradition and Platonic thought share a similar conception of "this world" (of appearances and images) as reflections of a higher and immutable reality. In what follows, I discuss the relation between the true and apparent within the framework of Nietzsche's "reversal of Platonism" and in Section 3, I move to Deleuze's view of the simulacrum in the wake of Nietzsche's re-

---

[67] Simulation refers to a process, an action, a relation, whereas the noun "simulacrum" (simulacra is the plural form) refers to a concrete object, which has undergone this process.

versal and, in section 4, I look at Baudrillard's genealogy of the orders of images and of simulacra.

The mission of Nietzsche's philosophy, according to Heidegger, is to overthrow Platonism: "the farther removed from true being, the purer, the finer, the better it is. Living in semblance as goal" (Heidegger 1991, 154). For Nietzsche, Plato's Socrates devalues the mutable realm of appearances in favour of an immutable realm of Forms.[68] The world of pure Forms is a phantasmagoria of an "another," a "better" life. In *Twilight of the Idols*, Nietzsche sees the task of philosophy as a "revaluation of values," which entails a dismissal of the realm of Forms as a chimera (Nietzsche 2005, 155). Does Nietzsche merely elevate what Platonism denigrates (i.e., appearances, becoming)?

Nietzsche's reversal of Platonism has been a central issue of debate in the treatment of his work and Heidegger argues that to reverse Plato's thinking without re-evaluating its overall structure is to fail to overcome it in a radical way. Given Nietzsche's rejection of Plato's true world of Forms, Heidegger claims that the reversal must not simply affirm the world of appearances if it seeks to avoid repeating the structural missteps of Platonic thought. The realms of both essence and appearance must be abolished in the manner in which they are seen within Platonic thought, along with the hierarchical structure "above and below" (Heidegger 1991, 201). A "reversal" must involve the destruction of both the world of essence and the world of appearance.[69]

According to Heidegger, the language of opposed realms of being is metaphorical. Socrates's discourse on the Forms in Plato's *Republic* implies the existence of a *single* realm that reveals and shows itself in two ways. The distinction between two "modes of

---

[68] It must be noted that "forms" are introduced in Plato's Republic without a formal argument for their existence.

[69] Heidegger critiques Nietzsche for being a metaphysician who only "inverted" the Platonic opposition between Being and Becoming by making Becoming, in the form of the endless flow of power, primary. Nietzsche awards Becoming the character of Being — that is the supreme will to power. I seek to show how Nietzsche overcomes the binary opposition in his attack of the Platonic tradition.

showing," John Sallis maintains, "is more fundamental than the distinction between the intelligible and the visible" (Sallis 1996, 385). The philosopher does not have access to a separate ontological realm, but rather penetrates the surface of a single realm of being and understands things as they are. For Heidegger, Nietzsche "completes" the history of metaphysics through the inversion of Platonism.[70]

Alan D. Schrift (1995, 22) rightly points out that Heidegger fails to acknowledge the extent to which Nietzsche breaks down privileged hierarchical relations. Nietzsche also reveals that the hierarchical opposition originates from the assignation of prior value that must be problematized. Concerning the genealogy of the "will to truth" for instance, Nietzsche first inverts the Platonic order of truth over falsity; secondly, he delves into the origin of the positive value placed upon truth and he finds it "simply a moral prejudice to affirm truth over error or appearances" (ibid., 22).

Nietzsche targets the unquestioning value of truth, the ascetic impulse to eradicate insecurity to a supposed truth, in whatever form a supposition may take, even an anti-metaphysical one (science) (Nietzsche 2007, 112). Truth for Nietzsche is dependent on our interest in truth. In the Third Essay paragraph 24 of *On the*

---

[70] The peculiarities of Nietzsche's "inversion" of Platonism is the focus of the concluding chapters of Heidegger's first lecture series on Nietzsche, Nietzsche. Volume One. The Will to Power as Art. Alan D. Schrift (1990, 44-45) says that "Nietzsche's inversion of the Platonist hierarchy is made on historical rather than theoretical grounds. That is to say, Nietzsche's inversion of the Platonist standards is grounded in history and the fundamental historical event of nihilism, that is, in the event of the highest values devaluing themselves. Nietzsche's overturning of Platonism is thus the result of his inquiry into the history of philosophy as the history of the devaluation of the highest values (nihilism) [...] Nietzsche's inversion of Platonism must be understood in terms of the overcoming of nihilism: the Platonist affirmation of the super-sensuous has, as a matter of historical fact, given rise to our present nihilistic situation and, if nihilism is to be overcome, we must, therefore, overcome the affirmation of the super-sensuous as the standard of the true." Alan D. Schrift, *Nietzsche and the Question of Interpretation. Between Hermeneutics and Deconstruction* (London: Routledge, 1990). As we shall see in Section 4, Baudrillard's phase of "simulation" and "hyperreality" brings Nietzsche's analysis of nihilism up to date.

Genealogy of Morals, Nietzsche says that the idea of *"presuppositionless* knowledge" is "unthinkable" (ibid., 112). A certain amount of "faith" is the precondition for any knowledge (ibid., 112.). Without a certain "faith," knowledge lacks "a direction, a meaning, a limit, a method, a *right* to exist" (ibid., 112.). Knowledge cannot be free of such (perspectival) limits. Nietzsche concludes the Third Essay of *On the Genealogy of Morals* by saying that science is not the obvious opponent of the (Christian) "ascetic ideal," because regarding the access to "truth," it also rejects unstable forces (Hatab 2008, 114). The "ascetic ideal" is transcendent: like truth, it is something that does not bear the features of the sensuous world. A genuine alternative to the ascetic ideal "tentatively" puts the value of (super-sensuous) truth "into question" (Nietzsche 2007, 112).

Nietzsche's early work "On Truth and Lying in a Non-Moral Sense" shows how he overcomes the dualistic and hierarchical order between illusion and reality by exposing the production of truth as an illusionary process. In this text, Nietzsche claims that "truths are illusions which we have forgotten are illusions" and that truth is nothing more than a "mobile army of metaphors" (Nietzsche 1999, 146). Nietzsche begins this important text by focusing on the human intellect's powers of deception and how this quality is crucial for human development. Deception (*Verstellung*) is the "means to preserve those weaker, less robust individuals, who, by nature, are denied horns or the sharp fangs of prey with which to wage the struggle for existence" (ibid., 142).

Humans overcome their physical weaknesses by devising subtle, deceptive intellectual strategies. We also find this idea in Nietzsche's story of the "slaves" in *On the Genealogy of Morals*. The slaves transform their physical weakness into strength through conceptual inventions such as the "free will" and "the subject." In addition, for Nietzsche, "the priestly caste" devises "the ascetic ideal" as precisely a compensatory strategy for their physical weakness. As Nietzsche puts it in the Third Essay paragraph 13: "the ascetic ideal is a trick for the preservation of life" (Nietzsche 2007, 88).

Returning to his earlier text "On Truth and Lying in the Non-Moral Sense," Nietzsche explains that a common feature of these "tricks" is that they are lies that the intellect produces to preserve itself by playing on the "surface of things" and producing favourable appearances (Nietzsche 1999, 142). Nietzsche regards such an "art of dissimulation" as necessary for the maintenance and development of human society (ibid., 143). Deception ranges from self-deception, deception of others to deception about the nature of the world. For Nietzsche, we misunderstand the intellect if we ignore that it is an organ of the will, and that man does not exist in order to know.

The question remains: where did the desire for truth come from? Nietzsche here points to the State because "man out of need and boredom wants to live socially and herdlike, he requires peace and strives to eliminate from his world at least the crudest *bellum omnium contra omnes*" (ibid., 143). Peace entails something that looks like a step toward understanding the urge for truth. Nietzsche identifies a transition from concealment towards a general "peace treaty" that establishes a common set of rules to avoid the "*bellum omnium contra omnes*" (Hobbes' expression for "a war of all against all" to describe the state of nature) (ibid., 143). The idea of universal truth was devised to enforce peace treaties, because the value of truth must be accepted by all.

This new concept of universal truth is an effect of the "legislation of language" (*Gesetzgebung der Sprache*), which creates a universal way of designating things that has "the same validity and force everywhere" (ibid., 143). The legislation of language gives order to the chaotic world. The boundaries between truth and lie are the rules by means of which a community structures and maintains a sense of itself. For Nietzsche, any concept is formed by reducing particularity in favour of a predicable world.

In addition, Nietzsche claims that it is only through "forgetfulness" that we come to imagine the possibility of truth as a perfect fit with things-in-themselves (ibid., 148). We forget that the relation between our words and concepts, on the one hand, and things themselves, on the other, is purely a metaphorical relationship. Metaphors are not inferior expressions of a superior pre-linguistic reality. Instead, they produce a reality-effect that we call the "world," which is then reviewed in terms of ideal truth and value.

Words are copies in images and sounds of "nervous stimulations" of the body and brain (ibid., 144). A metaphor is a translation from one realm to another; and Nietzsche will speak, in this context, of the differences between languages or the peculiarities of a particular language (ibid., 144). The arbitrary relation between words and things is obvious from the fact that different languages use different words to attribute various properties to the same objects.

Nietzsche reviews the relationship between metaphor and truth by regarding the "pure drive towards truth" as an effect of deception (ibid., 143). He challenges the idea that:

- truth is something good and error something evil;
- truth represents a world of eternal facts, and error, a world of becoming;
- truth is the opposite of error.

In this skepticism, 'error' becomes the metaphor for a world without vertical antitheses and distinctions between good and evil, being and becoming, beauty and ugly. Nietzsche's essay "On Truth and Lying in a Non-Moral Sense" provides an account of the origin and meaning of language in the style of a fable that is still reflected in his mature views on language. For instance, in a later text, "Reason in Philosophy," from *The Twilight of the Idols*, Nietzsche outlines the emergence of conceptual representation (Nietzsche 2005, 167). Reason requires that the real be other than what the senses bring forth, and reason demands that this other (Being/permanence) be grasped with a concept. Thus, the (merely) apparent world of sense experience, which reveals only becoming, is opposed to the real world (Being). "Being" is divided into true and untrue. Plato's philosophy for Nietzsche revolves around this hierarchically-based difference between true and apparent world.

The section on "Reason in Philosophy" is followed by "How the 'True World' Finally Became a Fable," which provides a brief account of a "history of an error." In six aphorisms, Nietzsche traces the trajectory of the "true" world, which was at first within grasp of thinkers, then promised to the faithful and then mobilized by the positivists; it then becomes unattainable, unknown, and finally useless. The "true" world is an idea that is no longer good for anything, not even obligating. The only thing worse than the "true" world and an all-encompassing regime of judgment (Platonic, Christian, Kantian, etc.), however, is finally not to have faith in any world.

The end of the longest error is the end of both truth and illusion — which is the "properly Nietzschean moment", as it represents the point of departure for interrogating the status of fiction (Lacoue-Labarthe 1993, 5). Neither reality nor appearance triumph, because both share the same realm, the midday of philosophy eliminates any such distinctions in an immanence with no more shadows — in Deleuze's words, the "terrifying models of the pseudos in which the powers of the false unfold" (Deleuze 1994, 128).

For Deleuze, modern philosophy must establish itself by reversing Platonism, as Nietzsche did in *Twilight of the Idols*. In his reading of Nietzsche's reversal, which will be discussed below, Deleuze champions a radical reign of simulacra, because the latter undermine the distinction between models and copies and the very foundations of Platonic thought. In the next section, I show how Deleuze seeks primarily to understand Plato's "motivations"[71] for banishing the simulacrum (the false pretenders) to the Idea. This search for the "motivations" overcomes the alleged "abstractness" of Nietzsche's reversal (Deleuze 2004, 291). I then discuss Baudrillard's simulacrum in Section 4.

---

[71] Individual signs are unmotivated, so a linguist must try to reconstruct the system. It is the system alone which motivates individual signs.

4.2 The Simulacrum and the Motivation for Plato's Method of Division

In the previous section, we saw how Nietzsche exposes the supposed truth behind language as a fiction. Concepts that supposedly refer to truth and reality are merely solidified metaphors that seek to provide categories for understanding. Nietzsche thereby sets the scene, as we shall see below, for Deleuze and Baudrillard's world of simulacra.

It is important to bear in mind that the simulacrum has long been implicated in the ancient theory of imitation (*mimesis*) and that it has also been part of the controversy concerning the legitimacy of images. Historically, simulacra have been regarded as equivalent to images, although in most cases their illusionary aspect is emphasized. The deceptive aspects of simulacra spring from their associations with the spheres of death and ghostly appearances.

The monotheistic prohibition against images that was philosophically supported by Plato's sharp critique of the image as "far removed from the truth" in Book X of *The Republic* would lead to the bloody wars during the Middle Ages and the Reformation. The Western world's rejection of the image took another turn in the 19th century with the arrival of Romanticism and Nietzsche. Nietzsche's philosophy, as we have seen, does not however merely champion illusion against Plato's critique of appearance, because for him the production of truth is an illusionary process.

The aesthetics of appearance makes its way to France thanks to the surrealist interest in the irrational, the unconscious, dreams, and phantasies.[72] The simulacrum (singular) is in this sense related to the Greek *phantasma*, which the ancient theories of perception used synonymously with simulacrum or *eidolon*. As a product of *phantasia* or the imagination, *phantasmata* are associated with

---

[72] The surrealist poet and ethnologist Michel Leiris published in 1925 a range of poems entitled *Simulacra*; André Breton the programmatic mastermind of surrealism (along with Paul Éluard) published *Essais de simulation* in 1930.

illusions and appearance, although to a lesser extent than with simulation.

The terms simulacrum and simulation become important within French theoretical discourse thanks to the Argentine poet Jorge Luis Borges as well as the artist and writer Pierre Klossowski who, in turn, influenced Deleuze and Lyotard. Roland Barthes regards the production of simulacra, that is to say the making of models, as the epistemological method of structuralism. Starting from the 1960s, Deleuze publishes essays on the simulacrum in Plato and Lucretius, which define a position close to Baudrillard's notion of simulation (Section 4). In Nietzsche's footsteps, both Deleuze and Baudrillard stress the inseparability of appearances and truth in simulacra.

Deleuze's reflections on the simulacrum are contained mostly in two texts: *Difference and Repetition* and the essay in his appendix to *The Logic of Sense*, namely "The Simulacrum and Ancient Philosophy." In what follows, I will focus on the latter text. For Deleuze, Plato's world of Forms is a Nietzschean idol, a myth constructed to legitimise Plato's ambition for philosophy as a path to truth. As Daniel Smith remarks, "[i]n the Platonic dialogues, according to Deleuze, myth functions as a narrative of foundation" (Smith 2006, 95). It is myth that makes the categorization of differences possible. Deleuze says the "myth constructs an immanent model or the foundation-test according to which pretenders should be judged and their pretensions measured" (Deleuze 2004, 293). Any truth-claim relies on myth and the production of truth is thus revealed as an illusionary process.

Smith explains that Plato created "the Idea of something pure, a pure quality. The Idea, as foundation, then allows its possession to be shared, giving it to the claimant (the secondhand possessor), on condition that the claimant pass the 'foundation' test" (Smith 2006, 96). Only the foundation itself, the Idea possesses something firsthand, for instance only Truth is true and only Justice just. The Idea "is what objectively possesses a pure quality, or what is nothing other than what it is" (Deleuze and Guattari 1994, 29-30).

The claimant adheres to the object of the claim only in so far as it is "modelled internally on the Idea, which comprehends the relations and proportions that constitute the essence" (Smith 2006, 97). It is on this condition that the claimant can rightfully participate in the Idea. Smith claims that the "Platonic conception of 'participation' (*metechein*, lit. "to have after") must be understood in terms of the role of this foundation: an elective participation is the response to the problem of a method of selection" (ibid., 96).

The Platonic meaning of representation is clear: all well-founded pretensions are re-presentations of the Idea. Even the ultimate "well-founded pretension" is subordinated to the founding Idea. The Idea is appealed to only as a basis of what is not "representable" in things themselves (Deleuze 2004, 296). Plato's tripartite structure, according to Deleuze, involves the ground (the unattainable Idea that provides the foundation for participation), the quality of the ground (the object for the test of foundation) and the claimants to the ground (those who participate unequally in the object). Platonic division establishes a hierarchy among the most faithful copies of the original Idea, but it also includes images that are only illusions of the founding model (simulacra). The real Platonic division lies not in the distinction between original and image, but rather lies between two types of images (*idoles*); good copies (*icônes*) that faithfully follow the principle of internal resemblance, and bad copies or simulacra (*phantasma*) that are false pretenders to the Idea.

Platonism seeks to banish the simulacrum to the "bottom of the Ocean," because its presence causes us to question the structure of intelligible model and sensible copy (ibid., 293-6). It even threatens to break down all foundations. The simulacrum thus indicates the way towards reversing Platonism. For Deleuze, Plato thus himself perceived the threat of the "simulacrum." In the *Sophist*, Plato distinguishes between two types of imitation: likenesses or similitudes (Greek: *eikon*) and semblances or simulacra (Greek: *phantasmata*). Plato proposes (in the voice of the Stranger) that the "perfect example" of a likeness "consists in creating a copy [of a statue] that conforms to the proportions of the original in all three dimensions and giving moreover the proper colour to every part" (Plato 1961, 235d-e).

On the other hand, simulacra are improper and manipulative imitations. Plato's example is of "colossal" works such as sculptures at the top of temples, the upper parts of which were out of proportion and exaggerated. In such works, the imitation "only appears to be a likeness of a well-made figure because it is not seen from a satisfactory point of view, but to a spectator with eyes that could fully take in so large an object [it] would not be even like the original it professes to resemble" (Plato 1961, 979). Simulacra fail to have the structural similarity that likenesses are said to have. As Deleuze explains, "simulacra are like false pretenders, built upon a dissimilarity, implying an essential perversion or deviation" (Deleuze 2004, 294). According to Deleuze (2004, 296), Plato is disturbed by the "non-productive" nature of the simulacrum as it

> "implies huge dimensions, depths and distances that the observer cannot master. It is precisely because he cannot master them that he experiences an impression of resemblance. This simulacrum includes a differential point of view; and the observer becomes part of the simulacrum itself, which is transformed and deformed by his point of view."

The simulacrum is built on an internal difference and is dissimilar to what it represents, but it still produces an "effect of resemblance" (Deleuze 2004, 295). This focus on "effects" underlines the future oriented, mutable aspect of the simulacrum. Identity and resemblance continue only as external effects of the internal differential dynamic of the simulacrum.

Plato rejects the simulacrum because it causes us to question the very notion of the model and the copy, and turns us away from the "good." In addition, the simulacrum generates confusion with regards to the possibility of selection and judgement. The simulacrum involves "the false as power, Pseudos, in the sense that Nietzsche speaks of the highest power of the false" (Deleuze 2004, 300). As a strange grey area, the simulacrum is neither a self-contained/containing ontology nor merely the reflection of an *a priori* ontology.[73]

Deleuze sees a connection between Nietzsche's "eternal return" and the simulacrum, because both involve a subversion of any ideal difference between the copy and the original, the past and the future. Here, according to David Lane, Deleuze follows Klossowski in regarding "the eternal return as a parodic play of mimesis" that overcomes the primacy of an original model and the very notion of origin itself" (Lane 2011, 105- 126, 11). For Klossowski, the eternal return is the "simulacrum of a doctrine" (Smith 2005, 16). Klossowski writes "[t]he simulacrum, in its *imitative* sense, is the actualisation of something in itself incommunicable and non-representable: the phantasm in its obsessional constraint" (Klossowski 1997, 76). Simulacra are *phantasma*, i.e., impulses and affects. For Klossowski, "*mimesis* is not a servile imitation of the visible, but the simulacrum of the unrepresentable" (ibid., 76).[74]

Likewise, according to Deleuze, to affirm the simulacrum and the "chaodyssey" (*chao-errance*) of the return is to deny Plato's transcendent plane of Forms, as well as "true being" (Deleuze 2004, 301). Deleuze focuses on Nietzschean "becoming," which has no model and fulfils no end. He concludes that to "reverse Platonism" is to undermine the world of representation — the "twilight of the idols" (ibid., 299).

In Nietzsche's *Twilight of the Idols*, we finally see that the "same and the similar no longer have an essence except as *simulated*, that is as expressing the functioning of the simulacrum [...] it is the triumph of the false pretender" (ibid., 299). As David La Rocca rightly points out, however, it is strange of Deleuze to insist on a "triumph" when the simulacrum is characterized by neutrality

---

[73] Jonathan S. Boulter, "Partial Glimpses of the Infinite: Borges and the Simulacrum," Hispanic Review, vol. 69, no. 3, pp. 355-377 (2001), 360.

[74] Smith ("Klossowski's Reading of Nietzsche: Impulses, Phantasms, Simulacra, Stereotypes," vol. 16, n. 11) claims that, unlike Baudrillard, Klossowski never doubts the real. For Klossowski, simulacra are no less real than phantasma or impulses. I agree with Butler (*Jean Baudrillard: The Defence of the Real*), who claims that Baudrillard's work focuses on the "real" as a problem and on how simulacra are responsible for the creation of a self-referential impasse. This will be discussed in Section 4.

and horizontality (La Rocca 2001, 326). A victory can only be proclaimed by defeating a rival (i.e., the icon and the copy) (ibid., 326). To regard simulacra as "rising" and "affirming" themselves implies a power struggle, the "rights" of simulacra conflict with the removal of hierarchy (Deleuze 2004, 299).

I agree with La Rocca's view that the point of Nietzsche's "reversal of Platonism" is not the "triumph" of one system for another. As he says, the "simulacrum has not replaced the icon: both have become possible aspects of perception."[75] In my view, Baudrillard, unlike Deleuze, is open to such an alternation. In what follows (section 4), I outline Baudrillard's genealogy of images and simulacra, which involves both Plato and Nietzsche.[76] In her study on Deleuze, Claire Colebrook (2002, 98) contrasts Deleuze's simulacrum with that of Baudrillard and she reads Baudrillard as "lamenting" the "loss of the real" in simulacra. Colebrook claims that in Deleuze's world of simulacra "each event of life is already other than itself, not original, a simulation" (ibid., 99).

Without a doubt, the Baudrillardian stance towards the simulacrum is more ambivalent than the Deleuzean one.[77] In my view, however, Rex Butler provides a more convincing analysis of Baudrillard than Colebrook: "Baudrillard's [...] problem is how to think the real when all is simulation, how to use the real against attempts by various systems of rationality to account for it" (But-

---

[75] David La Rocca, "The False Pretender: Deleuze, Sherman and the Status of Simulacra," Journal of Aesthetics and Art Criticism, vol. 69, no. 3 (Summer 2001), 327.

[76] Levin (*Jean Baudrillard. A Study in Cultural Metaphysics*, 82) calls Baudrillard a "perverse Platonist" and Julian Pefanis (*Heterology and the Postmodern: Bataille, Baudrillard and Lyotard*, 60) sees Baudrillard's work as "operating within, and on, the epistemological framework of [...] Platonic discourse." Yet Pefanis quickly also moves from the Platonic parallel to a Nietzschean one. Baudrillard's position is close to that of Nietzsche, because, for both thinkers, "the sham world is the real world, whereas the real world is the world of illusion" (Pefanis, *Heterology and the Postmodern: Bataille, Baudrillard and Lyotard*, 60).

[77] According to Sylvère Lotringer ("Remember Foucault," 20): "Deleuze probably regretted praising the simulacrum after Baudrillard used it to cancel every difference between the real and the referential, turning the entire system into Disneyland, a world-size simulacrum."

ler 1999, 17). Baudrillard seeks to challenge processes of simulation that try to bring about a real ("hyperreality"). Butler rightly claims that "Baudrillard's point is that each system he analyzes (and the work of any great thinker) creates its own reality, sets out the very terms in which it must be understood" (ibid., 54). Yet, in Baudrillard's work, there is another side to any attempt to bring about the real in simulation, a side which is the ultimate resistance to simulation.[78]

In what follows, I outline the "short" version[79] of the genealogy of images that Baudrillard provides in *Simulacra and Simulations* and, in the process, I discuss the parallels between Baudrillard's account and Nietzsche's *Twilight of the Idols*.

4.3 Baudrillard's Simulacrum

In section 2, we saw how Nietzsche questions the privileged (moral) status of truth over appearance and regards the "pure drive towards truth" as an "effect of deception" (Nietzsche 1999, 143). Nietzsche reverses Plato's affirmation of the super-sensuous as a standard of truth by exposing the production of truth as an illusionary process.

In section 3, we turned to Deleuze, for whom Nietzsche inaugurates a philosophy of the future for an era of simulacra. The simulacrum produces an "effect of resemblance" (Deleuze 2004, 295). It thereby completely undermines the distinction between the model and the copy. In this section, I turn to Baudrillard's genealogy of images and simulacra. By generalizing the simulacrum

---

[78] Butler (*The Defence of the Real*, 53) explains that "[i]t is this real, excluded by any attempt to speak of it, that is the limit to every system — it is the Platonic paradox that Baudrillard means by the real." The paradox first raised by Plato in his dialogue Cratylus. Derrida deals with Plato's Cratylus in *Plato's Pharmacy*.

[79] It is unclear, however, how the four-stage model outlined in *Simulacra and Simulations* relates to the three-stage model of *Symbolic Exchange and Death*. Baudrillard's "long" version of the genealogy of signs and simulacra is in *Symbolic Exchange and Death*. Baudrillard does not see a contradiction between the two models, because in his later text *Simulacra and Simulations* he refers to terminology developed earlier in *Symbolic Exchange and Death*.

to the whole societal realm, Baudrillard (like Nietzsche) emphasizes much more than Deleuze that simulacra involve social rapports and power.

According to the Baudrillard critic, Christopher Norris, Baudrillard's project is "a species of inverted Platonism" (Norris 2000, 364). For Norris, "Baudrillard's […] discourse […] systematically promotes the negative terms (rhetoric, appearance, ideology) above their positive counterparts" (ibid., 364). In the same vein, Drew A. Hyland says that one could see a kind of "reverse Platonism at work in Baudrillard. Instead of the supposedly Platonic degrees of reality metaphysics, we have a degrees of unreality doctrine" (Hyland 2014, 28).

Norris and Hyland do not, in my view, however, acknowledge the extent to which Baudrillard, like Nietzsche, breaks down privileged hierarchical relations altogether. Like Nietzsche, I show below that Baudrillard's analysis of the simulacrum does not simply involve the triumph of appearances and the false. In Baudrillard's view, there now only exists an "empty space of representation," which produces "effects of the real" (Baudrillard 1993, 70). Baudrillard calls this "the hyperreal." Hyperreality is a self-referential world composed of pre-established models or codes of simulacra that are grounded in no other "reality" than their own. "Hyperreality" puts an end to distinctions between object and representation, thing and idea.

To understand the full scope of this development, it is necessary to see how Baudrillard's work provides a theoretical link between structural linguistics and simulation. The precondition for any simulation is the disconnection from reality and this fits perfectly with the semiological paradigm. In Saussure's theory of the sign, a word is a sign, and a sign consists of a signifier and a signified; the signifier is the sound pattern of the word, e.g., c-a-t, and the signified is the meaning of the word, "furry animal with whiskers," which Saussure describes as a "mental image." The referent is the thing, the physical cat, which is simply left out of Saussure's structuralist account.

Saussure's contribution to the study of language was to show that the meaning of a word, the signified, is not determined by the referent – as Aristotle believes – but rather by its place in the system of signs and its relation to other signifieds: the meaning of a word is determined differentially or negatively, i.e., by its relation to other meanings. Saussure saw a relation of arbitrariness between signifiers, and between signifiers and their signified. The signification of words and phrases is neither based on verifiable facts or observations, so signification can only be expressed with a set of words or concepts that belong to a common language system.

For Baudrillard, in Saussure's model of linguistic signification, there is no significance outside the system (of significance) to serve as its (transcendent) assurance of significance – or, of its truth, because meaning is determined internally in the system of language, not through an external relation between language and reality. As Baudrillard says in the chapter of *Simulations* entitled "The Precession of Simulacra": "liquidation of all referentials ... artificial resurrection in the system of signs" (Baudrillard 1983, 2).

The concept of simulation refers to two aspects: firstly, to the disappearance of reality behind (its) signs and secondly, to the "effect" of reality. The first aspect is connected with the semiological method and can be derived from its premises or alternatively its radicalizations. The second aspect is related to the production of culture (in the broadest sense). Baudrillard's work therefore provides a theoretical link between semiology and simulation. For Baudrillard, structural linguistics not only presents us with a new theory of language; it also describes the social reality of late modernity (similarly, in chapter 1.2, I showed how for Baudrillard, Saussurean linguistics exemplifies specifically the consumer morality of late modernity).

The concepts of simulacra, simulation and hyperreality serve Baudrillard as tools to analyze current society and its "crisis of representation."[80] This crisis contains a dimension of historical depth that refers to a long history of images and signs. In *Simulacra and Simulations*, Baudrillard sketches four stages of the image:

---

[80] For more on the "crisis of representation" in relation to Baudrillard, see Pefanis (1991, 61).

1. It is the reflection of a basic reality. In this case, the real is represented by the image of the real, as a copy.
2. It masks and perverts a basic reality. Here the real is represented by an image that disfigures the real.
3. It masks the absence of a basic reality. At this stage, the real is replaced by an image, and the image conceals the fact that there is no reality. There is dissimulation or play: one pretends to have something (i.e., pretends not to have nothing, not to have no truth).
4. It has no relation to any reality whatsoever; it is its own pure simulacrum. In this final stage, the image eliminates the referential relation altogether.

Baudrillard names the four orders of the image — the order of the sacrament, the order of the malefice, the order of sorcery, and the order of simulation. He differentiates between signs and images that dissimulate something (the first two stages) and signs and images that dissimulate that there is nothing (stages three and four).

For Baudrillard, as for Nietzsche, the point is that there are no essential things-in-themselves that are perspective-free. According to Paul Hegarty (2004, 51), Baudrillard's stages of the image indicate that

> [t]here are always images, and the image removes the reality of whatever may or may not be there [...] [Baudrillard's] texts on simulation do not have a genuine reality as a necessary base, they deal instead with alterations in the perception of reality, and this perception is as much real as there is.

According to this quote, illusion is not opposed to reality. "Truth, i.e., the true as constant, is itself a kind of semblance that is a necessary condition of life" (Schrift 1990, 50). Both Nietzsche and Baudrillard, in my view, seek to overcome the hierarchical ordering between truth and illusion by exposing the production of truth as an illusionary process.

Baudrillard uses the example of religious iconography to argue that those iconoclasts who feel threatened by the images of God are the ones who recognize the real importance of religious simulations. Baudrillard accentuates the non-mimetic mode of simulation and he refers to simulation as the "divine irreference of images" (Baudrillard 1983, 3). Iconoclasts seek to destroy images "because they sense this omnipotence of simulacra, this facility they have of effacing God from the consciousness of men and the overwhelming destructive truth which they suggest: that ultimately there has never been any God, that only the simulacrum exists, indeed, that God himself has only ever been his own simulacrum" (ibid., 9). The implication of such "hyperreality" is that the supposed real, which they were once thought to be representations of, no longer exists. Images and signs precede reality due to the "precession of simulacra." The logical and temporal relation between the image and the real has been reversed.

As already mentioned above, simulation for Baudrillard is a process that consists of coded signs (and images) that refer to other signs in a model, not to an external referent.

As Charles Levin (1996, 191) rightly explains

> "Simulation refers to something deep but calculable in the real construction of actual technical, practical or social 'spaces'. Simulation is not so much an attempt to resemble something in 'appearance' as to *reassemble* it from 'within', algorithmically".

Simulation is often linked to computer technology and Baudrillard's concept comes close to these cybernetic associations, but it is also used in a much more general way. Following Levin's analysis in the above quote, the hypothesis of simulation is that the world can only be grasped as a simulation.
In the entry on "Simulacra," in the *Baudrillard Dictionary*, Pawlett (2010, 196) rightly sees the influence of Nietzsche and Klossowski on Baudrillard's theory of simulation. In addition, Pawlett claims that Baudrillard rejects a Platonic understanding of simulacra because Plato's understanding of the simulacrum focuses on the issue of falsity. For Baudrillard, simulacra are certainly not false images because the simulacrum claims to be true. The simulacrum is that which hides the truth's non-existence.

Baudrillard is therefore not in search of the truth "behind" simulacra. As Alexander Gungov rightly puts it "a simulacrum is not simply a false ideology that can easily be criticized, unmasked, and abolished forever...we live comfortably in a world organized by several prevailing codes, usually not suspecting this and being content with what we have available at hand" (Gungov 2006, 267).

To search for the truth is, according to Baudrillard, the intention of the critique of ideology. "Ideology corresponds to a corruption of reality through signs. It is always the goal of the ideological analysis to restore the objective process, it is always a false problem to wish to restore the truth behind the simulacrum" (Baudrillard 1994, 27). Any ideology critical[81] of representation, as Andreas Huyssen (1989, 9) points out "must continue to rely on some distinction between representations" — Baudrillard's last stage of the image collapses distinctions (i.e., the true/false) and "the viability of any ideology critique."

It must be emphasized, however, that Baudrillard's work still very much seeks to challenge processes of simulation that try to generate "effects" of the real and the true. Baudrillard's work follows a strategy of reversibility, which according to Butler means that the "basic axioms of the system" under examination must be pushed "to the point where they begin to turn upon themselves, to produce the opposite effects from those intended" (Butler 1997, 52). Reversibility is in tune with Baudrillard's rejection of any notion of linear progress and his Nietzschean view that systems have a built-in obsolescence and that systems self-destruct by their very functioning.[82]

According to Nietzsche's definition of nihilism, the highest values cannot resist their own devaluation and subsequent revaluation — their reversal. Nietzsche views the crisis of nihilism as a crisis in values. Judeo-Christian values are life-negating instead of

---

[81] According to Charles Levin (1996, 203), Baudrillard seeks to eradicate all traces of a sociological theory of ideology: "the theory of simulation seeks to abandon the mind-body split in sociology and absorb the problematic of ideology into a more all-encompassing metaphysical account of social being".

[82] In his entry on "Nihilism," Rex Butler (*The Baudrillard Dictionary*, 139) says "Nietzsche is one of Baudrillard's defining influences. He is one of the few thinkers whose presumptions are not turned against them," as Baudrillard did with Marx in *The Mirror of Production* and Saussure, as well as Freud in *Symbolic Exchange and Death*.

life affirming, because life is judged lacking in relation to something external, super-sensuous beyond it (what can be called Platonic "overvaluation"). Nietzsche identifies another form of nihilism, namely when these transcendent values are devalued, as in the case of the Enlightenment. Here, meaning and value are put into question. For Nietzsche, the celebration of life is the only proper response to nihilism, which suggests that nihilism refers to exhaustion and the denial of life.

Nietzsche claims that any philosophy must decide how to deal with these two problems (i.e., Platonic "overvaluation" and Enlightenment critical "devaluation"), which are integral to thought. Passive nihilism remains locked within the recognition that the world is without true foundation, ungrounded and meaningless. Active nihilism on the other hand, arises from the general insight that "the meaning and value of life depend on fictions that we must accept as true" (Winkler 2018, 105).

In section 2, we saw how Nietzsche problematizes the value of truth (without simply overturning the super-sensuous Platonic value structure, i.e., by privileging appearances). In the same way, for Baudrillard, as Butler (1997, 62) rightly puts it,

> the world can resemble itself, can realise itself, only because of or lead to an entirely 'other-worldly' explanation: the very difference between the world and itself, the real and its copy. It is this point — already two — at which absolute resemblance and absolute difference come together (death, symbolic exchange, seduction, reversibility, evil) that Baudrillard means by the real. It is this Platonic paradox — unrepresentable, unthinkable — that for Baudrillard is the most real thing in the world.

In the final phase of simulation there is no real to reflect or imitate, because simulation is a replacement. Simulation totalizes the world in its own image. In the order of simulation, the model and its internal system of relations generate phenomena. Although science demands an end to mimetic as well as to mythical thought, Baudrillard shows that this rejection is deluded. The demand for direct access is mythical but also fatal.

For Baudrillard, the rationality of the Enlightenment produces "the orders of simulacra" that destroy it. As Baudrillard puts it in *Fatal Strategies*, the "real does not efface itself in favour of the imaginary; it effaces itself in favor of the more real than real: the hyperreal. The truer than true: this is simulation" (Baudrillard 1990 FS, 11). The real has become its own simulation. Political and cultural events are inextricably linked to their mode of (re)presentation. In the same way, processes of simulation mistake reality with their reproduction.

In his study "Nihilism and the Sublime Postmodern," Will Slocombe rightly regards Baudrillard's simulation as arising "from the Enlightenment desire to attribute Reason as the measure of all things, to quantify and control by scientifically replicating the Real under laboratory conditions" (Slocombe 2006, 69). As Slocombe rightly points out, for Baudrillard (unlike Deleuze), simulation "is not an escape from Enlightenment rationality but the ultimate culmination of it" (ibid., 71). Enlightenment rationality destroys the value of truth that it produces, thus ironically inaugurating the "divine irreference of images" (Baudrillard 1994, 3).

Baudrillard follows Nietzsche's critique of the machinery that continuously revives the divine along with everything that gives meaning to a world and a humanity that finds itself produced through the character of that meaning. As David Allison puts it, Baudrillard's "oversaturated world of hyperreality […] [is] for Nietzsche, precisely the entire symbolic of the religio-moral idiosyncrasy" (Allison 1999, 183; spelling modified).

Conclusion

According to Nietzsche, Plato devalues the mutable realm of appearances in favour of an immutable, transcendent, true world of "Forms." As we saw however, Nietzsche does not simply invert the Platonic hierarchical order of truth over error or appearance, he also delves into the origin of the positive value placed upon truth and he finds it "simply a moral prejudice to affirm truth over error or appearances" (Schrift 1995, 22). In the wake of Nietzsche's "reversal of Platonism" and the concurrent "twilight of the idols," Deleuze and Baudrillard conceptualize simulacra and simulation not simply as a false portrayal (with no "real referent"). For Deleuze, the simulacrum is not derived from a prior identity. A simulacrum is "other" to that which it represents, but it still produces an "effect of resemblance" (Deleuze 2004, 295). This focus on "effects" is in tune with the future oriented, mutable aspect of the simulacrum. Identity and resemblance continue as external effects of the internal differential dynamic of the simulacrum. In Deleuze's world of simulacra, "each event of life is already other than itself," "not original," but rather, a "simulation" (Colebrook 2002, 99).

Unlike Deleuze's straightforward affirmation of simulacra, we have seen how Baudrillard's work seeks to challenge processes of simulation that try to generate "effects" of the real. Hyperreality, for Baudrillard, is a self-referential world composed of models or simulacra grounded in no other reality than their own. By means of his metaphor of "the precession of simulation," Baudrillard discusses how cultural models seem to circulate as "self-fulfilling prophecies" (Baudrillard 1998, 128). Social and geopolitical events repeat themselves in an endless cycle. In Baudrillard's work, simulation is not about emancipation, as in the case of Deleuze, but about control.

5. Hyperreality of Simulation

Introduction

Chapter 4 (section 1) discussed how Nietzsche overcomes Plato's affirmation of the super-sensuous as a standard of truth by regarding the "pure drive towards truth" as an effect of deception (Nietzsche 1999, 143). In section 2, we saw how, in the spirit of Nietzsche's reversal of Platonism, Deleuze conceives of a world of simulacra where "[t]here is no original life that is then varied and copied in different versions; each event of life is already other than itself, not original, a simulation" (Colebrook 2002, 99). In section 3, I briefly sketched Baudrillard's phases of the image, in which he accentuates the non-mimetic mode of simulation and refers to simulation as the "divine irreference of images" (Baudrillard 1994, 3). For Baudrillard, in the current phase, there now only exists an "empty space of representation", which produces "effects of the real"- "the hyperreal" (Baudrillard 1993, 70).

Unlike Deleuze's praise for the creative freedom simulacra offer (section 2), for Baudrillard, simulation is about a total systematization of life. Following Saussurean linguistics, simulation is a process which consists of coded signs that refer to other signs in a model not to an external referent or reality. The "hyperreal" world of simulation reassembles the real in the form of exclusively and universally determining codes of signification. The code permits opposition and alternation, but it is a pre-coded opposition, a pre-coded otherness.

In this chapter, I will take a closer look at how the real has become its own simulation and how this parallels Nietzsche's definition of nihilism: the highest values cannot resist their own reversal and devaluation.

In section 1, I start with Baudrillard's longer version of the genealogy of simulacra that he provides in his book *Symbolic Exchange and Death*. This will clarify how the rationality of the Enlightenment produces the third order of simulacra (the hyperreal) that leads to its own destruction. In section 2, I will go on to discuss the "structural law of value" which underpins the third order of simulacra (Baudrillard, 1993, 51) and I do so by further developing how Baudrillard's work provides a theoretical link between structural linguistics and simulation. In section 3, I look at the multiple causal factors that Baudrillard suggests for the third phase of simulacra as well as their Nietzschean resonances.

5.1 Genealogy of Simulacra

In the previous chapter section 1, we saw how in "Reason in Philosophy," from *The Twilight of the Idols,* Nietzsche (2005, 166) regards Plato as an icon or idol worshipper: reality is first transformed into the Idea of Being.[83] The real must be other than what the senses bring forth, and reason conceptualizes this other (Being/permanence). The decisive aspect of Plato's philosophy is the creation of the difference between true and apparent world. In section 2, I showed how for Deleuze, modern philosophy must establish itself by overturning Platonism as Nietzsche did in *Twilight of the Idols*. In his reading of Nietzsche's reversal, we saw how Deleuze champions a radical reign of false copies or 'simulacra' because simulacra undermine the very foundations of Platonic thought.

In section 3, I moved onto Baudrillard's four stages of the image. Here, Baudrillard outlines the demise of the real and the rise of simulation in a "rough chronological order" (Slocombe 2006, 69). I emphasized how secondary critics such as Allison

---

[83] "For thousands of years, philosophers have been using only mummified concepts; nothing real makes it through their hands alive. They kill and stuff the things they worship, these lords of concept idolatry [*Begriffs-Götzendiener*] – they become mortal dangers to everything they worship. They see death, change, and age, as well as procreation and growth, as objections, - refutations even. What is, does not *become*; what becomes *is* not…so they all believe, desperately even, in being. But since they cannot get hold of it, they look for reasons why it is kept from them. 'there must be some deception here, some illusionary level of appearances preventing us from perceiving things that have being: where is the deceiver? –'We've got it!' they shout in ecstasy, 'it is in sensibility! These senses *that are so immoral anyway*, now they are deceiving us about the *true* world" (Nietzsche 2005, 167).

(2013) and Hegarty (2004) point to crucial parallels between Nietzsche's 'How the 'True World' Finally became a Fable' from *Twilight of the Idols* and Baudrillard's own four-stage devolution into simulation.

In his study "Nihilism and the Sublime Postmodern", Will Slocombe rightly regards Baudrillard's simulation as arising "from the Enlightenment desire to attribute Reason as the measure of all things, to quantify and control by scientifically replicating the Real under laboratory conditions" (Slocombe 2006, 69). In order to show in greater detail that simulation is the culmination point of this Enlightenment rationality (and not an escape as Deleuze seems to claim), I will look at Baudrillard's longer analysis of the "orders of simulacra", which is to be found in *Symbolic Exchange and Death* (Baudrillard 1993, 71-103). Using Marxist political thought and Saussure's structural linguistics, Baudrillard provides a background to the order of simulation (the 'hyperreal') which runs parallel to the rupture with symbolic exchange.

A. Symbolic Exchange

> 1) involves the 'reversibility' and ambivalence of primitive societies
> 2) signs circulate within a rigid hierarchical system

B. Stages of Simulacra

> 1) Renaissance-classical period: nature/counterfeited nature
> 2) the industrial period: natural/ the produced counterpart (both 1 and 2 are based on the 'real')
> 3) post-industrial period: produced/simulated hyperreal mode

Baudrillard's three orders of simulacra are to be understood as specific historical logics of sign production, which form a society's horizon of meaning and give it a logical unity.[84] When

---

[84] Baudrillard develops his history of the order of signs with implicit reference to Michel Foucault's *The Order of Things* (1966) and its extensive history of *epis-*

Baudrillard, for example, discusses the "simulacrum of public opinion" (Baudrillard 1993, 67) he seeks to accentuate the fact that societies produce an overall image of themselves, through which they are able to recognize themselves and validate their sign productions – in this case, elections, opinion polls and other mechanisms are used to conjure up the image of a democratic bourgeois society.

For Baudrillard, archaic societies, antiquity and the Middle Ages are also sign systems. The concepts of simulacra and simulation, however, seem reserved for the modern order of signs. The pre-simulacra age, the symbolic age, prevailed during medieval and feudal times. At this time, signs are restricted in number and their function is not arbitrary:

> "Each [sign] retains its full value as prohibition, and each carries with it a reciprocal obligation between castes, clans or persons" (Baudrillard 1993, 50).

Before the Renaissance, signs (Baudrillard is referring here to signs of distinction like clothing, power insignias) were rigidly fixed because signs are bound to a social order of caste, rank or role: "There is no fashion in caste society, nor in a society based on rank, since assignation is absolute and there is no class mobility" (Baudrillard 1993, 50). This is the world of "transparent signs", a "strong symbolic order" (Baudrillard 1993, 50). "Let's be under no illusions," says Baudrillard, "this order has existed, and it was a brutal hierarchy, since the sign's transparency is indissociably also its cruelty" (Baudrillard 1993, 50). Yet the "transparency" of the symbolic order does not entail an unmediated real with direct ac-

---

temes, or orders of knowledge. Baudrillard however also deviates significantly from Foucault. On Foucault's influence on Baudrillard see Kellner (1989, 78), Zapf (2010, 136). Using a Foucauldian term Baudrillard speaks of the *dispositiv* and apparatus of simulation (1993, 2). Christa Karpenstein Essbach (2004, 158) on the other hand brings Baudrillard's concept of simulacra in conjunction with Lacan's concept of the symbolic order. Gary Genosko (1994, 44) relates the simulacrum to Charles Sanders Pierce as a logical succession of different classes of signs instead of a historical order.

cess to truth.[85] Baudrillard depicts symbolic exchange as a constant play of exchanges, of challenges, of appearances: masks, dances, feasts, rituals.

In the world of symbolic exchange, life is accepted as an illusion and there is no overarching problematic of 'reality' and no pretence to know or discover the natural scientific relationship between signs and what lies beyond the extraordinary effects they create. Signs are crucially not referential and not arbitrary:

> "the arbitrariness of the sign begins when, instead of bonding two persons in an inescapable reciprocity, the signifier starts to refer to a disenchanted universe of the signified, the common denominator of the real, towards which no-one any longer has the least obligation" (Baudrillard 1993, 50).

Arbitrary signs are 'counterfeit' because they are a "simulacrum of symbolic obligation" (Baudrillard 1993, 50). Arbitrary signs appear "bound to the world" but they are abstract, referential presentations of it. In conceiving of 'the world', on one hand, and the representational exchange of signs on the other, world and sign are separated: the sign and the referent. The link between sign and referent is one of convention, where signs actively represent the object. In symbolic exchange, this separation is not meaningful (Pawlett 2007, 75).

The feudal organizing principle is transformed in the early modern period, with the rise of the first order simulacra, which runs from the Renaissance to the Industrial Revolution. This is the start of open competition and signs begin to break out of rigid schemas. It is the

> "rule of the free and emancipated sign, in which any and every class will be able to participate. Competitive democracy succeeds the endogamy of signs proper to status-based orders" (Baudrillard 1993, 51).

---

[85] Transparency has more to do with a certain "trans-appearance" and a "phenomenology of absence" (Baudrillard 2008, 43). In an article entitled "The Violence of Images, Violence Against the Image" Baudrillard (2008, 45) plays with the French word "transparition" and he writes that the "secret rule of the image" is that of "coming into and going out of appearance [*Ce jeu de l'absence et de la transparition*]" (Baudrillard, 2008: 45). Baudrillard (2008, 43) claims here that "… the penalty for making the object appear [is] the disappearance of the subject".

The sign breaks free for the first time from the "reciprocal obligation" (Baudrillard 1993, 50) between the classes, castes and clans that marked feudal society and it begins to refer to some external reality. The sign is no longer (symbolically) exchanged from person to person but only exchanged through some common third element, which acts as the medium of exchange. Two signs can be compared to each other and are true only if they both refer to the same external reality. Here signs refer to the real through their difference from it. During this first stage of simulacra, the "counterfeit" had a central role in the organization of society and the signification of reality. The imitation of nature becomes the functioning paradigm in organizing the social and the representation of reality. The sign proliferates according to the "natural law of value" (Baudrillard 1993, 50).

What is imitated here is the previous regime of signs themselves: "the modern sign dreams of its predecessor and would love to rediscover an obligation in its reference to the real. It finds only a reason, a referential reason, a real and a 'natural' on which it will feed" (Baudrillard 1993, 51). Since the old stability of the (apparently) natural sign order has faltered, the absence of nature in the sign leads to a painful experience of loss. As a response to this rupture, there arises a "thriving nostalgia for the natural referent of the sign" (Baudrillard 1993, 50). In the Renaissance, therefore, one finds this idea of the rediscovery of nature in the realm of signs.

Baudrillard uses the Baroque stucco as the exemplary form, as it imitates nature via form. The flexible material of stucco is a "mirror" (Baudrillard 1993, 52) of all other materials and forms, which are duplicated according to the laws of resemblance. Each order of simulacra remodels the world to render it more intelligible, controllable and manageable. The counterfeit achieves this only "at the level of substance and form, not yet of relations and structures" (Baudrillard 1993, 53). Stucco, then, is used as a kind of "universal substance" that can model any shape or take any form – a principle of general equivalence, although of a very limited kind (Baudrillard 1993, 52).

The automaton is another example. "The automaton is an analogon of man" (Baudrillard 1993, 53), a metaphor of the human. "We must not be fooled by 'figurative' resemblance. Like God, the automaton questions nature (if not the mystery of the soul), the dilemma of being and appearance…" (Baudrillard 1993, 53). The automaton reveals something about the human by its difference from the human.

> "The difference is always maintained, as in the case of the automaton so perfect that on stage the illusionist mimicked its staccato movements in order that at least, even if the roles were reversed, confusion would be impossible. Thus, the automaton's questions remain open, making it an optimistic mechanics, even if the counterfeit always retains a diabolical connotation" (Baudrillard 1993, 54).

The second order simulacrum, "production," characterizes the time of the Industrial Revolution, and here there is a loss of the difference between sign and reality, copy and original. The industrial simulacrum, due to the development of production processes and industrial mass production, no longer brings forth artefacts in the form of imitations but rather in the mode of seriality, that is to say as identical mass products without original. Baudrillard (1993, 55) refers in this respect to Walter Benjamin's *The Artwork in the Age of Technical Reproduction* (2001). The term reproducibility is confusing because it still implies an opposition between original and copy. Baudrillard emphasizes, however, that there is no longer a relation of original to copy, also no question of analogy or mirroring, there is the rule of equivalence and indifference (Baudrillard, 1993, 56). At this stage, the sign does not refer to the real by means of its difference from it but aspires to be equivalent to the real.

The whole aim of the serial reproducibility of the industrial assembly line is that the first version of the thing (the model) and the last (the copy) cannot be distinguished. All products are equally original and unoriginal. They are not imitations because there is no real from which they derive.

> "In a series, objects become indistinct simulacra of one another and along with objects, of the men that produce them. The extinction of the original

reference alone facilitates the general law of equivalence, that is to say, *the very possibility of production*" (Baudrillard 1993, 55; italics in the text).

The robot for instance, unlike the automaton, seeks to be identical to the human, which abolishes any relationship between the two.

"The robot no longer questions appearances, its only truth is its mechanical efficiency...no more semblance or dissemblance, no more God or Man, only an immanent logic of the operational principle" (Baudrillard 1993, 54).

Each order of simulacra is defined by its modelling of the world through a law of value and a principle of general equivalence, which enables comparisons, classifications and ordered exchange between elements in the system.

The first order of simulacra, the counterfeit, as already mentioned, operates through the "natural law of value" and its principle of equivalence is use value. The second order is the order of production based on the "market law of value" or economic exchange value. The second order finds a general equivalent within class or market relations: the exchange of commodities in terms of economic exchange-value. Industrially produced or serial signs have no symbolic obligations. 'Origin' is not an issue for mass produced objects and industrial signs are "crude, dull, industrial, repetitive, echoless, functional and efficient" whereas signs of the first order are "magical, diabolical, illusionary... enchanting" (Baudrillard 1993, 57).

The age of production is "ephemeral" because it almost immediately moves towards the third order, but the age of production is still not yet for Baudrillard the age of simulation (Baudrillard 1993, 77). The idea of reference still remains. The central referential value of this era is human work (Baudrillard 1993, 28). The leading discourse of the order of production is political economy, which, due to Marxism, has become the main interpretative model of modernity. And it was this model that was the theme of Baudrillard's critique in *Mirror of Production* (1973; 1975). Three years after *The Mirror of Production* (with the publication of *Symbolic Exchange and Death* in French in 1976) this critique becomes obsolete for Baudrillard, because its object has disappeared:

we have arrived at "the end of production" (Baudrillard 1993, 9-12). Production is taken over by 'simulation' and the latter emancipates signs to their furthest point. Only the cybernetic digital 'code' and the model are the "signifier of reference" (Baudrillard 1993, 56).

During the first and second stages (of the counterfeit and production), the sign is still bound in some way to a real, but in simulation proper, which is the third order of simulacra, referential reality is effaced completely:

> "There is no more counterfeiting of an original, as there was in the first order, and no more pure series as there was in the second; there are models from which all forms proceed according to modulated differences" (Baudrillard 1993, 56).

In the third order, reality is replaced by simulation, a process which consists of coded signs that refer to other signs. Baudrillard presents the thesis that modern capitalism must be seen not as a mode of production but as a code dominated by the "structural law of value". The term is influenced by Marx's own law of value but here it goes beyond the economic boundary and becomes a mechanism which takes over all cultural spheres (Gane 1993, xi).

According to Charles Levin (1996, 110), Baudrillard sketches a "theory of modernity ... in which all human history appears as a ... translation of embodied experience into terms of value ...– a kind of 'liberation' of existence, permitting unrestricted selection and transformation of elements from a universal combinatory of possible phenomena".

To understand the full significance of the "structural law of value", and its "universal combinatory" (Levin 1996, 110), we need to return to Baudrillard's link between structural linguistics and simulation (introduced in the previous chapter 4.3). Even if it is accepted that 'referentiality' is only an illusion generated by the machine of language, as Baudrillard, following Nietzsche, does, the situation is transformed by the "liberation" of signifiers (characteristic of "structural" linguistics), that do not even have an illusionary external referentiality.

For Nietzsche, as for Baudrillard, the operation of language governs rational thought processes and it is this which underlies simulation. As we saw already in chapter 1 (section 3), in *On the Genealogy of Morals*, Nietzsche emphasizes the power of language to seduce us into accepting all kinds of metaphysical presuppositions such as the division between subject and object, cause and effects, and he asks us to question our grammatical habits.

The "double simulacrum" of the "merely 'apparent world' and the so-called 'real world'" are the result of a belief in discursive rationality or grammar (Allison 2013, 181). Reason is supported by an inherited grammar and it serves as the foundation for the belief in the true world. Yet that belief is already for Nietzsche, an illusion, a fable. And it is in Nietzsche's footsteps, that Baudrillard emphasizes how the hyperreality of our world is due to the vehicle of rationality, its signifying medium language.

In the next section, I will continue to delve deeper into Baudrillard's theoretical link between structural linguistics and simulation. Structural linguistics requires that we disregard the connection between language and reality; but once it has presented its theory of meaning – as determined differentially – the question returns: how does language understood in this sense link up with reality? Baudrillard is saying that it does not – that, in other words, as already seen in chapters 1 and 4, structural linguistics for Baudrillard, does not merely present us with a new theory of language, but also describes the social reality of late modernity, based on the "hyperreal", "structural law of value".

This section served as an overview of the genealogy of the orders of simulacra that Baudrillard provides in *Symbolic Exchange and Death*. In the next section, I will focus on how the third order of simulacra, the order of the "hyperreal", is run by the "structural law of value" and I will provide various examples. I will then move on to suggest some of the causes for the hyperreal.

5.2 The Hyperreal Structural Law of Value

In the previous section, we saw how the idea of reality emerges within the orders of simulacra. The different orders of simulacra are "entwined levels of simulation rather than a succession and seem to follow on from the (retrospective) lack of symbolic exchange that drives our culture to real-ize, for instance, all of the above are 'strategies of the real', our attempts to constrain ambiguity" (Hegarty 2004, 51). For Karlis Racevskis, the epistemological history of culture that Baudrillard sketches proceeds in a "spiral-like evolution" and, it has three distinguishable stages, "each new circle simply being a reflection, a repetition on a higher level of the system below" (Racevskis 1979, 34).

The first order of simulacra (with its distinctive binary oppositions of real/unreal and true and false) establishes the idea of reality and the idea reaches its height in the second order, where life, sex and work are the essential realities.

> "The second stage of simulacra is the locus of theoretical critiques of the social realm, the determinisms, objectifications and dialectics that purport to explain linguistic, economic, conscious and subconscious subjects. The third ... uses the second level systems as its referents and is thoroughly dominated by codes which have become its principles of reality" (Racevkis 1979, 35).

The emergence of the third order of simulacra is already contained in the very practice of industrial production. Each order contains the seed of its own destruction as well as its transformation. It is always ready to move to the next stage. For instance, the logic of production accelerates the production of commodities, but more importantly, it also needs to accumulate what makes production possible (i.e., capital) to such a degree that the system outpaces its own momentum and operations.

In this third stage, the productivist form codifies its operations (in terms of a purely formal purpose). As Baudrillard explains, "[a]s soon as dead work gains the upper hand over living labour (that is to say, as soon as the era of primitive accumulation ends), serial production yields to the generation by means of models" (Baudrillard 1993, 77). Automation renders manual labour increasingly superfluous and makes machines, computers and other technologies the main focus of production. The "model" signals the end of living work in favor of dead labour. Baudrillard uses the term "model" to depict a new order of social organization which now drives everything by modulating what is given to it according to the rule of "reproducing the same". The third order of simulacra is a social order that reproduces frenetically the apparent form of productivist organization which is now however emptied of its content.

The concept of simulation involves the disappearance of reality behind (its) signs, as well as an internally generated "effect" of reality. For Baudrillard, society moves from a "capitalist-productivist society to a neo-capitalist cybernetic order" (Baudrillard 1993, 60). The immanence of the code has taken the place of transcendent models ("God, Man, Progress and even History") (Baudrillard 1993, 60).

> "Life is now ruled by the discontinuous indeterminism of the genetic code, by the *teleonomic* principle [...] Finality is there in advance, inscribed in the code" (Baudrillard 1993, 59; italics in the text).

In the same way that language has codes or models that systematize communication and just as cells contain genetic codes, DNA, that structure experience and behaviour – society likewise operates according to codes and models which organize human life.

Hegarty (2004, 55) explains that "Baudrillard speaks of the general 'code' that replaces the quasi-Marxist term 'the system', as the code is what drives the system". Baudrillard's model of the code is DNA which programs various directions and constrains individual behaviour but which itself is invisible and which is subject to aleatory combinations and variations mixed with other social and environmental phenomena.[86]

---

[86] In *Forget Foucault,* Baudrillard (2007b, 47) says that the cellular form of power does not contain any revolutionary principle at all. Baudrillard suggests that precisely on the most microscopic level of the molecular, the DNA code dominates and controls behaviour. Baudrillard disagrees that micro-desires, small differences, unconscious practices, anonymous marginal elements constitute a new source of revolutionary action. Deleuze and Foucault are the main targets of Baudrillard's critique here – to fetishize a micropolitics of desire might be to advocate a politics of liberation in a sphere which itself may be controlled by coercive and in some cases unknown powers. It is unclear of the potential of the 'mass' as a silent majority and Baudrillard "vacillates between

> "After the metaphysics of being and appearance, after energy and determinacy, the metaphysics of indeterminacy and the code…Digitality is its metaphysical principle (Leibniz's God), and DNA its prophet…it is in the genetic code that the 'genesis of simulacra' today finds its completed form" (Baudrillard 1993, 57).

In the third order of simulacra, the model and its internal system of relations (which are cybernetically controlled) generate phenomena. The new operational formation is ruled by the machinery of the question and response process. The order of control is buried "in the depth of the 'biological' body" in "black boxes where all the commandments ferment" (Baudrillard 1976, 104; 1993: 58). This is the era of cellular programming, of molecular emission of signals.

> "Whether it is prison cells, electronic cells, party cells, or microbiological cells, we are dealing with, we are always searching for the smallest indivisible element…even space is no longer linear or unidimensional but *cellular*, indefinitely generating the same signals like the lonely and repetitive habits of a stir crazy prisoner" (Baudrillard, 1993, 58; italics in the text).

At this locked-in ('cell'-ular) level there is no transcendent purpose or meaning. All that is recognized is the arbitrary mix of elements in this cellular, reflex world – everything is ready to be decoded. Binary combination is the framework; the mode of decoding it through the zero and the one (0/1). Baudrillard refers to Jacques Monod as the "strict theologian" of this era (Baudrillard 1993, 59).[87] Social theory must now be reconsidered in view of genetic programmes. For Baudrillard, the digital code and its dual form regulates society.

This code is the blueprint for processes of simulacra. For example, the media provides models that structure various activities within daily life. Yet, the society of simulations also severely limits an individual's range of reaction and behaviour. For Baudrillard, social control is based upon codes (not powerful individuals or

---

cynicism and approval" (Huyssen 1989, 14). This ambiguity is however also a key feature of Nietzsche's treatment of the 'master' in *On the Genealogy of Morals* as we saw in chapter 1 (section 3).

[87] Baudrillard plays with the (French) acronym for DNA: 'ADN' and 'ADoNaï' – the latter means God in Hebrew.

interest groups) and programming becomes the principle of social organization. Individuals respond to pre-arranged repertoire of messages in the realm of economics, politics, culture and everyday life (Baudrillard 1993, 63).

As already mentioned in chapter 1 (section 2), consumers have a range of choices and the code tries to embrace contingency, incorporate a certain variety and accept an unpredictable outcome. But this all arises thanks to the code. There is no independent, external real, as in the first order of simulacra, but a real that arises (like usefulness and function in *The System of Objects*) only as an effect of the code (Butler 1999, 39).

This is a world of simulated "tests" and programmed differences. Tests, polls, elections, consumer purchases, media and so forth are all part of a system of binary regulation stabilized by two political parties, two opposing classes, two (or more) choices at every moment.[88] 'Public' and 'opinion' are, for Baudrillard, simulation models as is their combination (public opinion): "We see the "impossibility of obtaining a *non-simulated* response to a *direct(ed)* question" (Baudrillard 1993, 67).

Responses are structured in a binary system of affirmation or negation: every advertisement, political candidate and poll is a test to which one is to respond. Through the selection among alternatives on offer, individuals are absorbed in a coded system of similarities and dissimilarities of identities and programmed differences. The codes send signs and continually test individuals, inscribing them into a simulated order. Different political parties, products, life styles and so forth are intended to manage and deter demands for radical social change. For Baudrillard (1993, 69):

> "duopoly is the completed stage of monopoly. It is not that a political will (State intervention, anti-trust laws etc.) shatters the market's monopoly: any unitary system if it wants to survive must find a binary regulation ... power is only absolute if it is able to diffract into various equivalents, if it knows how to divide in order to become stronger".

---

[88] The regulation is binary: "it is always the 0/1, the binary scansion that is affirmed as the metastable or homeostatic form of contemporary systems. It is the core of the processes of simulation that dominate us" (Baudrillard 1993, 69).

As a symbol of this stabilized society of simulations, Baudrillard refers to the Twin Towers of the New York World Trade Centre (WTC):[89]

> "The two towers of the WTC are the visible sign of the closure of the system in the vertigo of doubling, while the other skyscrapers are each of them the original moment of a system continually surpassing itself in a perpetual crisis and challenge" (Baudrillard 1993, 70).

Everything is reduced to binary regulation: Two supposedly dominant poles (0/1) maintain a self-regulating, self-reproducing system. Oppositional, outside or threatening elements to the system are functional parts of a society of simulation. They are mere 'alibis' which only enhance social control. Digitization and cybernetic control are a universalizing cultural power because they reduce "the concept 'opposite' to a pure form without content, comparable to exchange value. The ones and zeros are an irresistible general medium of equivalence" (Levin 1996, 177).

Simulation is a system of differences in which one cannot speak of something outside the system.[90] For Rex Butler (1999, 24), the point is that:

---

[89] In his article, "In the Shadow of McLuhan: Jean Baudrillard's Theory of Simulation", Huyssen (1989, 8) explores Baudrillard's "appropriation" of McLuhan's work, as well as the "hidden referent of Baudrillard's media theory, which in its political and social implication was always much more than a theory of images and image perception". From his discussions of Disneyland, Pop Art, and the Twin Towers of the World Trade Centre, to Baudrillard's (1987) book *Amérique* – "the ultimate hidden referent of Baudrillard's discussion on simulation is the imaginary United States", according to Huyssen (1989: 13). "America is the paradigm and telos for the theory of simulation just as it was the paradigm and telos in McLuhan's theory of the electric age. But the parallel goes further...in *L'Echange symbolique et la Mort* and then in 'Precession of Simulacra' Baudrillard reads history in terms of the successive stages of the simulacrum, just as McLuhan read history as a function of changes in media technology" (Huyssen 1989, 13).

[90] According to Huyssen (1989, 10) "If an outside of simulation is no longer possible, then the question of the real becomes like the question of God or the question of truth: not provable, but also not to be disproven, or not to be represented, therefore in desperate need to be simulated to conceal the truth that there can be no truth". Baudrillard's simulation according to Huyssen (1989, 10) is to be seen as "a strategic point of articulation of ... cynicism, an enlight-

135

> "simulation ... is not an empirical phenomenon... Baudrillard is very well aware of the paradox that in so far as the simulation he is describing exists, it makes it any way of verifying it as impossible... [t]he very real which we say is lost in simulation and against which we compare it is only conceivable in simulated form."

The challenge Baudrillard sets himself, according to Butler is to describe simulation when it is not possible to compare it to anything else (Butler 1999, 24). The world can only be grasped as a simulation.

In the first paragraph of his book *Simulacra and Simulation,* in the chapter "The Precession of Simulacra", Baudrillard (1983, 1-2) discusses the difference between the second and third orders of simulacra by means of a brief analysis of Jorge Luis Borges' very short story *"On Rigor in Science"*, a 'story' of a map so detailed that it totally covers the territory it depicts: the story is about how the real is displaced by its representation. Borges' writing attempts to provoke a questioning of the very nature of origins, of originality. Yet Baudrillard regards Borges' tale of the simulacrum of the territory as "having nothing but the discrete charm of the second order simulacra" (Baudrillard 1983, 1). Borges' description of the simulacrum is merely that of the "map, the double, the mirror of the concept" (Baudrillard 1983, 1) this description is still based upon an external reality.[91]

In the third order of simulacra, "the map precedes the territory – a "precession" of simulacra. So now it is the 'real' territory that slowly rots away with the vestiges here and there, this is the desert of the real" (Baudrillard 1994, 1). There is no longer a "sovereign difference" between the map and the territory (Baudrillard 1981, 10). There is no gap between the real and its representation

---

ened false consciousness, which Peter Sloterdijk has cogently analysed as a dominant mindset of the post sixties era" (Sloterdijk 1987).

[91] "The coefficient of reality is proportionate to the reserve of the imaginary that gives it its specific weight. This is true of terrestrial as well as space exploration: when there is no more virgin, and hence available to the imaginary, territory, when the map covers the whole territory, something like the reality principle disappears. In this sense, the conquest of space constitutes an irreversible threshold on the way to the loss of terrestrial references" (Baudrillard 1993, 86f).

that leads to the artificial revival of the real of the third order of simulacra, its re-introduction of difference to maintain a functioning reference, but it is a real that is possible because of the model or code. Simulation generates a real from models (that precede any experience or perception of the real). This model is not closed in the sense that it does not interact with its environment; it is closed in the sense that it functions on its own terms, free of the supporting environment.

Following to a certain extent Roland Barthes' notion of "*the effect of the real*" (Barthes 1986, 141-148)[92] Baudrillard also speaks in this context of a reality effect, of an effect of the real (Baudrillard, 1993: 62). It is therefore, as Pawlett (2007, 41) rightly says, to misread Baudrillard to claim as Callinicos (1989, 145) or King (2000, 264)[93] do, that we live in a world of free-floating, independent signs or signifiers that mean nothing, or alternatively anything. Instead, for Pawlett (2007, 41; italics in the text) "[s]ignifiers *simulate* the effect of meaning and reference" and a reality effect is produced. This is what Baudrillard refers to as hyperreality.

---

[92] For Barthes, "reality" and the "real" refer to the lived world as something that finally resists any representation and meaning (Barthes, 1986a, 146). See Butler (1999: 27) on the differences between Baudrillard and Barthes.

[93] According to Anthony King (2000, 264) in his article 'A Critique of Baudrillard's Hyperreality', Baudrillard's epistemological notion of hyperreality "refers to a culture based upon foundationless representations" (King 2000, 260). For King "Baudrillard's theory of the hyperreal is Cartesian" (King, 2000: 261) because it consists of an ocular fixation. "The general framework and basic assumptions on which hyperreality rest are Cartesian" (King 2000, 261). According to King (2000, 262), for both Descartes and Baudrillard, "the ocular sensation of external material objects is the starting point... Baudrillard and Descartes share the same representationalist paradigm but whereas Descartes sees the mists of nihilism descending the moment one considers how we might verify the representations we see, Baudrillard historicizes this moment of doubt to the mid-1970s, arguing that the classic epistemological problem of representation and skepticism emerges for a society as the television attains a position of cultural dominance" (King, 2000: 266). My above discussion on the intrinsic links between semiology and simulation show that for Baudrillard language is not supplementary to the ocular experience but radically constitutive of it. For an excellent discussion of Baudrillard and Descartes, see Butler (1999, 144-146).

Disneyland is one essential example that Baudrillard refers to. Disneyland is one component of the "double simulacrum" that constitutes "hyperreality" because the alleged real world, which it is supposed to make a (distorted) reference to, is also a simulacrum. In Baudrillard's eyes Disneyland, is sectioned off as a place of childhood, in order to show that the rest of America is by contrast 'grownup'. "Disneyland is there to conceal the fact that it is the 'real' country, all of real America, which is Disneyland (just as prisons are there to conceal the fact that it is the social in its entirety, which is carceral)" (Baudrillard 1994, 12).

Baudrillard combines the idea that prisons hide that we are incarcerated in society, with the idea that Disneyland is there to make the rest of America look real. We believe in our freedom because we lock criminals away and we believe in the real thanks to official places of "make-believe" like Disneyland. The construction of such a double simulacrum, diverts us from seeing the structural similarities between the two realms.

"The Disneyland imaginary is neither true nor false; it is a deterrence machine set up to rejuvenate in reverse the fiction of the real" (Baudrillard 1983, 25). Baudrillard refers here to the process 'deterrence' from nuclear deterrence, which takes the place of full-blown war. Deterrence is "the neutral, implosive violence of metastable systems or systems in involution...the balance of terror is the terror of balance" (Baudrillard 1994, 31).

For Baudrillard, all binary systems are deterrence models in which radical change is ruled out since the very fact of an option acts as a deterrent against a demand for change. The system creates distinctions, puts forward an "other" side so that it is proved all the more. This 'other' however, is generated by the code. We do not have the system but the world in its very abstract indifference can only be explained because of it.

Baudrillard calls this binary system "hyperreality" because the real itself is defined only in terms of our broader social codes. "Hyperreality" is the semiotic effect of a more real than real (beyond the distinction real/unreal – Nietzsche's "Twilight of the

Idols"). Hyperreality is both the aesthetic and epistemological form of simulation (Baudrillard 1993, 70-6).[94] As Levin sees it, hyperreality "is a way of presenting and receiving reality – in brief, it is reality conceived without otherness. In a sense, it abolishes the space within which the 'scene' of reality can be represented" (Levin 1996, 274).

Hyperreality is reality pushed to an extreme. There is no more distance, but rather a surplus of reality, with no more secrets, or illusions of interiority.

> "Irreality no longer belongs to the dream or the phantasm, to a beyond or a hidden interiority, but to the *hallucinatory resemblance of the real to itself*. To gain exit from the crisis of representation, the real must be sealed off in pure repetition. Before emerging in pop art and painterly neo-realism, this tendency can already be seen in the *nouveau roman*. Here the project is to create a void around the real, to eradicate all psychology and subjectivity from it in order to give it pure objectivity" (Baudrillard 1993, 72).

In the above paragraph, Baudrillard moves towards providing a literary and aesthetic dimension to hyperreality. He sees hyperreality at work not only in the setup of our larger social scheme but also at play within such artistic movements such as the French

---

[94] Levin (1996, 274) sees "a thematic connection between the hyperreality of simulation and Heidegger's *Gestell* (the framing of our experience of Being through technology) which can be articulated most effectively through consideration of the enhanced deconstructive, reproductive and, reconstructive capacities of digital technologies". *Gestell* is a Heideggerian term for the technological system, as he described in his 1953 lecture *Die Frage nach der Technik*. According to Günter Figal (1992, 160): "Das Wesen der Technik, das 'Ge-stell', ist nichts anderes als die herausfordernde, sich in keinem Ziel vollendende Dynamik der Weltbeherrschung und Naturausbeutung". The word *Gestell* is not used by Baudrillard, "but the influence of Heidegger's reading of 'Western Metaphysics' is everywhere in his work" (Levin 1996, 273). The *Gestell* of metaphysics and technology is problematic because "it screens out anything resistant to codification in rational form" (Levin 1996, 273). For Heidegger, this means that 'Being' is reduced to 'being' (mere phenomena). Levin also mentions that "Baudrillard was one of the first to elaborate Heidegger's theory of technology… particularly in his 'critique of the political economy of the sign', his analysis of the digitalism of the 'third order' of simulation, and the structural revolution of value" (Levin 1996, 273).

"nouveau roman".[95] The *nouveau roman* describes a movement of experimental French writers who reject elements of novel writing such as a linear, sequential plot, as well as the analysis of characters' motives or the notion of a central protagonist. There is an attempt to maintain a neutral register and explore surfaces. The *nouveaux romanciers* saw a close relation between fiction and theory. Relatedly, there is an attempt towards a rational approach, which seeks to emphasize the self-conscious nature of writing fiction.

In addition, Baudrillard refers to hyperreality within the context of American pop art. In *Consumer Society*, Baudrillard (1998, 115-121) theorizes pop art as a turning point in the history of art – the point at which art becomes simply the reproduction of signs of consumer society, which is primarily as we have seen, a system of signs.

> "Pop art signifies the end of perspective, the end of evocation, the end of testimony, the end the creative act and, last but not least, the end of the subversion of the world and the curse of art. Its aim is not merely the immanence of the 'civilised' world, but its total integration into that world. There is in this a mad ambition, the ambition of abolishing the whole splendours (and foundations) of a whole culture, the culture of transcendence. And there is in it perhaps quite simply also an ideology" (Baudrillard 1970, 34; 1998, 116; translation modified).

It is clear from the above section in *Consumer Society* that Baudrillard's intention is not to criticize pop art for a naïve Americanism, an overt commercialism, or a flatness and banality. For Baudrillard, pop art reproduces the very logic of contemporary culture. Pop art does not oppose the world of objects, it is an art of "collusion" (Baudrillard 1998, 121). It is the first art form to explore its own status as an art object which is "signed" and "consumed" (Baudrillard 1998, 117). Pop art is the triumph of signs over the referent and the end of re-presentational art. It is an en-

---

[95] An important feature of the new novel or *nouveau roman* is their involvement in literary theory and criticism; from the 1950s onwards the novels themselves have been accompanied by a discussion of the "evolution of fiction as a genre, realism, and the political role of literature" (Britton 1992, 1).

capsulation of hyperrealist simulation because it collapses the distinction between reality and fiction.

By leaning on the examples of Warhol's pop art, Baudrillard identifies three modalities of simulation.

> "Tout Andy Warhol est là: les répliques multipliées du visage de Marilyn sont bien en meme temps la mort de l'original et la fin de la représentation (Baudrillard 1976, 108) ".[96]

In this above quote we see, firstly, that the basic form of hyperreality involves a model (i.e., Marylin Monroe's digitized and reproduced face), the binary code and digitality (0/1). Secondly, there is the immediate close up 'reading' of the object, along with the splitting of the object and its serial reduplication.

It must be kept in mind, that the concept of the hyperreal (the dissolution of real and imaginary into a code) depends on the technical mechanism (*dispositif*) of the mass media. Edgar Morin already saw the mass media's tendency to collapse reality and fiction in his book *L'Esprit du Temps* (1962). For Morin:

> "In mass culture, the imaginary and real are more intertwined than in religious myths or fairy tales. The imaginary projects itself not towards the sky but towards earth. The gods – the celebrities, athletes – and the demons – criminals, murderer – are among us, made of our flesh and blood, and are mortal as we are. Mass culture is realistic" (Morin 1998, 219; *my translation*).

If the content of mass culture is realistic then the fictitious potential of the medium is not exhausted. Instead, there is a focus on the real – that is to say what is considered to be real.

> "It is this excess of reality that makes us stop believing in it. The saturation of the world, the technical saturation of life, the excess of possibilities, of actualisation of needs and desires. How do we believe in reality once its

---

[96] The English translation by Iain Hamilton Grant is: "Every Andy Warhol does this: the multiple replicas of Marilyn Monroe's face are of course at the same time the death of the original and the end of representation" (Baudrillard 1993, 70). It is rather strange to 'pluralise' Andy Warhol ("Every Andy Warhol does this"). Perhaps "All of Andy Warhol is here" or "The essence of Andy Warhol is here" is a clearer rendition of what Baudrillard has in mind. Iain Hamilton Grant is perhaps reproducing the serialized 'logic' that Baudrillard is discussing here.

production has become automatic? The real is suffocated by its own accumulation. There is no way for the dream to be an expression of a desire since its virtual accomplishment is already present" (Baudrillard 2005, 19).

In addition to art, Baudrillard uses metaphors drawn from science especially physics[97] to exemplify the "confusion of the fact with its model" (Baudrillard 1994, 17). He speaks of the "implosion of antagonistic poles" (Baudrillard, 1994, 17), "short circuits" (Baudrillard 1994, 217) and a "Moebius strip" (Baudrillard 1993, 36). The real and the imaginary but also the two poles of "cause and effect" merge and exterminate (Baudrillard 1994, 122) each other in an "uninterrupted circulation without reference" (Baudrillard 1994, 6).

Baudrillard plays mischievously with the above-mentioned scientific concepts (and others) by generalizing them as social processes. For example, the Moebius Strip is used as a metaphor for the proliferation of models and simulations in society at large. Just as a Moebius Strip when cut in half, produces more complex spiralled structure, so simulations form a spiralling and circular system with no beginning and no end, they multiply infinitely.

> "If the entire circle of any act or event is envisaged in a system where linear continuity and dialectical polarity no longer exist, in a field unhinged by simulation, then all determination evaporates, every act terminates at the end of the cycle" (Baudrillard 1994, 31).

Baudrillard refers to black holes, entropy, DNA and genetics, digital codes and information theory, satellites and cybernetics in or-

---

[97] In his 1952 essay *'Pataphysics,'* Baudrillard said that "the pataphysic mind is the nail in the tire" (Baudrillard 2005, 213). The so-called pataphysical was invented by Alfred Jarry and his science of 'imaginary solutions' represents an obverse and parodic mirror to the philosophically and scientifically serious (Pefanis 1991, 9). Pataphysics reveals that science is not as lucid as it appears, since science must often ignore the arbitrary status of its own axioms. According to the pataphysical view, poetry must draw its rules of metaphor from a genre that rules out metaphor. Science inspires poetry. Jarry does not borrow scientific concepts so much as scientific conceits, doing so, in order to imagine a 'counterdynamic' (Jarry 1965, 253).

der to 'illustrate' his theory.[98] Kellner regards Baudrillard's writing as "perhaps the first radical high-tech, new wave social theory" (Kellner 1989, 84) and very rightly goes on to explain that Baudrillard provides "perhaps the first self-consciously produced science fiction social theory to project futuristic anticipations of the world to come, the world right around the corner" (Kellner 1989, 84). [99]

Baudrillard immerses himself and reproduces the features and the limits of the social order he describes and sometimes attacks. Levin regards Baudrillard as a social philosopher who in his writing, enacts 'implosions', collapsing binary polarities:

> "Baudrillard appropriates the academic languages of social theory – even the technical languages of molecular biology, wave mechanics, catastrophe theory, chaos theory – and applies them illegitimately, collapsing the normal distance between the signifier and the signified, the sign and the referent, so that abstractions and intellectualisations are pressed into dimensions of lived experience, words become things, models become material infrastructures" (Levin 1996, 82).

In the spirit of Nietzsche, Baudrillard seeks to knock down idols and reduce the 'seriousness' of abstract concepts by supplementing them with narrative provocations and "literalizations". This is in tune with his Nietzschean reversal of the opposition between truth and lie, dealt with in the previous chapter. In the incipit of *Simulacra and Simulation* (1994: 1), Baudrillard "quotes" the Old Testament book of *Ecclesiastes*: "The simulacrum is never that

---

[98] For a critique of Baudrillard's use of scientific metaphors see Sokal and Bricmont (2000) and for a general critique of Baudrillard's writing and thought see Zima (2010).

[99] Kellner asks whether Baudrillard's texts are to be seen as mere "simulations of social processes which are implicated in the object of critique so much that radical critique dissolves in the reproduction of its object? Or do his texts actually illuminate the transition to a new type of society and provide perspectives that might be useful for critical social theory and for projects of political transformation?" (Kellner 1989, 84). Kellner concludes that Baudrillard's theory lacks sufficient empirical description which is why it fails to be useful for radical critique. Mike Gane, in his introduction to Baudrillard's book *Symbolic Exchange and Death*, claims that there is a sense in which Kellner's relation to Baudrillard is one of "repulsion and attraction" (Gane 1993, ix)

which conceals the truth – it is the truth which conceals that there is none. The simulacrum is true." This is a completely fictious reference to a book which purports to be a book of wisdom. Neither the word "simulacrum" or the word "truth," appears in *Ecclesiastes*.

Baudrillard's insights are valuable not because they are accurate depictions of lived experience. As Levin rightly puts it: "if Baudrillard is in some sense right about all this, then what he has to say will seem obvious (if ineffectual), and soak into the texture of our conventional understanding of ourselves, as so many of his ideas indeed already have done" (Levin 1998, 208).

Baudrillard's work should not be judged according to models of accuracy or whether his analysis is "right" or "wrong".

In chapters 1, 2 and 3, I related Baudrillard's work to Nietzschean genealogy and I emphasized that Baudrillard's aim (like that of Nietzsche) is to change our current moral pre-judices regarding the right and the wrong and he performs a critically motivated art of drastic presentation in order to show that such divisions are always con-textually driven.

Anthony King confirms this when he says:

> "the importance of Baudrillard lies in the fact that he both demonstrates the most extreme symptoms of contemporary intellectual malaise and simultaneously provides the cure of that disease…no other individual represents both critical and pessimistic moments quite so dramatically. It is in this contradiction that the lasting importance of Baudrillard's work resides" (King 1998, 106).

Baudrillard speaks dramatically of the "trauma" (Baudrillard 1994, 31) of simulation and describes a psychotic stage of culture. Baudrillard suggests a series of possible causes, but no final answers.

This section has provided an outline of hyperreality, with some examples and metaphors to illustrate the "double simulacrum" that makes up hyperreality (such as Disneyland). In the next section, I now look at the multiple causes he provides.

5.3 The Causes of Simulation

We have discussed Baudrillard's notion of the hyperreal and how its (double) simulacrum unfolds by means of a (binary) code. In this section, I will go through some of the possible causes that contribute to the collapse into hyperreal simulation. I call it a collapse into the hyperreal because for Baudrillard, the inauguration of an age of simulation constitutes a fundamental turning point in comparison with the previous history of signs. Baudrillard speaks dramatically of the "hell of simulation" (Baudrillard 1994, 14) and describes a deranged stage of culture.

Baudrillard suggests a series of possible causes for his diagnosis, yet, as we have seen, his work also seeks to overturn conventional social scientific views of motivation, origin and determination.[100] Organisational hierarchies, conceptual distinctions, 'reality' and other topologies, are, as Levin says "empirical – they can be described – but their causal and functional 'explanations' have been bracketed or undermined" (Levin 1996, 203). By means of a genealogical analysis (e.g., of the consumer society and simulation), Baudrillard, in the footsteps of Nietzsche, problematizes direct, and linear causality in order to reveal transformations at multiple levels.

As emphasized in chapter 1, Baudrillard, like Nietzsche, brings attention to the fundamental changes, psychological, moral inventions that arise within specific material and cultural contexts. Nietzsche and Baudrillard do not, however, simply oppose themselves to the search for origins. Baudrillard does want to show how the past inheres in the present. A search for origins must accept the discovery of an origin that challenges our existing worldview. In what follows, I reconstruct some of the possible causes for the hyperreal. These range widely, as we shall see, from economic causes (the floatation of currencies) to technological, cultural ones and finally I turn to a metaphysical cause (Nietzsche's Death of God).

---

[100] Baudrillard problematizes 'motivation' by focussing on consumer society's myth of 'needs'.

5.3.1 Simulation as an economic effect

In *Symbolic Exchange and Death*, Baudrillard discusses economic factors for the emergence of simulation. Baudrillard connects the flotation of currencies to the flotation of signs, which he sees as parallel processes (Baudrillard 1993, 7; 23). The flotation of currencies is linked to the demise of the "gold standard" in economics and the flotation of signs is due to the structuralist dismissal of the referent in the realm of linguistics (Baudrillard 1993, 10).

This parallel between linguistics and economics can be seen in terms of the Marxist 'base and superstructure' model, whereby the (cultural) superstructure of signs reflects and represents a specific development at the economic base. At times, Baudrillard indeed seems to advocate such a classical reading of simulation, when he speaks of simulation as driven by the processes of capital (Baudrillard 1993, 6-7) and when the history of simulation is seen as "parallel to the mutation of the law of value" (Baudrillard 1993, 57). The influence of capital manifests itself especially with the introduction of an abstract code, i.e., the law of value.

> "Because in the end, throughout history, it was capital that first fed on the destructuration of every referential, of every human objective, that shattered every distinction between true and the false, good and evil, in order to establish a radical law of equivalence and exchange, the iron law of its power. Capital was the first to play at deterrence, abstraction, disconnection, deterritorialisation, etc, and if it is the one that fostered reality, the reality principle, it was also the first to liquidate it by exterminating use value, all real equivalence of production and wealth, in the very sense we have of the unreality of the stakes and the omnipotence of manipulation. Well, today it is this same logic that is even more set against capital. And as soon as it wishes to this disastrous spiral by secreting a last glimmer of reality, on which to establish a last glimmer of power, it does nothing but multiply the signs and accelerate the play of simulation (Baudrillard 1994, 22).[101]

On the other hand, Baudrillard breaks through the logic of base and superstructure when he writes that fashion is far ahead of

---

[101] Simulation theory thus comes close to Debord's economic theory of the spectacle even if Baudrillard (1994, 30) proclaims that we are now "beyond the spectacle".

money and the economy in terms of its general commutation (Baudrillard 1993, 56). The superstructure consumes in certain ways the base and as a result the two concepts lose their meaning (Baudrillard 1993, 18). One should not try to "search for the secret of the code in technique or economy" (Baudrillard 1993, 56) because in the time of simulation and the "loss of determination of the economic, we also lose any possibility of conceiving the [economic] as the determinant agency" (Baudrillard 1993, 9). Political economy itself is for Baudrillard a redundant paradigm and has been taken over by simulation.

Baudrillard now classifies (with hindsight) his own previous theory of the sign economy[102] terminologically provisional (Baudrillard 1993, 8). According to Levin, Baudrillard's "general theory of simulation resists the functionalist (and 'materialist') tendency to accord 'superstructural', secondary status to semantic processes and dynamics in society" (Levin 1996, 203).

5.3.2 Simulation as media effect

Even as the aforementioned section denies the importance of the economic as well as the technological ("superstructural") spheres, many critics regard developments outlined by Baudrillard in (media) technology as the main cause of simulation. [103]

The development of the process of simulation is indeed unthinkable without media technologies such as television (Huyssen, 1989).[104] The theory of simulation is largely a theory of the mass media age. But are the mass media, television, newspapers, advertising, the internet to be seen as the cause of simulation? Is it due to the technological stucture's "onesided" communication (with-

---

[102] As demonstrated in Baudrillard's early studies on the *System of Objects* (1968) *Consumer Society* (1970) and *For a Critique of the Political Economy of the Sign* (1981b).

[103] See Huyssen (1989) and for a critique of the 'media'-based causes for simulation see also Zapf (2010, 118).

[104] According to Huyssen (1989: 11): "...if there is a technological determinism, media determinism in Baudrillard, it is more sophisticated than McLuhan's in that it does not simply ignore the discourses of social theory and political economy, but claims to have worked through them".

out response), its "unilateralness", which Baudrillard emphasizes in his article "Requiem for the Media" (Baudrillard 1972, 200-208)? But in a Renaissance art work there is just as much "speech without response (*parole sans réponse*)" (Baudrillard 1972, 228). What is so new in today's media?

At times, Baudrillard's theory of simulation is in tune with a model based on resemblance, which involves optical illusions, techniques of deception, immersion and *trompe -l'oeil*. Dieter Mersch for instance (2006, 157) sees Baudrillard as a theoretician of media illusions. According to this view, the particularly modern achievement of the media lies in allowing images to come so close to their object to the extent that the audience can no longer be certain whether or not that which is shown is a reproduction or not. According to Anthony King (2000, 263) "Hyperreality occurs … when the relationship between the object and the representation is called into doubt. The television screen, from which individuals derived their notion of reality, has no verifiable or direct connection with the outside world".

Baudrillard's concept of hyperreality, however, goes beyond mere perspectival doubt, illusion and confusion (this belongs more to the first order of simulacra). Crucially, Baudrillard seeks to show that simulation involves precisely a loss of illusion: "[T]he 'realising' of the world, through science and technology, is precisely what simulation is – the exorcism of the terror of illusion by the most sophisticated means of the realisation of the world" (Baudrillard 1993 BL, 184).

There are three powerful factors of modern mass media that can be identified from Baudrillard's scattered remarks: transparency, acceleration and proliferation. In the 1980s, Baudrillard thematises the phenomenon of technical acceleration with his friend Paul Virilio. Thanks to electric media, information circulates at the speed of light. In *Fatal Strategies* (1990 FS) Baudrillard claims that simulation leads to a kind of blindness (i.e, an undifferentiated, 'blurred' perspective), which the frenzy and acceleration of signs, generates.

Inextricably linked to this is also the issue of proliferation. The quicker signs replace each other, the more they need to be produced (and vice versa):

> "Nothing (not even God) now disappears by coming to an end, by dying. Instead, things disappear, because of extenuation or extermination or as a result of the epidemic of simulation, as a result of their transfer into secondary existence of simulation. Rather than a mortal mode of disappearance, then a fractal mode of dispersal" (Baudrillard 1993 TE, 4).

The transfer of the world into secondary existence of simulation means "we live amid the interminable reproduction of ideals, phantasms, images and dreams which are now behind us, yet which we continue to reproduce in a sort of inescapable indifference" (Baudrillard 1993 TE, 4).

The overflow of images in the media is linked to a third moment the transparency of images. The world becomes a huge image because the mass media raises everything to the surface of the screen nothing is spared from this visual over presence of images where there is nothing left to see.

When the world can only be experienced through the media apparatus there can be no meaningful comparison between the image and the real. The image forfeits the tension between the signifier and the signified; behind the surface of images there no longer opens any imaginary dimension:

> "Gone is the very imagination of the image, its 'optical illusion', since in this synthetic operation the referent no longer exists, nor is there any time for reality to take hold when it straight away becomes virtual" (Baudrillard 2008, 42).

The media do not worship images for Baudrillard. Instead, there is a subtle rebellion against the image, a new form of hostility. Modern iconoclasm writes Baudrillard lies no longer in the destruction of images but in the unlimited production of images (where there is no longer anything to see). If one side of the image and reality equation topples, then the other side will also be destabilized. When the world has become an image, and the image no longer has anything to show, nothing remains of the world.

According to Zygmunt Bauman, we should simply switch off our televisions and go outside. This would make us realize that not everything is hyperreal or simulated (Bauman 1995, 87). Bauman has a point that the phenomenon of simulation is largely due to the excess of information of the mass media. For Baudrillard, the mass media indeed transform events into information and make events lose their sense of reality for the observer. But this is only one aspect of Baudrillard's theory of simulation, even though it is the aspect that has been focused upon by secondary critics and has also been the most influential.

5.3.3 Simulation and the Death of God

In chapter 4 (section 3), we saw how Baudrillard names the four orders of the image – the order of the sacrament, the order of the malefice, the order of sorcery, and the order of simulation and he differentiates between signs that dissimulate something (the first two) and signs that dissimulate that there is nothing.

Nietzsche (1988: 3; my translation) characterizes the modern condition best when he claimed that "what is new about our current position to philosophy is the conviction, that no other time had, that we do not possess the truth." Nietzsche proclaimed the "death of God" and was thereby able to encapsulate the core condition of the era like no other.[105] The death of God and the entrance of simulation are possibly related phenomena.

Baudrillard himself relates the death of God to the desperate modern search for the real: "it is when one is no longer sure of the existence of God or when one has lost the naïve faith in a self-evident reality that it becomes absolutely necessary to believe in it" (Baudrillard 2005, 19).

It is finally the authority of God, who guarantees the stability of the pre-modern sign order.

> "All Western faith and good faith became engaged in this wager on representation: that a sign could refer to the depth of meaning, that a sign could be exchanged for meaning and that something could guarantee this ex-

---

[105] Regarding the death of God in Nietzsche see especially *Also Sprach Zarathustra* (1883-1885).

> change – God of course. But what if God himself can be simulated, that is to say can be reduced to the signs that constitute faith? Then the whole system becomes weightless, it is no longer itself anything but a gigantic simulacrum – not unreal, but a simulacrum, that is to say never exchanged for the real, but exchanged for itself, in an uninterrupted circuit without reference or circumference" (Baudrillard 1994, 5-6).

The death of God collapses fixed distinctions between the real and the apparent, true and the false, good and evil, which are the very structuring principles of Platonic, Christian and scientific thought. Science, like religion is based upon the split between the true and the false and they both establish a hierarchy between terms. 'Enlightened' from superstition, science cannot access the real world because the real world was part of the fable.

Nietzsche's "History of an Error" in *Twilight of the Idols* is the genealogy of an Idea (of the true world). For Nietzsche, some ideas simply fade when they become fetishes (significantly overinvested or in Baudrillard's terminology: hyperreal), no longer even a mechanism of exchange; they are hollow-out and disinvested (Allison 1999, 182).

The "true world", for Nietzsche, encapsulates Western metaphysics: it covers everything from religion to science, morality, and teleology among others. Nietzsche's critique of the true world (as a world of pure fiction) attacks the entire apparatus of intelligibility, which defines the discourse of the West and the Judeo-Christian universe. In *The Antichrist*, Nietzsche claims that such a fictional world is driven by a hatred of the natural, the sensible world, as is Baudrillard's digital code of hyperreality. As David Allison (1999, 183) rightly puts it, Baudrillard's "oversaturated world of hyperreality… [is] for Nietzsche, precisely the entire symbolic of the religio-moral idiosyncrasy".[106] "Let us represent monotono-theism by adopting the manner of a gravedigger! And above all, away with the body, this wretched *idée fixe* of the senses, disfigured by all the fallacies of logic, refuted, even impossible,

---

[106] Heidegger calls this the Western tradition of "ontotheology" and Nietzsche calls it monotono-theism (Allison 1999, 183).

although it is impudent enough to behave as if it were real!" (Nietzsche 1968b, 479-80).

Conclusion

In this chapter, I gave an exposition of Baudrillard's third stage of simulacra, the hyperreal. This order of simulacra differs from the previous two, because it involves a dissolution, an implosion of poles, into the code. For Baudrillard, the digital code regulates society. This code rules processes of simulacra and it is based upon a pre-coded opposition, a pre-coded otherness. In the third order of simulacra, the model and its internal system of relations generate phenomena. Signs refer to other signs in a model not to an external referent or reality. Although science demands an end to mimetic as well as mythical thought, Baudrillard shows that this rejection is deluded. The demand for direct access is mythical but also fatal.[107]

In the footsteps of Nietzsche, Baudrillard's work provides a fatal optimism about the "reversibility" of systems. This means that the basic codes of a system must not be opposed, subverted or inverted but rather pushed to the point where they begin to turn upon themselves and collapse to reveal their hollowness (to philosophize in Nietzschean fashion, with a hammer).

---

[107] In his book, *Seduction*, Baudrillard (1990 S) recounts the myth of Narcissus, who mistakes his own reflection for another (his beloved Echo). Baudrillard emphasizes the role of the mirror as the key explanatory figure for the myth. It allows the essential confusion of Narcissus' reflection with another's but cannot itself be reflected. Baudrillard sees the mirror as a figure of seduction in the story: "Seduction cannot possibly be represented because in seduction the distance between real and its double, the same and other is abolished" (Baudrillard 1990 S, 102). Seduction, Rex Butler (1999, 101) explains, is the "distance between things that allows for their resemblance or the distance that arises when their resemblance is pushed too far". As already mentioned in chapter 4 (section 2), it is this real, excluded by any attempt to speak of it, that is the limit to every system – it is the Platonic paradox that Baudrillard means by the real" (Butler 1999, 53). The paradox was first raised by Plato in his dialogue *Cratylus* (1875, 257) and was treated by Derrida in his essay *Plato's Pharmacy*.

Reversibility is central to what Baudrillard calls "objective irony" – the "strong probability, verging on a certainty, that systems will be undone by their own systematicity" (Baudrillard 2000, 78). What Baudrillard calls reversion is this cyclical process of presence negated by absence. It marks ontology as a process of Nietzschean "becoming". Things are inherently ambivalent and what something 'is', is inseparable to what it 'is not'. In the "Preface" to *Symbolic Exchange* Baudrillard (1993, 4) writes "[p]erhaps death and death alone, the reversibility of death, belongs to a higher order than the code". Death can dissolve the code, which stands for all terms valued in opposition within the system. For Baudrillard, the separation of life and death, as we shall see in the next chapter, is the founding condition of hyperreality.

Death radically revaluates all values in Nietzschean fashion, beyond good and evil. It obliterates the difference in value between the true and the false, the signifier and the signified and exposes the metaphysical presuppositions of such valuations. In the next chapter, I will explore Baudrillard's view of death and relate it to Heidegger's analysis of human existence as constituted by death.

6. Baudrillard and Heidegger: Towards a Genealogy of Death

Introduction

Nick Hanlon (2004, 516) in an article entitled "Death, Subjectivity, Temporality in Baudrillard and Heidegger"[108] sees "essential correlations" between Heidegger's and Baudrillard's views of death and he emphasizes how Baudrillard's position is closer to Heidegger's than Baudrillard admits. According to Hanlon, both Baudrillard and Heidegger seek to highlight the centrality of death for our existential situation, which, for them, has been sidelined in conceptions of existence and society. For Hanlon, Baudrillard's problematization of the separation between life and death in *Symbolic Exchange and Death* recalls Heidegger's analysis in *Being and Time* of human existence as constituted by its relation to death.[109]

Following up but also departing from Hanlon's comparative study, my aim in this chapter is to show how Baudrillard's and Heidegger's conceptions of mortality might be linked further. For both Baudrillard and Heidegger, death is a domain in which the tension between the individual and society becomes pertinent. Cultivating an "authentic" relation to death, according to Heidegger, shatters one's unquestioned absorption in the public world of das Man.

I will begin with some background concerning Baudrillard's engagement with Heidegger, as well as a general overview of Heidegger's conception of human mortality in section 1. Leaning on Hanlon's article, I focus on the questions of subjectivity that death raises. I discuss the direct observations Baudrillard made in *Symbolic Exchange and Death* regarding a certain subject-

---

[108] This is the only in-depth study available I know of that systematically researched the relation between Heidegger and Baudrillard's view on death.

[109] I wish to thank Thaddeus Metz for his suggestions and helpful comments while working on this chapter.

centredness in Heidegger's view of death which he contrasts with his own position. Baudrillard critiques the "singularizing" aspect of the Heideggerian concept of "authenticity" as well as the *Jemeinigkeit* (mineness) of death.

In section 2, I move to Baudrillard's "genealogy" of death. I show how Baudrillard's mode of genealogy, in the footsteps of Nietzsche's *On the Genealogy of Morals*, and to a certain extent Foucault's method of genealogical problematization,[110] functions by setting up a contrast between modern, individualized, rational, 'natural' conceptions of death and the role of death in "primitive societies". In primitive societies, Baudrillard claims that death is always a shared, collective event and the dead continue to be active partners in symbolic exchange. Death is crucially not regarded as a mere biological process or individual fatality.

In section 3, I return specifically to Hanlon's analysis on Baudrillard and Heidegger. According to Hanlon, on the matter of death, Baudrillard's analysis suffers from a structural deficit and his approach revolves around pure critique. In my view and contra Hanlon, Baudrillard's "genealogical" critique does propose alternative scenarios, in the form of symbolic exchange, which are open to critique.

Finally, I argue that the constructed and fictionalized hypothetical primal scenes of subjectivity that genealogies use against the current self-understandings are meant to multiply perspec-

---

[110] I rely on Colin Koopman's (2013) book "Genealogy as critique: Foucault and the problems of modernity" in this regard. I do not however agree with Koopman's (2013, 62) claim that Nietzsche unambiguously sets out to denounce Christian slave morality or that he is "normatively ambitious". For Koopman, Nietzsche and Foucauldian genealogy diverge because Nietzsche uses "genealogical histories to generate normative justifications" (Koopman 2013, 61). I have argued in chapter 1 that Nietzsche does not seek to lament a lost origin and Nietzsche makes it clear that without Christian "slave" morality, humanity would have remained an unreflective beast and would not have attained the height of culture that derives from controlling spontaneous instincts, which is why the aim of his 'contempt' for Christian morality is more likely to be rhetorical rather than substantive, i.e., independent of the content. Nietzsche's aim is to describes different types of life. Nietzsche does not elevate the "aristocratic, master" morality as a straightforward ideal (Nietzsche 2007, 21). Baudrillard's notion of symbolic exchange is also similarly an ambivalent, rhetorical tool.

tives. Baudrillard's genealogical narratives (in the footsteps of Nietzsche's *On the Genealogy of Morals*) about social power seek to denaturalize the assumed social neutrality and universality of moral values. He specifically problematizes the abnormal status of the dead in modern rationalist western culture and questions the seemingly natural fatality that we take death to be. He uses "primitive societies" to make this point. In addition to providing a new understanding of Baudrillard's genealogical approach to death, this chapter, while not defending Baudrillard's account of death, provides reasons to take it seriously as a supplantation of Heidegger.

6.1 Death and Subjectivity

Death is one of Baudrillard's core concerns along the lines of "being-toward-death" (*Sein-zum-Tode*) in Heidegger or the death drive (*Todestrieb*) in Freud. It certainly occupies the same position in Baudrillard's work as "symbolic exchange", "ambivalence", "seduction", to name but a few. These terms play very specific roles within his theoretical framework. Like Heidegger, Baudrillard never ceases to reflect on the question of death in direct and indirect ways (e.g., consumption, sacrifice, destruction, terrorism) throughout his intellectual career.

In the thought of Baudrillard, as will be shown below, death turns out to be neither a natural phenomenon whose essence can be proved through empirical observation, nor an entity of the metaphysical, transcendent order. There is something elusive about death, and Baudrillard, for his part, tries to forge an understanding of death from the standpoint of a genealogy of power (dealt with in detail in section 2).

William Pawlett explains that

> "the system of power and control is founded on a particular construction of the relationship between life and death, one which separates and opposes them, making death the absolute termination of life. Baudrillard explores an alternative understanding of death in 'symbolic' or 'primitive' cultures: death as a social, cyclical and reversible position in symbolic exchange ritual" (Pawlett 2010, 46).

Pawlett importantly emphasizes that Baudrillard questions death from the standpoint of the power relations that shape individuals in society. Baudrillard seeks to bring attention to the importance of death for our social and personal situation which has now become repressed in conceptions of existence and society. As I shall develop further below, this view resonates with Heidegger's critique of "das Man" [111] and its "covering up" of death.

For Heidegger, confronting death in an authentic manner can shatter an unquestioned, blind immersion in existing social conceptions and attitudes towards death. Dasein[112] must realize its lostness in das Man and be brought "face to face with the possibility of being itself... in an impassioned freedom towards death – a freedom which has been released from the illusions of das Man" (Heidegger 1962, 311). Death here seems to be a relatively independent resource, emerging spontaneously from outside the dominant structures of das Man.

Before going any further into Heidegger's analysis of death in *Being and Time* and possible connections to Baudrillard's view of death, it is important to make a few general observations regarding Baudrillard's direct references to Heidegger. In a book of interviews collected as *D'un fragment l'autre,* Baudrillard (2001, 11) said the following about his relationship to Heidegger:

> "Heidegger, que j'ai lu certes mais pas en allemand, et par fragments."

With these words, Baudrillard seeks to distance himself from Heidegger.[113] As a result, as Hanlon points out in his article, we

---

[111] The German term "das Man" is similar to the English 'one'. It expresses views or actions without reference to an agent. Heidegger uses das Man to indicate a system of social norms and conventions that cover over the authentic self. Das Man is part of the ontological structure of Dasein. Some secondary critics use English translations of the term such as the "they"' (Macquarrie and Robinson) but I use the German.

[112] Dasein is the distinctive way in humans are "there" (Da means "there" in German) in being (Sein) – as "being in the world" as well as "being with others" or "Mitsein" (Heidegger 2001, 325).

[113] As a trained Germanist and a reviewer of German and Italian literature, Baudrillard translated into French major works by German playwrights, social anthropologists and political philosophers. The fact that Baudrillard was orig-

must assume that Baudrillard's view of Heidegger is influenced by the French translation and reception of Heidegger's work, especially Sartre's interpretation of Heidegger.[114] The implicit influence of Levinas[115] on Baudrillard is also important because of Levinas's critique regarding the "singularizing" aspect of the Heideggerian notions of *Jemeinigkeit* and also "authenticity". *Eigentlichkeit* (authenticity) derives, etymologically speaking, from the adjective *eigen* meaning 'own', 'separate', yet also 'strange', e.g., *Eigenartig* which have been critiqued by Levinas (1948, 24; 89).

This critique of Heidegger's subjective focus is forcefully evident in the following footnote in Baudrillard's book *Symbolic Exchange and Death*:

> "La raison dialectique s'effondre chez Heidegger: elle prend un tour subjectif et irrationnel, celui d'une métaphysique de l'absurde et du désespoir, qui ne cesse pourtant pas d'être la dialectique d'un sujet conscient, qui y retrouve une liberté paradoxale" (Baudrillard 1976, 228-29).[116]

In this quote, Baudrillard identifies "un sujet conscient" in Heidegger. Yet, the somewhat ironic French phrase "un tour subjectif"[117] also acknowledges the subjective 'tension' within

---

inally a Germanist makes his avoidance of reading Heidegger *dans le texte* more remarkable.

[114] Sartre was one of the major channels of Heidegger's reception in France and overall an important figure in France for much of the twentieth century (both within and without intellectual circles). Baudrillard's book reviews in the early sixties were published in Sartre's journal *Les Temps Modernes*.
For an overview of Heidegger's reception in France (with no mention of Baudrillard however) see Tom Rockmore, *Heidegger and French Philosophy*. London: Routledge, 1995.

[115] Nick Hanlon also emphasizes the influence of Blanchot and in particular Levinas. See Emmanuel Levinas *Le Temps et l'autre* (Paris, PUF, 1948).

[116] "With Heidegger, dialectical reason falls into ruin, taking a subjective and irrational turn towards a metaphysics of despair and the absurd which, however, does not prevent it from continuing to be the dialectic of a conscious subject finding a paradoxical freedom in it: 'Everything is permitted, since death is insurmountable' (quia absurdum: Pascal was not so far from the modern pathos of death)" (Baudrillard 1993, 190).

[117] The French expression "jouer un tour à quelqu'un", for instance means to play a trick on someone.

Heidegger's work more than the English translation does ("subjective turn") and Hanlon for his part emphasizes this tension between Heidegger's presentation of Dasein, the importance placed on *Jemeinigkeit* as well as his critique of Cartesianism (anti-subjectivity).

Baudrillard claims that in Heidegger:

> "la mort est distillée comme négativité à doses homéopathiques. Même les philosophes modernes de l'être pour la mort ne renversent pas cette tendance: la mort y sert de relance tragique au sujet" (Baudrillard 1976, 228).[118]

Baudrillard's image of Heideggerian death as a disease (treated in minute doses) can be seen as a further critique of Heidegger's 'internal' (*Jemeinig*) focus of death. In this quote, through death, Heidegger is linked to negativity and subjectivity. This is a view, according to Nick Hanlon (2004, 518), that could have been influenced by Sartre's analysis of Heidegger. Sartre connects *Jemeinigkeit* in Heidegger with the Cartesian "cogito"; he also translates "Dasein" here as "réalité-humaine" (a common translation in the late 1940s) "thereby giving it a distinctly anthropological bias" (Hanlon 2004, 518). As Nick Hanlon points out, this is also in tune with Corbin's original translation.[119] In Baudrillard's version of a passage from *Being and Time* in the footnote in *Symbolic Exchange and Death*, Baudrillard (1976, 229) uses "l'homme" instead of Corbin's "réalité-humaine". This still follows the already strong anthropocentric interpretation with a diluted and generalized twist.

---

[118] The current French translation (1976) of *Sein und Zeit* renders "Sein-zum-Tode" as l'être-vers-la mort whereas Baudrillard here employs "l'être –pour-la-mort" (following Corbin's translation which has been used by Heidegger critics including Levinas). The "pour" rather than "vers" gives a different impression of "Sein-zum-Tode": "pour" has less a sense of a movement towards and also allowing possible connotations of exchangeability and being in "favor of" both of which could be seen to inflect Baudrillard's conception of Heidegger on death.

[119] A translation that Derrida calls a "traduction monstrueuse" (Derrida 1972, 136).

Overall, Heidegger's treatment of death does indeed contain many examples of "subjectivism". On Heidegger's account in *Being and Time*, 'my' death is my ownmost possibility that is of vital concern to me and a distinctive possibility which no one can take away from me. Death stands before us (*Bevorstand*) (Heidegger 1962, 294) in a very special way. The concept of "unrepresentability" (*Unvertretbarkeit*) is important in this regard (Heidegger 1962, 239-240; Kellner, 1986: 86). Representability characterizes social existence, our being-with-others (*Mitsein*). In the everyday possibilities of the world (das Man) another person can always represent me.

In division two, chapter I of *Being and Time,* Heidegger explains that while it is possible to substitute for one another in social roles, this is not the case with death. My death is irrevocably *mine*.

> "[D]eath, as the end of Dasein, is Dasein's ownmost (*eigenste*) possibility – nonrelational, certain and as such indefinite, not to be outstripped. Death is, as Dasein's end, in the being of this entity towards its end" (Heidegger 1962, 303; italics in the text).

In the above quote, we see clearly how for Heidegger, death's singularizing effect on Dasein severs its links to the world and its relations to others ("non-relational"). Death exposes the mineness (*Jemeinigkeit*) that constitutes Da-sein. It is not merely the case that death presupposes a self; rather, there is no I 'before' death. From death, myself, being-in-the-world and being-with-others proceed (Heidegger 1996, 274). Dasein is given the certitude of its death as its only ineluctable possibility. As a result, death is not only certain, but the source of certitude (*Gewissheit*) and thus also of conscience (*Gewissen*).

It is most "certain" yet "indefinite" because we do not know when the inevitable fact of our death will occur. Heidegger's aim is not to focus on the moment of demise which is phenomenologically inaccessible. Instead, Heidegger focuses on our forerunning (*vorlaufen*) towards death. Dasein's existence is characterized as 'being-towards-death'. As a result, Dasein's temporal structure is framed as essentially futural and the Heideggerian notion of projection is key here. In this projection of itself towards its future, by making projects and future plans, Dasein also projects itself towards death, which is the possibility of "no longer being there".

As Rafael Winkler explains: "Dasein is drawn to a future or absence, its future absence, which is without measure, incalculable" (Winkler 2016, 410). In answer to the question as to how Dasein can "own" that which is "not yet" and "that which is not a determinable entity", Winkler, in his article "Time, Singularity and the Impossible: Heidegger and Derrida on Dying" proposes to read Heidegger's claim that "death is in every case mine" "not in the strict sense that Dasein owns its death, but that death is something like a principle of singularization. Not a principle of individuation. Dasein is not an individual, an indivisible or simple atom, whether soul, substance, ego or person" (Winkler 2016, 211). This highlights again the tension that exists in Heidegger (and Baudrillard, as will be discussed further in section 3) between a certain lingering subjectivity and a general critique of subjectivity (or anti-Cartesianism).

Without denying that Heidegger has an "individuated notion of death", Havi Carel (2006, 135) in her book on "Life and Death in Freud and Heidegger", also emphasizes that Heidegger's rendition of Dasein has contradictory tendencies within it. "Dasein" must be viewed in terms of "Mitsein" (being-with-others), which means that the structure of Dasein is "inherently relational, and contains alterity within it, which is what speaks in the 'call of conscience'. Dasein contains otherness in it, and is not closed off by individuation" (Carel 2006, 137).

In her book, Carel (2006, 68) does point out the limitedness of Dasein's relational structure however by arguing that Heidegger restricts his analysis of death to 'freedom from das Man', which is the condition of Dasein's potential authenticity. In addition, he does not discuss the possibility of sharing death or having an authentic experience with the death of another. Every Dasein must die its own singular death and tackle this in a reflexive way. Heidegger relies heavily on the difference between the first and third person perspectives. For Heidegger, my own death is different from the death of any other Dasein, because from my perspective, my death represents the radical closure of all possibilities of existence, whereas the other person's death is one more event in my life. The death of others cannot be experienced authentically (Heidegger 1962, 284).

This position creates for Havi Carel (2006, 68) "an unjustified identification between individuation and authenticity" and she seeks to "reformulate the strong opposition between my death and the death of another". Carel therefore explores the possible ways in which Dasein may experience the death of another and demonstrates that this experience may be authentic. According to Carel (2006, 67), das Man is an important yet conflictual dimension of Dasein's structure, not merely an external obstacle. In Carel's reviewed analysis of das Man, Dasein acquires new openness towards others and is thereby able to experience authentically the death of another. This allows for a new understanding of being-towards-death as relational, by moving away from the primacy of "mineness" as the condition for authenticity.

In my view, Carel's analysis resonates with Baudrillard's relational focus on death (she does not mention him in her book) and this side of "living with the death of others" will be dealt with more in the next section on Baudrillard, who claims that in our current death denying society, the dead are precisely not integrated but rather expelled from the centre of society. In Baudrillard's view, this severely impacts the meaning of our own impending deaths. Baudrillard is unconcerned with questions of 'authenticity' (due to its subjective (i.e., *eigen*) implications but also due to its association with truth)[120] towards questions of meaningfulness.

---

[120] Baudrillard radically problematizes truth throughout his work, for instance in a chapter of *Symbolic Exchange and Death* entitled the "Order of Simulacra", Baudrillard sketches a genealogy of the orders of simulacra. I tackled Baudrillard's concept of the simulacrum in chapters 4 and 5. Baudrillard's genealogy of simulacra parallels Nietzsche's early essay "On Truth and Lying in a Non-Moral Sense" *(1873)* as well as his later his text "How the 'True World' Finally became a Fable" in *The Twilight of the Idols*. Here, Nietzsche subjects the history of truth formation also to genealogical analysis. Nietzsche rejects the idea that concepts and truths are timeless (i.e., as supra-sensuous Platonic "Ideas"). It must be emphasized though that following Nietzsche, both Heidegger and Baudrillard turn their backs on eternal truth.

In this section, the important (and problematic) role of subjectivity in Heidegger surrounding death has been outlined and it becomes central when I discuss Baudrillard's critique of Heidegger further in section 3. I will first go on to show how Baudrillard claims that death involves first and foremost a relation to others (Baudrillard 1993, 20).

6.2 Baudrillard (Re-)socializing Death

In the previous section, we saw how Heidegger highlights the tension between the individual and society with regards to death. According to Heidegger, das Man aims at pacification and evasion, and it is the task of Dasein to free itself from this tranquilization and engage with death in an authentic way. The attitudes advocated by das Man are based on a denial of death that cultivate an indifference towards it or attempt to minimize its importance for life. Such lulling encourages a "constant fleeing in the face of death" (Heidegger 1962, 298). The social attitude to death detaches Dasein from its singular relationship to its death by discouraging an existential understanding of it, all of which renders Dasein inauthentic.

As we shall see below, like Heidegger, Baudrillard seeks to emphasize the central role of death. For him, the "extradition" of death from social life has consequences not only for the individual but for the whole social realm (Baudrillard 1993, 127). Importantly and unlike Heidegger, he proposes an alternative, reconfigured social role for death in the form of (primitive) "symbolic exchange". Instead of recoiling towards a merely reflective relation to one's death against the social's death denial, Baudrillard proposes a different social relation to death.

In his "genealogy" of death, Baudrillard explicitly refers to Foucault, who in *Madness and Civilisation* (1961; 1967) also speaks of the internment of the mad at the beginning of modernity in clinics. The development of reason is linked to the excommunication of "others". Foucault's genealogical study argues that "madness" is a category erected by modern Enlightenment thought as it defines what is normal and subsequently separates it from the abnormal. Madness and reason are two sides of the same coin of modern discourse. Enlightenment thought "judged human experience in relation to scientifically defined 'norms', thereby actually producing categories of 'abnormality'. The 'abnormal' are then confined to asylums and subjected to further scientific scrutiny" (Pawlett 2007, 56).

In the medieval period, on the other hand, a far wider range of behaviour was permitted. As Foucault explains:

> "in the Renaissance, madness was present everywhere and mingled with every experience by its images or its dangers. During the classical period, it was also on view, but on the other side of bars . . . in comparison to the incessant dialogue between reason and madness that had marked the Renaissance, classical confinement had been a silencing" (Foucault 1961, 145; 1967, 497).

Colin Koopman (2013, 157) rightly argues in his book *Genealogy as Critique: Foucault and the Problems of Modernity* that Foucault's genealogies display the emergence of "purifications". With reference to Foucault's *The History of Madness*, for instance, Koopman writes,

> "Purification can be taken as describing a process in which two kinds of practices rigorously isolate themselves from one another, such that the purification of madness and reason amounts to the simultaneous production of both madness and reason in such a way that they cannot admit of admixture with one another" (Koopman 2013, 157).

Koopman explains that genealogies are histories of emergence and what emerges is specific in time. Neither rationality nor madness are static and ahistorical. The point for Foucault, as Koopman argues, is not that some essential primitive reality of madness is one-sidedly subjugated by reason, but rather that madness and reason in their modern forms are simultaneously produced as opposed to one another through a process of purification. Foucault's study of madness aims to

> "go back toward the decision that simultaneously links and separates reason and madness; it must aim to uncover the perpetual exchange, the obscure common root, the original confrontation that gives meaning to the

unity, as well as to the opposition, of sense and non-sense" (Koopman 2013, 166). [121]

On top of denaturalizing a phenomenon, according to Koopman, Foucault's method of genealogy, therefore, also tries to show *how* that which is so easily taken as natural was made into the natural-seeming thing that it is.

In *Symbolic Exchange and Death,* Baudrillard (1993, 195) refers to several of Foucault's major works citing them as "masterful analysis of the true history of our culture, the Genealogy of Discrimination". Baudrillard's book also resonates with Foucauldian notions of disciplinary society, the normalization of the body. Yet, Baudrillard identifies an extradition that is more radical than that of the mad, the children or inferior races – that of the dead and of death. The "extradition" of the dead is at the "core of the 'rationality' of our culture", says Baudrillard (1976, 195). In modern society *"it is not normal to be dead and this is new"* (Baudrillard 1976, 196; 1993, 126; italics in the text). According to modern, rational standards of normality and abnormality, for Baudrillard life and death become radically opposed and separated out across linear time. Birth is placed at the beginning and death is at the end of biological existence.

In addition, death in modern society is regulated by institutions like hospitals and professionals such as doctors (in Heidegger's sense of das Man) that mediate our relation to death. It occurs behind closed doors, and here a "natural" death is the "ideal and normal form of death" (Baudrillard 1993, 126).

In *Symbolic Exchange and Death,* Baudrillard works on a phenomenology of social discontent with an existential analysis of social practices. These include concepts such as immortality; but also institutions such as funerals, cemeteries and hospitals and ways of treating the sick and old. In these practices, life is stripped of ambivalence, which means that life and death can no longer be "symbolically exchanged". All these practices are based on the

---

[121] Foucault (1961, xxxiii) and as quoted in Derrida (1963, 43); this passage can be found in the recently translated longer version of *Histoire de la Folie* but not in the abridged *Madness and Civilization* publication.

opposition between "life as accumulation" and "death as due payment [*échéance*]" (Baudrillard 1993, 159), thus instituting the primal separation of life and death as the general structure underlying more specific forms of "alienation" and "abstraction" (Baudrillard 1993, 130). Baudrillard speaks here of an outright extradition of the dead into a ghetto and states that there is a social discrimination against the dead (Baudrillard 1993, 127).

(Implicitly) following Nietzsche's *On the Genealogy of Morals*, Baudrillard describes how during the course of history, religious "priest castes" emerged to establish themselves within the social realm where once there was a symbolic exchange with death. Everyone who wants to take up contact with the dead is dependent on these "healing experts" as mediators who now have a "monopoly on death" (Baudrillard 1993, 130). The fundamental rupture of symbolic exchange between the living and the dead enables the emergence of social and political power, first of the priesthood and later of the secular state. The control of a symbolic exchange between life and death is, for Baudrillard, the foundation of social power.

In chapter 2, within the context of consumer society, we saw how Baudrillard draws upon Nietzsche's genealogical account of church practices and I made the link between the Nietzschean priest and the advertiser in Baudrillard's consumer context. In the Third Essay of *On the Genealogy of Morals*, Nietzsche discusses how the priest explains the 'meaning' of the slave's unhappy suffering and his power is forged by making suffering more "bearable". Priests secure their power by propagating eternal, fixed or otherworldly "ascetic ideals".

At the end of *On the Genealogy of Morals*, Nietzsche goes on to identify the presence the "ascetic ideal" in non-religious domains, like science (in chapter 3, I also discussed the possible continuation of the ascetic ideal and its "life negating" qualities in relation to Baudrillard's analysis of consumer society) and that in modern times yet another version of the ascetic ideal dominates: the scholar's dedication to 'truth'. In the footsteps of Nietzsche, Baudrillard disputes the purely individual, natural and biological conception of death that is propagated by the high 'priests' of science.

Baudrillard's genealogy of death, in my view, seeks to answer the question: "how was our view of death contingently constructed as separated from life"? And to answer this question, he sketches a genealogy, namely something that inquires into the history of the ex-tradition of death and the ex-communication of the dead. It is natural for us to take our death and that of others as a final biological end and destiny. Baudrillard's point is to show that death is more than biology, more than natural.[122] Baudrillard also claims that we must be sensitized to how death became a seemingly individual fatality. As mentioned earlier, he draws on examples from "primitive symbolic societies" to provide an alternative perspective. I will focus on this "symbolic" alternative to death in the next section.

6.3 Beyond death as natural fatality

In the previous section we saw how Baudrillard identifies a social discrimination of the dead. In the chapter "The Political Economy and Death" of *Symbolic Exchange and Death*, Baudrillard claims that

> "[s]avages have no biological concept of death. Or rather, the biological fact, that is, death, birth or disease, everything that comes from nature and that we accord the privilege of necessity and objectivity, quite simply has no meaning for them" (Baudrillard 1993, 131).

In this quote, Baudrillard problematizes the "biological fact" of death, which we moderns elevate to the level of an unquestionable "necessity and objectivity". This idea is according to Baudrillard non- existent and senseless in primitive society. Here, death is first and foremost a *"social relation"* (Baudrillard 1993, 131: italics in the text).

---

[122] According to the trans-humanist view, technology can solve all problems, including death. Death is thus a temporary, soon to be surmounted obstacle. In the section "My Death is Everywhere, my Death Dreams" in *Symbolic Exchange and Death*, Baudrillard (1993, 177; note 40) shortly mentions "cryonics". In addition, it is also important to note the repetition here of the personal pronoun "my". It exemplifies that Baudrillard underlines the centrality of both the personal as well as the social dimension towards death. Baudrillard does not privilege the social dimension at the expense of the personal as Hanlon claims.

It must be stressed that for Baudrillard, death is a threat to any social order, be it for capitalist modernity or primitive culture:

> "... every thanatopraxis, even in contemporary societies, is analyzed as the will to ward off this sudden loss of signs that befalls the dead, to prevent there remaining, in the asocial flesh of the dead, something which signifies nothing" (Baudrillard 1993, 181; italics in the text).

According to Baudrillard, in this quote, the problem is not the 'real', 'biological fact' of death; it is rather the asociality of signs, which is the most threatening aspect of death. The body of the (recently) deceased is rich with a network of signs and social meaning, but on the other hand there is decay which threatens to be a sign signifying nothing. It is then always a matter of signs and social meaning, not the biological 'reality' of death.

Baudrillard goes so far as to claim that death is the first and most important object of "symbolic exchange" in primitive society. Baudrillard uses examples from anthropology and primitive societies to "argue for the centrality of death within human experience and to assert its reality against all efforts to deny or rationalise it" (Butler 1999, 98). In contrasting primitive societies to capitalism, Baudrillard again draws on the anthropological works of Mauss and Sahlins on the gift (discussed in chapter 3.1.). Baudrillard privileges the gift economy against capitalism because in the gift economy, exchanges are always symbolic.

Importantly, primitive societies did not only exchange gifts among each other, they also exchanged with death through sacrifices and ritual offerings. Here death is more than a mere final event. In a world where all actions and events involve active players or agents, death is also an active partner in exchange.

> "With the primitives, there is no 'natural' death: every death is social, public, collective, and it is always the effect of an adversarial will that the group must absorb (no biology)" (Baudrillard 1993, 164; italics in the text).

Baudrillard here clearly envisions death in primitive society as an active opponent with whom one must communicate and negotiate. Every death involves a collective attempt to come to grips with an opposing "will" (Baudrillard 1993, 164). This confrontation (or *'Aus-ein-ander-setzung'*) takes place in rituals and feasts. Baudrillard also refers to the initiation rituals in the Central African tribe called Sara, to whom the ethnologist Robert Jaulin (1967) dedicated a study in *La Mort Sara* (Baudrillard 1993, 131). In this tribe there is an "exchange between ancestors and the living" in which a social relation between partners comes into being, an important circulation of gifts and counter gifts, like the circulation of luxury goods and women – an "incessant play of responses where death can no longer establish itself as end" (Baudrillard 1993, 131).

This play of exchange in initiation rituals is necessary, because in the logic of symbolic exchange, life itself is a gift that must be reciprocated. "'Natural' death is devoid of meaning because the group has no longer any role to play" (Baudrillard 1993, 164). Just as there is no 'natural' (unilateral, abstract, anonymous, irreversible, fixed) death there is also no 'natural' birth.

> "In the symbolic order, life, like everything, is a crime if it is a one-sided operation, if it is not given and received, taken and destroyed, if it is not 'returned' to death" (Baudrillard 1993, 132).

Life is a gift that must be returned, a gift with the same magnitude as death. The initiation is according to this perspective, a kind of second birth, through which the first gift is returned in a ritualized cycle and in the symbolic order of the universe, the equilibrium of gifts is again established. This relation of life and death is formulated, for instance in the Hindu Veda: "a man being born is a debt; by his own self he is born for Death, and only when he sacrifices does he redeem himself from Death" (Graeber 2011, 56).

Initiation takes the form of a symbolic death, an acceptance of and into the realm of the dead, who are still among the living. The initiate has been with the dead and is now back, this means that the dead are accessible and have a vital role in initiating the start of adult life. In tribal societies, death is not understood as a static destination or end, which in turn resonates with Heidegger's view of death: "Death is a way to be" (Heidegger 1962, 289). By leaning on primitive societies, Baudrillard shows how a process of exchange can be opened between the living and the dead, a play of continual reciprocity. Out of this cyclical reversibility springs the ambivalence that characterizes the symbolic. In this case, it emerges as the radical indeterminacy between life and death.

According to Baudrillard, the bureaucratization of death establishes the first and basic form of political power and domination. The repression of death and the "emergence of survival" is at the same time the "birth of power" (Baudrillard 1993, 129). This serves Baudrillard as the starting point for his own genealogy of power. Through the spreading of the social jurisdiction on death, individual groups are unable to directly exchange with the dead. This loss has serious political consequences: the "manipulation and administration of death" weakens the group dynamic in democracy, because collective rituals with the dead are also a form of sovereign self-management of the group (Baudrillard 1993, 130).

The ex-communication of the dead from the centre of society is instigated by a 'bar'[123] or line of social demarcation. The bar that separates life and death also joins them. For Baudrillard,

> "[w]hen one says that power *tient la barre*, this is not a metaphor: it is this bar between life and death, this decree which interrupts the exchange of life and death, this tollgate and this control between the two sides" (Baudrillard 1993, 130).

The bar represses death and it has the social power to do so; *tenir la barre* means to take control. The power bar between life and death is the "archetype" of all the separations (Genosko 1994, 1). Life and death are reunited when the bar has been lifted in favour

---

[123] The concept of the bar (la barre) is taken from Jacques Lacan's reading of Saussure (Lacan 1977, 149). Jacques Lacan places the signifier over the signified, the former exercises power over the latter (*avoir sur barre*). Baudrillard does not apply the theories of Lacan systematically; rather, he draws some basic insights from the writings of Lacan, such as the tri-polar arrangement of the Symbolic, the Imaginary and the Real, but this paradigm is used differently by Baudrillard. There is unfortunately little space to discuss this further here. Importantly for my purposes however, regarding the 'bar' of social demarcation, Pawlett (2007, 58) says that in Baudrillard's work, the "'Real and the Imaginary' function as binary oppositions, each implying the other in a tactical, coded relationship...the 'real' does not precede it as ontological essence". As already mentioned, Baudrillard, following Nietzsche, rejects essential (perspectival-free) things-in-themselves,

of a fluid process of symbolic exchange. In terms of power relations, the separation and opposition of life and death creates the hierarchical structures of authority that are the fundamental mechanisms of social control. In temporal terms, when life and death are separated, time becomes linear rather than cyclical. Death becomes the final, irreversible event in the life of the individual. Baudrillard critiques the current rationalization of existence and how, as a result, death is at the opposite pole of social life.

In stateless, tribal societies, power relations have not yet been solidified into differentiated state apparatuses. Power relations are fluid and reversible. A form of power does indeed emerge in such societies, but power is not a possession (Baudrillard 1993, 43). Prestige is attained through the loss or giving of wealth: chiefs may live in destitution. It is important to note that societies based on symbolic exchange for Baudrillard actively avoid the accumulation of any surplus and institute its destruction through, for example, ritual encounters.

In these societies, prestige is a temporary effect determined by gift-giving within networks of kinship relations, it is not the property of individuals. There is no locatable economic infrastructure; instead, there is an endless cycle of giving, and it is this that determines the course of social hierarchy and authority, kinship relations and religious practices. Gift exchange is the expression of societies without the demarcation into the spheres considered as politics, economics, religion, sexuality and culture. Building on this perspective, Baudrillard sees a rupture in the history of human society. He follows the line separating centralized state societies from pre-state societies, *acephale* or capital-less/head-less societies, where power is dispersed, flexible and not accumulated, economized and fixed at one pole.

According to Baudrillard (1993, 127), when life is separated from death it can no longer be meaningful, as it is based on "the indifferent fatality of survival". This separation of life from death is not beneficial for life. Life might be protected from death, but life is reduced to a deferral of death (survival, living-on and ascetic self-preservation). Even though death is denied, it touches life.

The negative term retains a certain power over the positive term, just as the meaning of "sanity" still depends upon "insanity". Once such binary thinking dominates, 'otherness' is only thought of according to a binary opposition based on what is known or similar (Pawlett 2007, 56). Symbolic exchange on the other hand, is not based on a pre-coded relation.

For Anthony King, "[t]he symbolism of exchange means that it always represents the individual and his relations" (King 1998, 91). It does not fix terms in advance by means of rigid binary opposition and is rather characterized by ambivalence (Pawlett 2007, 56).

As mentioned in chapter 1, certain secondary critics on Baudrillard's work critique Baudrillard's apparent "nostalgia" or "essentialism" towards a society based symbolic exchange (Lyotard 1993, 103-127; Kellner 1989, 45). It must be emphasized again that Baudrillard does not idealize[124] a specific symbolic order. Baudrillard uses symbolic society to multiply perspectives into our conception of death. The central point for Baudrillard in my view (following Koopman's explanation regarding 'purification' discussed in the previous section) is to show how death and life in their modern forms are simultaneously produced as opposed to each other by a bar of social demarcation.

Life and death can however neither be fully purified (or separated) from one another nor can they be totally assimilated to one another. It must be remembered that, according to the logic of symbolic exchange, life and death are linked despite being separated. Symbolic exchange between life and death is barred, but separated from the symbolic, death is meaningless and simply reduced to an "unprogammable" horror, an "unthinkable anomaly" (Baudrillard 1993, 126).

As a result, for Baudrillard (1993, 127) our culture is a "culture of death": by being silenced, death makes its symptomatic

---

[124] As Charles Levin (1996, 88) puts it: "While apparently joining Rousseau to denounce historical civilisation as a perversion, however, Baudrillard has demonstrated no particular faith in the innate 'goodness' of human nature. In this respect, he is Nietzschean (and Freudian) to the core".

mark everywhere. The power of the bar is to block and control an (inescapable) relational tension in which there is an incessant obligation to give, to receive and to return, and thus to enter into symbolic communication (Genosko 1994, 1). Baudrillard aims to restore a space for interaction where life and death could freely converse.

For Baudrillard, humanism, democracy and even revolution "bar" symbolic exchange through binary oppositions. Equality also continues the structural nature of binary oppositions. Political movements based on improving conditions for the repressed and marginalized side (in terms determined the dominant power) cannot, for Baudrillard, be revolutionary: rather, "the revolution can only consist in the abolition of the separation of death, and not in equality of survival" (Baudrillard 1993, 129).

Baudrillard claims that primitive societies "concede the dead their difference" (Baudrillard 1976, 275; 1993, 181). Through their "difference", the dead remain partners of social exchange. Difference ventilates and enables symbolic exchange. Hegarty explains it well when he says that instead of an opposition, which reduces and pre-codes the difference between life and death, societies of symbolic exchange

> "inscribe the loss, waste and absence among the movements of symbolic exchange, which occur at the 'real' level of language, ritual formulae, and as the effect both have on the society as a whole. All of these elements together mean symbolic exchange is occurring and slipping between the real and the unreal, true and false, self and other, all 'mediated' by death" (Hegarty 2004, 44–45).[125]

In a section of *Symbolic Exchange and Death*, entitled "Death in Bataille", Baudrillard praises Bataille for recognizing the central role of death and for overcoming the life and death opposition. As He-

---

[125] Hegarty does not think that Baudrillard envisions symbolic death as an "Outside" that should be privileged (Hegarty 2004, 45). Ambivalence is inherent to structure, each act as a fuel and discharge of the other. Non-categorical and non-reductive thought is namely also an illusion. "The symbolic is neither a concept, an agency, a category, nor a "structure" but an act of exchange and *a social relation which puts an end to the real* and at the same time puts an end to the opposition between the real and the imaginary" (Baudrillard 1993, 133).

garty (2004, 44) explains, Bataille expresses the role of death beyond "the rationalist logic of exclusion" (Hegarty 2004, 44). Bataille regards death as "excess, ambivalence, gift, sacrifice and paroxysm" (Baudrillard, 1976, 237; 1993, 154). Death involves a relation to others, because it "is another expression of the loss of subject and object in intimacy" (Hegarty 2004, 44). Both death and eroticism have the sense of expenditure, waste, festival. Both seek to temper the ambitions of rationality, use-value and the linear system of economy.

Due to sections 2 and 3, we now see how Baudrillard sets up a contrast between "symbolic death" on the one hand, and natural, "brute" biological death in the rationalist West, on the other. In my view, symbolic exchange is presented as an "imaginary solution" to the problem of death (that has not yet been posed).[126] Baudrillard's notion of symbolic exchange has no "truth value". In the next section, I return to my discussion on Baudrillard's relation to Heidegger by considering the issues of subjectivity and temporality (raised by Nick Hanlon's article) within the overall frame of death.

6.4 (Re-) Situating Heidegger and Baudrillard

Before I started exploring Baudrillard's genealogy of death and the extradition of the dead in modern society (provided in the above sections), I noted that Baudrillard regards Heidegger's position as subject-oriented (in Heidegger, according to Baudrillard, "la mort y sert de relance tragique au sujet"). A view, according to

---

[126] The influence of the playwright Alfred Jarry (1873-1907), in whose writings the so-called 'science' of pataphysics originated, is very much in evidence throughout Baudrillard's oeuvre. Alfred Jarry (1960, 131) says (in the guise of Doctor Faustroll) that "(P)ataphysics will be above all the science of the particular ...it will investigate the laws that govern exceptions, and it will explain the universe supplementary to this one; or, less ambitiously, it will describe a universe that one might envision – and that perhaps one should envision – in place of the traditional one. DEFINITION: Pataphysics is the science of imaginary solutions, which symbolically attributes to their lineaments the properties of objects described by their virtuality."

Nick Hanlon (2004, 518), that could have been influenced by Sartre's appropriation of Heidegger.[127]

For Hanlon (2004, 518), "Baudrillard's analysis of Heidegger raises the problem of subjectivity in *Being and Time,* a problem crucially connected with death". Hanlon (2004, 518) goes on to claim however that the issue of subjectivity "remains just as problematic in Baudrillard's theorizing as in Heidegger's". Hanlon recognizes that Baudrillard is similarly attempting to overcome the subject-centredness of contemporary epistemology. In *Symbolic Exchange and Death,* Baudrillard writes:

> "Contre cette torsion qu'imprime le sujet à sa propre perte, il n'est de désaisissement que dans la mort violente, inattendue, qui restitue la possibilité d'échapper au contrôle névrotique du sujet" (Baudrillard 1976, 269).[128]

Here, Baudrillard thinks that a violent, un-natural abrupt death might overcome the structure of a calculated subjectivity built on self-preservation. Yet, Baudrillard also does emphasize the central role of the "will" in accidental death:

> "In the fatal accident, the artificiality of death fascinates us. Technical, non-natural and therefore *willed* (ultimately by the victim him- or herself), death becomes interesting once again since *willed* death has meaning" (Baudrillard, 1993: 165; italics in the text).

According to Hanlon (2004, 521), Baudrillard's discussion of accidental, violent death serves to support his point that Baudrillard avoids theorizing death according to a temporal "situatedness", as this would lead to a Heideggerian subjectivism which he criticizes. Yet in Baudrillard's emphasis on "*willed* death" there is a Nietzschean (and Bataillean) "subjectivity-effect" through 'expenditure', loss and 'excess'.

---

[127] See for example Piotr Hoffman's essay "Death, Time, History: Division II of Being and Time" in the Cambridge Companion to Heidegger, edited by Charles Guignon (Cambridge, University Press, 1993), pp. 195-214 where he concludes that Dasein's link up with a historical community does not remove from Dasein's structure, its dimension of subjectivity (Guignon 1993, 213).

[128] "Against this distortion that the subject stamps upon its own demise, there is no divestment except in violent, unexpected death, which alone restores the possibility of escaping the subject's neurotic control" (my translation).

Regarding the issue of subjectivity, as mentioned earlier in section 1, Baudrillard (and others, such as Levinas) identifies in Heidegger a tension between an anti-Cartesianism and the presence of a certain subjectivity. According to Tilottama Rajan (2002, 258) this tension is one that may also be found in Baudrillard's own work. Baudrillard tries to

> "capture death through a duel between psychoanalysis and anthropology. In the process death is de-ontologised, it is primitivised and drained of its ambivalence. Death, rather than being the cogito's ungraspable double, figures Baudrillard's own mastery over his epistemic others. This mastery in turn has two sources. First, Baudrillard objectifies death as 'that of which he speaks' rather than 'that out of which'... Second, he encloses death within anthropology – a discipline newly masculinized and virilized by being associated not with the gift but with sacrifice and sovereignty" (Rajan 2002, 258).

Although I cannot dismiss the argument that Baudrillard's use of violence and death is in some way masculine, a 'deconstructive' reading reveals precisely the non-necessity of such limitation on the gender of the Baudrillardian subject. In my view there is no definitive answer to the position of 'woman' in Baudrillard's writing and I do not have sufficient space here to develop the intricacies of Baudrillard's provocations in this regard, as my focus here is only on the tension between the individual and the social that the issue of death raises and especially Baudrillard's critique of Heidegger in this regard.

In my view, the point is that Baudrillard rejects a pre-constituted masterful subject in favour of one that is capable of incorporating many experiences, perspectives and being transformed by them. Baudrillard importantly does not see an inert world, that is then ordered and 'represented' by a subject. Throughout his work, Baudrillard seeks to emphasize the power of the object-world and the inadequacy of the subject. Yet Baudrillard also provides a dynamic, practical conception of subjectivity, that is to say, a theory of historical variables, practices and procedures, rituals (for instance with the dead) that give rise to subjectivity. Practices (for example initiation rituals mentioned above in section 3) are arenas that constitute the self.

In his book *Jean Baudrillard: The Defence of the Real*, Rex Butler (1999, 9-10) explains "the miracle of writing [for Baudrillard] is that, although it is completely of this world, a reflection of it, it ends up destining or determining the world, making it a reflection of his writing". According to Butler (1999, 9-10) writing is for Baudrillard an exercise in transformation. It expresses a power that seeks to open a new context, a new perspective (e.g., on death). All life is a process of creating differences and possibilities that then require a response. Baudrillard uses language as an active formation, as the creation of styles and possibilities: "[w]riting ends up preceding life, determining it. And life ends up conforming to a sign, which was initially quite cavalier. This is no doubt why so many are afraid to write" (Baudrillard 1990 CM I, 202). Baudrillard reflects on the indifference of the world: but he also transforms this indifference, and he "actively strives to bring it about", knowing that "it does not exist without being willed" (Butler 1999, 9).

As Rafael Winkler (2016, 410) rightly puts it:

> "If authorship entails ownership, the reverse is not always the case. I am not the author of my existence and I may not be the author of my current thoughts or experiences. Nevertheless, an existence that does not belong to someone, a 'who' an experience or thought that is not someone's experience or thought is hardly thinkable. Except of course, when this belongingness-to me, this ownership, is neutralised by *das Man*, and existence, experience and though, along with death, appear as impersonal causal events in nature or as culturally mediated significations. Properly considered, however, existence and death, experience and thought are characterised by first-person ownership, mineness, even if their authors are not even identifiable".

There is some freedom to play within the object world which in many senses thinks us rather than vice versa. Nick Hanlon emphasizes that "Baudrillard's writings and his publishing of autobiographical fragments" (in his *Cool Memories*) is a further indication "of an element of subjectivity or individuality in his work: evidence, one might say, of Baudrillard's glossing over the presence of *Jemeinigkeit*" (Hanlon 2004, 521).

In my view, Baudrillard does not avoid ('gloss over') subjectivity or individuality, rather he strongly advocates an 'effect' of subjectivity. In my view, subjectivity is problematic for Baudrillard to the extent that it is abstracted and (pre)conceived as separate from social life and when the subject is barred from achieving meaningful community bonds. For Baudrillard, death becomes radical when it is resocialized and stripped of its biological and irreversible and individual "fatality":

> "In our culture…everything is done so that death is never done to anybody by *someone* else, but only by 'nature', as an impersonal expiry of the body. We experience our death as the 'real' fatality inscribed in our body only because we no longer know how to inscribe it into a ritual symbolic exchange" (Baudrillard 1993, 166).

This quote shows that Baudrillard seeks to move away from a purely impersonal (biological) relation to death. Neither radically individuating (Heidegger) or straightforwardly antithetical to singular personhood, death obtains sense between or amongst persons.

According to Hanlon, it is Baudrillard's interpretation of Heidegger as too subjective that leads him away from the situatedness (*Befindlichkeit*) entailed in the *Jemeinigkeit* of death. Baudrillard provides an "immanent" conception of temporality (where all history occurs within a transitory, immanent field of flux) which neglects the "situatedness" of our Being.[129] Yet Hanlon claims that Baudrillard does end up situating himself in a temporal context because his texts tackle "topical" events (e.g., the Gulf War, 9/11 etc.).

This leads to a broader question regarding Baudrillard's non-structural approach (especially in his later work after *Symbolic Exchange and Death*).[130] His own critiques on Heidegger show how

---

[129] In *L'Illusion de la fin* Baudrillard writes: "Toute transcendance sociale, historique, temporelle, est absorbée par cette masse dans son immanence silencieuse" (Baudrillard 1992, 15).

[130] Rex Butler's *Jean Baudrillard: the Defence of the Real* (1999, 7) demonstrates that while Baudrillard's earlier works (until *Symbolic Exchange and Death*) were more empirical and scientific his later works have become increasingly pataphysical and self-referential. His philosophy has become its own commentary, a self-enclosed system with its own preferred metaphors, which no

his arguments tend to rely on the categories of the thinker he defines himself against. In fact, as Charles Levin (2000, 200) rightly observes, Baudrillard is a "counter-dependent thinker" and is "against" any thinker whose ideas he takes seriously. According to Hanlon, Baudrillard's approach is one of one-dimensional critique, as it does not propose alternative structures, which are open to critique.

As mentioned in section 3, Baudrillard does propose an alternative perspective based on symbolic exchange. Symbolic exchange is presented as a form or principle, rather than as the specific 'content' of cultural practices. Baudrillard's notion of symbolic exchange is a figure of speech that serves to enable us to make sense of what we do and what we believe.

In the words of Rafael Winkler, I regard Baudrillard, like Nietzsche as a thinker "of the limit of metaphysics" (Winkler 2018, 88). According to Winkler (2018, 87) Nietzsche does not aim to "neutralize metaphysical characterizations of the world whether as reality or appearance, being or becoming". Winkler claims that Nietzsche proposes a "new practice of self-discipline", whose aim is

> "to incorporate the insight that the totality of propositions that has defined Western humanity's self-understanding since Plato rests on simplifications, errors or fictions. The principal question here is not *Is that insight true?* but, rather, *What would that insight do to me, how would it transform me, if it were true?* and *Am I able to overcome resistances to it?* In Nietzsche's eyes, what remains at the end of metaphysics, once the distinction between the supersensuous and the sensuous worlds has collapsed in the general insight that our most cherished and prized truths rest on illusions, is a practice that uses these so-called truths as a means and tests of self-overcoming. Nietzsche is, like Heidegger, a thinker of the limit of metaphysics" (Winkler 2018, 88).

In my view, genealogy is mobilized by Baudrillard as such a practice at the limit of metaphysics. For Baudrillard (1993, 159) "[t]he subject needs a myth of its end, as of its origin, to form its identity". Science demands an end to mythological thought. Nietzsche, Heidegger and Baudrillard criticize the attempt of science to re-

---

> longer point to something in the real world because they have been transformed into meta-objects.

gard subjects, objects and practices as examples of scientific laws; as unilateral irreversible facts; as universal and interchangeable.

Conclusion

In the above chapter, we have seen that Baudrillard (1993, 166) claims we are "hostages" to a system that attempts to define, control, administer and absorb our death. Baudrillard critiques the rationalization, economization and compartmentalization of death, along with its separation from life. Death in modern society is separated from social life and is regulated by impersonal institutions. It is regarded as a private, individual occurrence. "Natural" death is the "ideal and normal form of death" (Baudrillard 1993, 126). Baudrillard problematizes the "biological fact" of death, which we moderns elevate to the level of an unquestionable "necessity and objectivity" (Baudrillard 1993, 131).

As shown in sections 2 and 3, Baudrillard offers us genealogies of our present that articulate some of our current problems; he does not need to tell us directly how to address them. Genealogy might serve as a tool for political change, but does not itself come normatively pre-scribed. Baudrillard first and foremost seeks to alert us to death's extradition, and how it is placed at the opposite pole of life and made a seemingly natural fatality (destiny).

On the other hand, Baudrillard presents to us with a problematic situation: the extradition of the dead severely impacts the meaning of our own impending deaths. This provokes us to think about alternatives. The most important rhetorical or stylistic element of a genealogy is its hyperbolic, polemical character.[131] This renders the hypothesis regarding the invention of subjects urgent and makes us think about possible alternatives to our ways of living and thinking. Baudrillard's problematization of death in mo-

---

[131] Baudrillard follows Nietzsche in regarding all interpretation as polemical: to support one view is to combat another view. The subtitle of Nietzsche's *On the Genealogy of Morals* is *A Polemic* and a characteristic of Nietzsche's genealogical study is that it combats interpretations which claim to be self-evident, beyond dispute, necessary and eternal.

dernity does not amount to a denunciation of the present or a one-dimensional critique (as Hanlon claims he does).

Baudrillard elaborates a conception of death in terms of symbolic exchange, in terms of the gift and the counter-gift, couched in an anti-economic, symbolic obligation to return what one has received. As Gary Genosko (1994:94) rightly puts it "[e]ven the gift of death, issued from the statistical indifference of an anonymous system may be socialized in a radical gesture."[132] To articulate death socially is a mortal danger to the dominant system because it reveals the extent to which it is already administered by the system. Death is a social relation between persons, established through ceremony and artifice.

Leaning on Hanlon's (2004) article, I showed the ways in which Baudrillard investigates the social role and place of death away from a certain subject-centred-ness which he identifies in Heidegger's conception of death (Baudrillard 1976, 228-29). For Hanlon, this means that Baudrillard ends up theorizing death outside any structural conceptions of temporality or subjectivity.

In my view, however, Baudrillard hypothesizes on the constitutive relation between subjectivity and structures of power. What genealogies show is that different regimes (e.g., of power) structure human behavior and self- understanding. We cannot regard our development as an external object of disinterested and neutral observation and therefore a certain "distancing" from our past is necessary, which according to the genealogical hypothesis, is always a history of social relations along with their struggles (e.g., for status or power). Baudrillard's genealogies are interested in constructing "imaginary solutions" that serve as a contrast to current self-understandings. The constructed and fictionalized hypothetical primal scenes of subjectivity that genealogies use

---

[132] How do we respond to the symbolic challenge of death and the dead, the challenge they pose to our conscious experience? This is for Baudrillard the question of September 11 2001. Political economy is the most rigorous attempt to put an end to death (the system's unilateral gift of life) so for Baudrillard only death (suicide terrorism) can put an end to political economy. See "The Baudrillardian Symbolic, 9/11, and the War of Good and Evil" by Bradley Butterfield (2002).

against the current self-understandings are imaginary (not strictly factual) because they are less concerned with the past and more concerned with the not-yet historical present.

Genealogy, as practiced by Baudrillard, is a critically motivated art of drastic presentation, which should help us transform our current views of the world and ourselves. Baudrillard exposes the myths surrounding biological, natural, impersonal death and he draws on examples of "symbolic exchange" from "primitive societies" to provide alternative perspectives.

Concluding Remarks and Summary of the Study

This study started by emphasizing that explicit references to Nietzsche are rare in Baudrillard's works. In interviews, Baudrillard speaks of Nietzsche as an "ingrained memory" (Baudrillard 2004, 1) and as "the author beneath whose broad shadow I moved, though involuntarily and without really knowing what I was doing" (Baudrillard 2004, 2). Nietzsche is crucial to Baudrillard's work, but not as a direct point of reference.

In chapter 1 section 1, I made general observations regarding Baudrillard's relation to Nietzsche. I provided a short review of the fragmented and scattered secondary literature available on the relation between Baudrillard and Nietzsche. I noted that no scholar has specifically tried to reconstruct how certain critical elements, strategies and figures within Nietzsche's *On the Genealogy of Morals* resurface in Baudrillard's work.

In section 2, I started my investigation into how Baudrillard's work specifically re-actualizes Nietzsche's mode of genealogy. In line with Nietzschean genealogy, Baudrillard, in his early work on consumer society, does not attempt to offer a foundational account of morality, but rather, like Nietzsche, he treats morality as a contingent historical creation whose value can be taken as an object of critical reflection. I showed how Baudrillard (in the footsteps of Nietzsche) scrutinizes the differential relations that are responsible for the creation of values. In addition, I looked at how 'personalisation' functions in consumer society. Consumers construct a "a synthetic individuality", a "personality" through the manipulation of "marginal differences", which constitute the sign system (Baudrillard 1998, 88).

Baudrillard is interested in understanding the structures of consumer society and how there is nothing inevitable or natural about them. Baudrillard applies the critical tools of genealogy to Saussurean linguistics, and in Nietzschean fashion, he analyzes concepts as indicators of the powers that have become dominant.

For Baudrillard, Saussurean linguistics presents us with a theory of language and it describes the consumer morality of late modernity. Baudrillard argues that neither structural linguistics nor our current morality of consumption is universal or natural. They are historical and contingent.

In section 3, I moved on to an account of perspectivism and how genealogy, as practiced by Nietzsche and Baudrillard, reminds readers not only of the contingency of their perspectives but proposes different perspectives. Nietzsche and Baudrillard put forward fictional accounts of noble and symbolic societies as ways of problematizing and undermining a morality that people share and find binding. Our own development is not an external object of disinterested and neutral observation, and therefore a certain "distancing" from our past is necessary, which according to the genealogical hypothesis, is always a history of power.

In chapter 2, I focussed on how Baudrillard's exploration of the construction of subjects in consumer society resonates with Nietzsche's own view in *On the Genealogy of Morals*.

In section 1 (against the backdrop of Baudrillard's discussion of 'personalisation' in consumer society) I explored how Nietzsche's "psychological" processes such as *ressentiment,* bad conscience and guilt mark out the different origins of the subject. For Nietzsche, the subject has multiple origins and is divided at the origin, and therefore cannot properly serve the purpose of unification or identification.

In section 2, I brought Nietzsche and Baudrillard's views together regarding the technological invention of the human. I did so by focussing on the *systems of mnemonics* that are at work in Nietzsche's *On the Genealogy of Morals,* as well as in Baudrillard's consumer society.

In section 3, I brought Baudrillard's figure of the advertiser together with Nietzsche's figure of the ascetic priest. Just as Nietzsche's priest reduces all events to a moment of divine reward and punishment, Baudrillard's advertiser reduces all desire to a fixation for sign-objects on offer. The ascetic priest invents a fictional explanation for why we suffer in the form of the ascetic ideal which gives the world a re-assuring, yet life-negating, supersensuous, transcendent meaning. According to the ascetic priest, we suffer because we cannot live up to the ascetic ideal.

In chapter 3, I went on to discuss the extent to which consumption, as it is outlined by Baudrillard, rests on the principle of the ascetic ideal.

In section 1, I started by showing how several themes in Nietzsche, but also Mauss and Bataille play a central role in Baudrillard's critique of consumer society. I suggested that Nietzsche's views on excess and the will to power are at work in Baudrillard's (re)view of the true function of excessive expenditure and waste.

Against this back drop, in section 2, I unpacked the impoverished and indefinitely exasperated desire that characterizes consumer society. In consumer society, the source of value and meaning remains endlessly deferred. I showed how for Baudrillard, a social relationship (and a social logic) based on the wealth of symbolic exchange is required, rather than one based on "luxurious and spectacular penury" (Baudrillard 1998, 68). Consumer society hollows out individual experiences and relationships – this, I argue is an extension of Nietzsche's analysis of the ascetic ideal.

In section 3, we saw how Baudrillard gives the short novel *Les choses* by Georges Perec a crucial place in the *System of Objects*. Baudrillard's discussion of the novel seeks to show the extent to which consumer society impoverishes life. Baudrillard gives the final word of his book to a work of fiction, as a way of triggering a perspectival change on the part of his reader.

In this section, we also saw how consumer society is run by pseudo-events and pseudo- objects, which are beyond the true and the false. This allowed me to introduce the concept of simulation (the theme of chapters 4 and 5). I showed how in consumer society, no distinction between fact and fiction is possible because consumer society "no longer produces myth ... it is itself its own myth" (Baudrillard 1998, 193). Consumer society is self-referential and self-legitimizing; it establishes the terms for its own evaluation.

In chapter 4 section 1, I continued to set the scene for the concepts of "simulacra and simulation" by discussing Nietzsche's "Reversal of Platonism". In his early essay "On Truth and Lying in a Non-Moral Sense" *(1873)* as well as his later his text "How the

'True World' Finally became a Fable" in *The Twilight of the Idols*, Nietzsche subjects the history of the 'concept' and truth formation to genealogical analysis. Nietzsche thus problematizes the idea that concepts and truths are fixed or that they represent unchanging supra-sensuous Platonic "Forms".

In Nietzsche's work, the 'twilight of the idols' and the 'reversal of Platonism' rupture the illusion of an ordered and stable opposition between the real and the apparent, the true and the false. The "death of God" collapses any fixed distinctions between good and evil, the very structuring principles of Platonic and Christian thought. Science, like religion, is based upon a distinction and hierarchy between the true and false, reality and illusion, good and evil. Science, freed and 'enlightened' from superstition, cannot grasp the 'real' world because 'reality' is part of the enchantment. In his essay "On Truth and Lying in the Non- Moral Sense" (1873) Nietzsche regards the "pure drive towards truth" as an "effect" of deception and he exposes the production of truth as an illusionary process (Nietzsche 1999, 143).

In section 2, I moved on to Deleuze's view of Nietzsche's reversal of Platonism. For Deleuze, Nietzsche's reversal inaugurates a world where simulacra (false pretenders to the Idea) have at last prevailed over immutable Platonic Forms. Deleuze affirms and endorses the simulacrum's disruptive and chaotic power, as well as its "effect of resemblance" (Deleuze 2004, 295). On the other hand, the problem Baudrillard sets himself is how to speak against this simulation when there is nothing outside of it or when the outside can only be imagined and judged on its terms.

In section 3, I moved to Baudrillard's genealogy of the orders of the image. For Baudrillard (1993, 70) the collapse of the real and apparent worlds into simulation (the 'twilight of the idols' and the reversal of Platonism) means that there now only exists an "empty space of representation", which produces "effects of the real". Baudrillard (1993, 70) also calls this "the hyperreal". Unlike Deleuze, in Baudrillard's work, simulation is clearly not only a matter of creative emancipation; it also involves systematic control.

In chapter 5, I went into further detail regarding Baudrillard's concept of "hyperreal simulation". This required that I scrutinize Baudrillard's "longer version" of the orders of simulacra that he provides in *Symbolic Exchange and Death*.

In section 1, I discussed Baudrillard's detailed genealogy of simulacra and its culmination in 'simulation', which is a process consisting of coded signs that refer to other signs that operate according to an internal model not according to an external referent or reality. The self-referential "hyperreal" world of simulation reassembles the real in the form of exclusively and universally determining codes of signification. The code permits opposition and alternation, but it is a pre-coded opposition.

In section 2, I explored how this third order of simulacra is ruled by the "structural law of value" (Baudrillard 1993, 51). I showed how Baudrillard's work thereby seeks to provide a theoretical link between structural linguistics and simulation.

In section 3, I looked at the multiple causal factors that Baudrillard suggests for the third phase of simulacra as well as their Nietzschean parallels. Nietzsche's "History of an Error" in *Twilight of the Idols* is the genealogy of an idea, and as Allison (2013, 182) rightly puts it, for Nietzsche, some ideas simply lose their relevance in a signifying system when they become fetishes or in Baudrillard's terminology "hyperreal" i.e., no longer instruments of exchange; they are overinvested and subsequently disinvested.

The "true world" for Nietzsche is a record of Western metaphysics: it covers everything from religion to science, morality, and teleology among others. Nietzsche's critique of supersensuous truth attacks the entire apparatus of the "true world" (which defines Western and the Judeo-Christian discourse). In *The Antichrist*, Nietzsche claims that such a fictional world is motivated by a hatred of the actual and the sensible. Baudrillard's digital code of simulation along with the "oversaturated world of hyperreality… [is] for Nietzsche, precisely the entire symbolic of the religio-moral idiosyncrasy" (Allison 2013, 183).

Like Nietzsche, Baudrillard is optimistic about the "reversibility" of systems. It is futile to directly oppose the basic codes of a system; one must push codes to the point where they begin to turn upon themselves and collapse to reveal their hollowness (this is what it means to "philosophize," in Nietzschean fashion, "with a hammer"). What Baudrillard calls reversion is this cyclical process of presence overcome by absence. It marks ontology as a process of Nietzschean "becoming". Things are inherently ambivalent. What something 'is' is inseparable to what it 'is not'. In the "Preface" to *Symbolic Exchange*, Baudrillard (1993, 4) writes:

> "[p]erhaps death and death alone, the reversibility of death, belongs to a higher order than the code".

To understand the "reversibility of death" and how Baudrillard seeks to problematize the separation between life and death, I dedicated chapter 6 to Baudrillard's genealogy of death. Death, as a metaphor, revaluates all values in Nietzschean fashion, beyond good and evil. It obliterates the difference in value between the true and the false, the signifier and the signified and reveals the metaphysical presuppositions of such valuations.

In chapter 6 section 1, I found it necessary to show that Baudrillard's problematization of the separation between life and death recalls Heidegger's analysis in *Being and Time* of human existence as constituted by its relation to death.

In section 2, the differences between Heidegger and Baudrillard's views of death were however made apparent. Baudrillard pays more attention than Heidegger to anthropological attitudes towards death among primitive tribes. Baudrillard sketches a Nietzschean genealogy of death to challenge current conceptions of biological and natural death.

I showed that according to modern rational standards of normality and abnormality, life and death are no longer enclosed in cycles of (symbolic) exchange. Instead, they are detached across linear time. Life is at the beginning, and death is placed at the end of biological existence. The binary opposition of life and death cannot progress beyond the logic that life is not death and death is not life.

We saw how Baudrillard regards the separation of life and death as the founding condition of binary thinking. The 'bar' between life and death creates power: the hierarchical structures of authority that drive social control.

Baudrillard is self-consciously radical, our culture is a culture of death: by expelling that which cannot be expelled, death makes its symptomatic mark everywhere. The separation of life from death does not result in a profit increasing for life.

Death for Baudrillard must not come to one from an abstract impersonal force (such as science or the state). Death is a social relation between persons (beyond Heideggerian mineness or *Jemeinigkeit*), established through ceremony and artifice. To articulate death socially is a mortal danger to the dominant system because it reveals the extent to which it is administered by the system.

Baudrillard elaborates his conception of death in terms of symbolic exchange, in terms of the gift and the counter-gift. Even the gift of death, issued from the statistical indifference of an anonymous system, may be socialized in a radical act.[133] The system manifests its superiority by defining death, in giving a gift that cannot be returned (Baudrillard 1993, 243- 82).

In section 3, leaning on Hanlon's (2004) article, we saw how Baudrillard's analysis of Heidegger raises the problem of subjectivity, a problem crucially connected with death. Baudrillard investigates the social role and place of death away from a certain subject-centred-ness which he identifies in Heidegger's conception of death. He thereby seeks to critique all economization and compartmentalization of death.

For Hanlon, Baudrillard theorizes death outside any structural conceptions of temporality or subjectivity. In light of the conclusions reached from previous chapters however, Baudrillard does leave room for a practical conception of subjectivity. In my view, Baudrillard, like Nietzsche, puts forward a certain historical point of view of the subject. He hypothesizes on the constitutive

---

[133] Unfortunately, I did not have the space here to elaborate on the radical gestures Baudrillard proposes, e.g., terrorism. Overall, following in Nietzsche's footsteps, Baudrillard's hyperbole serves to move the audience towards thinking differently.

relation between subjectivity and structures of power. The most important rhetorical or stylistic element of Baudrillard's Nietzschean-inspired genealogy is its hyperbolic, polemical and fictional character. This ensures an urgency to the hypothesis regarding the invention of subjects.

This style also connects with Baudrillard's and Nietzsche's engagement with the concept of truth as perspectival (chapter 1 section 3). Baudrillard's genealogical analysis, like that of Nietzsche, seeks to effect a change in perspective or ethical orientation on the part of the audience. This is achieved by means of its dramatic mode of presentation and not only due to its contents, which includes hypotheses and speculations about origins and ends.

By emphasizing a dual movement of anticipation and transformation in Baudrillard's relation to both Nietzsche and Heidegger, I sought to maintain the particularity of their views, as well as the singularity of all their contributions. In his work, Baudrillard repays his special debt to Nietzsche, not by means of a consciousness of guilt (which is for Nietzsche the Christian model: the debt can never be repaid in this life) but rather he reciprocates excessively and luxuriously i.e., beyond the current, accepted scientific academic standards of referencing, which are ascetic and part of the will to truth.

7. Bibliography

Acampora, Christa Davis. 2006. "On Sovereignty and Overhumanity Why it Matters How We Read Nietzsche's Genealogy II: 2". In *Critical Essays on the Classics: Nietzsche's On the Genealogy of Morals*, edited by Christa Davis Acampora. New York: Rowman & Littlefield Publishers.

Allison, David. 1999. "Iconologies: Reading Simulations with Plato and Nietzsche". In *Nietzsche, Epistemology, and Philosophy of Science II*, edited by Babette Babiche. Kluwer Academic Publishers.

Allison, David. 2013. "Iconologies: Reading Simulations with Plato and Nietzsche". In *Nietzsche, Epistemology, and Philosophy of Science: Nietzsche and the Science II*, edited by Babette Babiche. Springer Science & Business Media.

Alexandre, Marc. 1969. 'Sur la société de consommation' *La Nef*, 37. 26e année, avril-août

Allsobrook, Chistopher. 2009. "Contingent Criticism: Bridging Ideology Critique and Genealogy". In *Nietzsche, Power and Politics: Rethinking Nietzsche's Legacy for Political Thought*, edited by Herman W. Siemens and Vasti Roodt. De Gruyter.

Anderson, Lanier R. 2005. "Nietzsche on Truth, Illusion and Redemption". *European Journal of Philosophy*, Vol. 13, No. 2. Oxford: Oxford University Press.

Ansell-Pearson, Keith. 1992. "Who is the Übermensch? Time, Truth, and Woman in Nietzsche". *Journal of the History of Ideas*, Vol. 53, No. 2. (Apr.- Jun)

Ansell-Pearson, K., 2007. 'Introduction: on Nietzsche's Critique of Morality'. In *On the Genealogy of Morals* by Friedrich Nietzsche, edited by Keith Ansell-Pearson. Translated by Carol Diethe. Cambridge University Press.

Barthes, Roland. 1986. "The reality effect". *The Rustle of Language*, translated by Richard Howard. New York: Basil Blackwell.

Bataille, Georges. 1967. *La part maudite, précédé de la notion de dépense.* Paris: Éditions de Minuit.

Bataille, Georges. 1991a. *The Accursed Share.* New York: Zone Books.

Bataille, Georges. 1991b. *The Accursed Share, Vols. II and III: The History of Eroticism and Sovereignty.* New York: Zone Books.

Baudrillard, Jean. 1968. *Le système des objets.* Paris: Gallimard.

Baudrillard, Jean. 1970. *La société de consommation.* Paris: Gallimard.

Baudrillard, Jean. 1973. *Le miroir de la production: ou l'illusion critique du matérialisme historique*. Tournail: Casterman.

Baudrillard, Jean. 1975. *The Mirror of Production*, translated by Mark Poster. St. Louis: Telos Press Ltd.

Baudrillard, Jean. 1976. *L'échange symbolique et la mort*. Paris: Gallimard.

Baudrillard, Jean. 1979. *De la séduction*. Paris: Galilée.

Baudrillard, Jean. 1981. *Simulacres et Simulations*. Paris: Galilée.

Baudrillard, Jean 1981b. *For a Critique of the Political Economy of the Sign*, translated by Charles Levin. St Louis: Telos Press.

Baudrillard, Jean. 1983. *Simulations*, translated by Paul Foss, Paul Patton and Philip Beitchman. New York: Semiotext(e).

Baudrillard, Jean. 1987. *Amérique*. Paris : Grasset.

Baudrillard, Jean. 1990 FS. *Fatal Strategies*, translated by Philip Beitchman and W.G. J Neisluchowski, New York: Semiotext(e).

Baudrillard, Jean. 1990 CM. *Cool Memories 1*, translated by Chris Turner. London: Verso.

Baudrillard, Jean. 1990 S. *Seduction*, translated by Brian Singer. New World Perspectives.

Baudrillard, Jean. 1992. *L'illusion de la fin*. Paris: Galilée.

Baudrillard, Jean. 1993. *Symbolic Exchange and Death*, translated by Ian Hamilton Grant. London: Sage Publications.

Baudrillard, Jean. 1993 TE. *Transparency of Evil*, translated by James Benedict. New York: Verso.

Baudrillard, Jean. 1993 BL. *Baudrillard Live: Selected Interviews*, edited by Mike Gane. London: Routledge.

Baudrillard, Jean. 1994. *Simulacra and Simulation*, translated by Sheila Faria Glaser. Ann Arbor: University of Michigan Press.

Baudrillard, Jean. 1996. *System of Objects*. London: Verso.

Baudrillard, Jean. 1998. *The Consumer Society. Myths and Structures*, translated by J.P. Mayer. Sage Publications.

Baudrillard, Jean. 2000. *The Gulf War Did Not Take Place*, translated by Paul Patton. Sydney: Power Institute.

Baudrillard, Jean. 2001. *D'un fragment l'autre,* Paris: Albin Michel.

Baudrillard, Jean. 2002. *The Spirit of Terrorism*, translated by Chris Turner. New York: Verso.

Baudrillard, Jean. 2004. *Fragments: Conversations with Francois L'Yvonnet*. New York: Routledge.

Baudrillard, Jean. 2005. *System of Objects*, translated by Benedict James. New York. Verso.

Baudrillard, Jean. 2007. *Exiles from Dialogues*. Cambridge: Polity Press.

Baudrillard, Jean. 2007b. *Forget Foucault*. Translated by Nicole Dufresne. New York: Semiotext(e).

Baudrillard, Jean. 2008. "The Violence of the Image", translated by Paul Foss. *Art US*. Foundation of International Art Criticism. Summer. Vol. 23.

Baugh, Bruce. 2000. "Death and Temporality in Deleuze and Derrida". *Angelaki. Journal of Theoretical Humanities*. 8/1/2000.

Bauman, Zygmunt. 1995. *Ansichten der Postmoderne*, translated by Nora Raethel. Hamburg: Argument Verlag.

Bauman, Zygmunt. 2000. "The Sweet Smell of Decomposition". In *Jean Baudrillard*, edited by Mike Gane. Sage Publications.

Belsey, Catherine. 2003. *Poststructuralism: A Very Brief Introduction*. Oxford: Oxford University Press.

Belting, Hans. 2001. *Bild-Anthropologie. Entwürfe für eine Bildwissenschaft*. München: Wilhelm Fink.

Benjamin, Walter. 2001. *The Work of Art in the Age of Mechanical Reproduction*, translated by J.A. Underwood. Penguin.

Bogard, William. 1990. 'Closing down the Social: Baudrillard's Challenge to Contemporary Sociology'. *Sociological Theory*, Vol. 8, No. 1 (Spring, 1990), pp. 1-15.

Boldt-Irons, Leslie Anne. 2001. "Bataille and Baudrillard. From a General Economy to the Transparency of Evil". In *Angelaki. Journal of the Theoretical Humanities*. Vol 6, No.2. August.

Bolz, Norbert. 1991. *Eine kurze Geschichte des Scheins*, München: Fink Verlag.

Boorstin, Daniel J. 1992. The Image: A Guide to Pseudo- Events in America. New York, Vintage.

Borges, Jorge Luis. 1999. *Collected Fictions*, translated by Andrew Hurley. Penguin.

Boulter, Jonathan S. 2001. "Partial Glimpses of the Infinite: Borges and the Simulacrum". *Hispanic Review*, Vol. 69, No. 3. pp. 355-377. University of Pennsylvania Press.

Britton, Celia. 1992. *The Nouveau Roman: Fiction, Theory and Politics*. New York: St. Martin's Press.

Butler, Rex. 1997. "Reading In the Shadow of the Silent Majorities as an Allegory of Representation." In *Art and Artefact*, edited by Nicholas Zurbrugg. London: Sage Publications.

Butler, Rex. 1999. *Jean Baudrillard: The Defence of the Real*. London: Sage Publications.

Butler, Rex. 2010. *The Baudrillard Dictionary*, edited by Richard D. Smith. Edinburgh: Edinburgh University Press.

Butterfield, Bradley. 2002. "The Baudrillardian Symbolic, 9/11, and the War of Good and Evil". *Postmodern Culture* – Vol. 13, No. 1, September. The Johns Hopkins University Press.

Callinicos, Alex. 1989. *Against Postmodernism. A Marxist Critique*. Cambridge: Cambridge University Press.

Carel, Havi. 2006. *Life and Death in Freud and Heidegger. Contemporary Psychoanalytic Studies* 6. Amsterdam: Editions Rodopi B.V.

Chen, K.H. 1987. 'The masses and the media: Baudrillard's implosive post-modernism', *Theory, Culture and Society* (4) 1; 71-88

Cohen, Richard A. 2006. 'Levinas: Thinking Least about Death – contra Heidegger.' *International Journal of Philosophy and Religion*. Vol. 60.

Colebrook, Claire. 2002. *Gilles Deleuze*. New York: Routledge Critical Thinkers.

Colebrook, Claire. 2006. *Deleuze: A Guide for the Perplexed*. London: Continuum.

Culler, Jonathan. 1975. *Structuralist Poetics: Structuralism, Linguistics and the Study of Literature*. London: Routledge.

Dastur, Françoise. 1996. *Death: an Essay on Finitude*, translated by John Llewelyn. London: Athlone Press.

Debray, Régis. 1992. *Jenseits der Bilder: Eine Geschichte der Bildbetrachtung im Abendland*. Rodenbach : Avinus.

Deleuze, Gilles. 1969. *Logique du Sens*. Paris: Les Éditions de Minuit.

Deleuze, Gilles. 1994. *Difference and Repetition*, translated by Paul Patton. New York: Columbia University Press.

Deleuze, Gilles. 2004. *Logic of Sense*, translated by Mark Lester with Charles Stivale. London: Continuum.

Deleuze, Gilles 2006. *Nietzsche and Philosophy*. London: Athlone

Deleuze, Gilles and Félix Guattari. 1994b. *What is Philosophy?* Translated by Hugh Tomlinson and Graham Burchell. New York : Columbia University Press.

Derrida, Jacques. 1963. "Cogito et histoire de la folie". *Revue de Métaphysique et de la Morale*, 69 (4), 425-473.

Derrida, Jacques. 1972. *Marges de la philosophie*. Paris: Les Éditions de Minuit.

Drochon, H., 2016. *Nietzsche's Great Politics*. New Jersey: Princeton University Press.

Elgat, Guy, 2017. Nietzsche's Psychology of Ressentiment : Revenge and Justice in 'On the Genealogy of Morals'. London: Routledge.

Figal, Günter 2007. *Martin Heidegger. Zur Einfuhrung*. Hamburg: Junius Verlag.

Flaxman, Gregory. 2012. *Gilles Deleuze and the Fabulation of Philosophy*. Minneapolis: University of Minnesota Press.

Foucault, Michel. 1961. *Folie et déraison: Histoire de la folie à l'âge classique*. Paris: Libraire Plon.

Foucault, Michel. 1963. *Naissance de la Clinique*. Paris: Presses Universitaires de France.

Foucault, Michel. 1967. *Madness and Civilisation*, translated by Richard Howard Tavistock Publications.

Foucault, Michel. 1973. *The Order of Things*. New York: Random House.

Foucault, Michel. 1990. *History of Sexuality Vol 1: An Introduction*, translated by Robert Hurley. New York: Vintage Books.

Freerks, Vanessa. 2019. "Nietzsche's Reversal of Platonism and the Simulacrum". *Sofia Philosophical Review*, Vol XII, No. 2.

Freudenberger, Silja and Hans Jörg Sandkühler (eds.) 2003. *Repräsentationen. Krise der Repräsentationen, Paradigmenwechsel. Ein Forschungsprogramm in Philosophie und Wissenschaften*. Frankfurt: Peter Lang GmbH, Internationaler Verlag der Wissenschaften.

Fuchs, Werner. 1969. *Todesbilder in der modernen Gesellschaft*. Frankfurt a.M.: Suhrkamp.

Gallop, Jane. 1989. 'French Theory and the Seduction of Feminism'. In *Men in Feminism*, edited by Alice Jardine and Paul Smith. London: Routledge.

Gane, Mike. 1991. *Critical and Fatal Theory*. New York: Routledge.

Gane, Mike. 1991b. *Baudrillard's Bestiary: Baudrillard and Culture*. New York. Routledge.

Gane, Mike. 1993. 'Introduction'. In *Symbolic Exchange and Death*. London: Sage Publications.

Gasché, Rodolphe. 1987. "Readings in Interpretation Hölderlin, Hegel, Heidegger". *Theory and History of Literature*, 26. Minneapolis: University of Minnesota Press.

Genosko, Gary. 1994. *Baudrillard and Signs: Signs Ablaze*. London: Taylor and Francis.

Genosko, Gary. 1998. *Undisciplined Theory*. London: Sage.

Genosko, Gary. 1999. *McLuhan and Baudrillard: masters of implosion*. London: Routledge.

Gogan, Brian. 2017. *Jean Baudrillard: The Rhetoric of Symbolic Exchange*. Southern Illinois University Press

Goulimari, Pelagia. 2015. *Literary Criticism and Theory: From Plato to Postcolonialism.* New York, Routledge.

Grace, Victoria. 2000. *Baudrillard's Challenge: A Feminist Reading.* London: Routledge.

Graeber, David. 2011. *Debt: The First 5,000 Years.* New York: Melville House.

Guay, Robert. 2011. 'Genealogy and Irony'. *Journal of Nietzsche Studies.* Vol.41, No 1 (Spring).

Gungov, Alexander. 2006. "Simulacra in the Age of the New World Order," *Proceedings of the Twenty-First World Congress of Philosophy*, vol. 2 Social and Political Philosophy, 267.

Gutting, Gary. 1989. *Michel Foucault's Archaeology of Scientific Reason.* Cambridge: Cambridge University Press.

Gutting, Gary. 2001. *French Philosophy in the Twentieth Century.* Cambridge: Cambridge University Press.

Hanlon, Nick. 2004. 'Death, Subjectivity and Temporality in Baudrillard and Heidegger'. *French Studies.* LVIII, No. 4. 513-525. Society for French Studies.

Hatab, Lawrence J. 2008. "How Does the Ascetic Ideal Function in Nietzsche's Genealogy?" In *Journal of Nietzsche Studies*, 35/36 (Spring-Autumn). PA: Penn State University Press, 2008.

Hegarty, Paul. 2004. *Jean Baudrillard: Live Theory.* London: Continuum.

Heidegger, Martin. 1962. *Being and Time,* translated by John Macquarrie and Edward Robinson. London: Blackwell.

Heidegger, Martin. 1991. *Nietzsche: Volumes One and Two,* translated and edited by David Farrell Krell. New York: Harper Collins.

Heidegger, Martin. 2001. *Sein und Zeit.* Achtzehnte Auflage. Tübingen: Max Niemeyer Verlag.

Huyssen, Andreas. 1989. "In the Shadow of McLuhan: Jean Baudrillard's Theory of Simulation". *Assemblage*, 10 (December).

Hyland, Drew A. "Simulate This! The Seductive Return of the Real in Baudrillard," *Subjects and Simulations: Between Baudrillard and Lacoue-Labarthe,* ed. Anne O'Bryne, and Hugh J. Silverman (Lexington Books: 2014), 28.

Jarry, Alfred. 1965. *Selected Works of Alfred Jarry.* Roger Shattuck and Simon Watts Taylor, New York: Grove.

Joseph, John E. 2000. *Limiting the Arbitrary: Linguistic naturalism and its opposites in Plato's 'Cratylus' and modern theories of language".* John Benjamins Publishing Company.

Karpenstein-Essbach, Christa. 2004. *Einführung in die Kulturwissenschaft der Medien*. München: Fink Verlag.

Katona, George. 1964. *The Mass Consumption Society*. New York: McGraw-Hill.

Kellner, Douglas Mackay. 1986. *Heidegger's Concept of Authenticity*. New York: PhD thesis Columbia University.

Kellner, Douglas Mackay. 1989. *Jean Baudrillard. From Marxism to Post Modernism and Beyond*. Cambridge: Polity Press.

King, Anthony. 1998. "Baudrillard's Nihilism and the End of Theory". *Telos*, Issue 112.

King, Anthony. 2000. "A Critique of Baudrillard's Hyperreality: Towards a Sociology of Postmodernism". In *Jean Baudrillard*, edited by Mike Gane. Vol.11. Sage Publications.

Klossowski, Pierre. 1997. *Nietzsche and the Vicious Circle*, translated by Daniel W. Smith. Chicago: University of Chicago Press.

Klossowski, Pierre. 2007. *Such a Deathly Desire*, translated by Russell Ford. Albany: State University of New York Press.

Kofman, Sarah. 1993. *Nietzsche and Metaphor*. London: The Athlone Press.

Koopman, Colin. 2013. *Genealogy as Critique: Foucault and the Problems of Modernity*. Indiana: Indiana University Press.

Krämer, Sybille. 1994. 'Vom Trugbild zum Topos. Über Fiktive Realitäten'. In: Stefan Iglhaut/Florian Rötzer/Elizabeth Schweger (Hg.). 1995. *Illusion und Simulation. Begegnung mit der Realität*. Hatje Cantz, Ostfildern.

Kroker, Aurthur. 1991. *The Postmodern Scene. Excremental Culture and Hyper-Aesthetics*. Macmillan.

Lacan, Jacques. 1977. *Écrits. A Selection*, translated by A. Sheridan, W. W. Norton. New York.

Lacoue-Labarthe, Philippe. 1993. *The Subject of Philosophy*, translated by Thomas Trezise, Hugh Silverman, Gary M. Cole, Timothy Bent, Karen McPherson and Claudette Sartiliot, edited by Thomas Trezise. Minneapolis: University of Minnesota Press.

Lane, Richard J. 2009. *Jean Baudrillard*. 2nd Edition. London: Routledge.

Lane, David. 2011. "Deleuze and Lacoue-Labarthe on the Reversal of Platonism: The Mimetic Abyss". *SubStance* 3125, Vol. 40, No. 2.

La Rocca, David. 2001. "The False Pretender: Deleuze, Sherman and the Status of Simulacra". *Journal of Aesthetics and Art Criticism*, Vol. 69, No.3 (Summer).

Leiris, Michel. 1925. *Simulacre: poèmes et lithographies*. Éditions de la Galerie Simon.

Leiter, Brian. 2002. *Routledge Philosophy Guidebook to Nietzsche on Morality*. London: Routledge.

Lepers, Philip. 2009. "Baudrillard und Nietzsche: vademecum, vadetecum". In *Nietzsche und Frankreich*, edited by Clemens Pornschlegel and Martin Stingelin. Berlin: De Gruyter.

Levin, Charles. 1996. *Jean Baudrillard. A Study in Cultural Metaphysics*. Hertfordshire: Prentice Hall Europe.

Levin, Charles. 2000. "Baudrillard, Critical Theory and Psychoanalysis." *Jean Baudrillard*, edited by Mike Gane, IV, 198-216. London: Sage Publications.

Levinas, Emmanuel. 1948. *Le Temps et l'Autre*. Paris: PUF.

Levinas, Emmanuel. 1993. *Dieu, la mort et le temps*. Paris: Grasset.

Lotringer, Sylvère. 2008. "Remember Foucault". *October*, 126 (Fall).

Lyotard, Jean Francois. 1993. *Libidinal Economy*, translated by Iain Hamilton Grant. London: Athlone.

Major-Poetzl, P. 1986. 'Postmodernism and popular culture'. *Journal of Communication Inquiry*. Vol.10, No. 2: 108-16.

Marx, Karl. 1977. *Capital. Vol 1*, translated by Ben Fowkes, New York: Penguin.

Marx, Karl and Friedrich Engels, 1978. "The Communist Manifesto". In *The Marx-Engels Reader*, edited by R Tucker. New York: Norton.

Marx, Karl. 2018. *Das Kapital*. Köln: Anaconda Verlag.

Mauss, Marcel. 1950. "Essai sur le don: forme et raison de l'échange dans les société archaïques". In *Sociologie et Anthropologie*. Paris: Presse Universitaire de Paris.

Mauss, Marcel. 1990. *The Gift: The Form and Reason for Exchange in Archaic Societies*, translated by W. D. Halls. Routledge, London.

Mauss, Marcel. 2002. *The Gift: The Form and Reason for Exchange in Archaic Societies*, translated by W. D. Halls. Routledge, London.

May, Simon. 1999. *Nietzsche's Ethics and his 'War on Morality'*. Oxford: Clarendon Press.

McLuhan, Herbert Marshall. 1962. "Review of The Image". *Canadian Forum*, 42. (July).

McLuhan, Herbert Marshall .1964. *Understanding Media: The Extensions of Man*. New York: McGraw-Hill.

Merrin, William. 2005, *Baudrillard and the Media*. London: Sage.

Mersch, Dieter. 2006. *Medientheorien zur Einführung*. Hamburg: Junius.

Moore, Gerald. 2011. *Politics of the Gift: Exchanges in Poststructuralism*. Edinburgh: Edinburgh University Press.

Morin, Edgar. 1998. *L'Esprit du Temps*. Paris: Grasset.

Morris, Meaghan 2000. "Room 101 or A Few Worst Things in the World" in Jean Baudrillard, edited by Mike Gane. Vol 3. London: Sage Publications.

Nehamas, Alexander. 1985. *Nietzsche: Life as Literature*. Cambridge, Mass: Harvard University Press.

Nietzsche, Friedrich. 1967. *Beyond Good and Evil*, translated by Walter Kaufmann. New York: Random House.

Nietzsche, Friedrich. 1968. *The Will to Power*, translated by Walter Kaufmann and R.J. Hollingdale: New York: Random House.

Nietzsche, Friedrich. 1968b. *The Portable Nietzsche*, translated by Walter Kaufmann. New York: Viking.

Nietzsche, Friedrich. 1988. *Nachgelassene Fragmente 1880-1882. Kritische Studienausgabe* (KSA), Bd. 9. München: De Gruyter/Dtv.

Nietzsche, Friedrich. 1999. *The Birth of Tragedy and Other Writings*, translated by Ronald Speirs. New York: Cambridge University Press.

Nietzsche, Friedrich. 2005. *The Anti-Christ, Ecce Homo, Twilight of the Idols, and Other Writings*, edited by Aaron Ridely, translated by Judith Norman. New York: Cambridge University Press.

Nietzsche, Friedrich. 2007. *On the Genealogy of Morals*, translated by Carol Diethe, edited by Keith Ansell-Pearson. New York: Cambridge University Press.

Norris, Christopher. 2000. "Lost in the Funhouse: Baudrillard and the Politics of Postmodernism". *Jean Baudrillard. Sage Masters of Modern Thought*, edited by Mike Gane, 1. London: Sage Publications.

Oniki, Yuji. 1995. "Perec, Marx, and Les Choses". *Qui Parle*. Vol.9, No. 1. Fall/Winter.

Owen, David. 2007. *Nietzsche's Genealogy of Morals*. New York: Routledge.

Pawlett, William. 2007. *Jean Baudrillard. Against Banality*. London: Routledge.

Pawlett, William. 2010. "Simulacra + Simulacrum". In *The Baudrillard Dictionary*, edited by Richard G. Smith. Edinburgh: Edinburgh University Press.

Pawlett, William. 2010. Death. In *The Baudrillard Dictionary*, edited by Richard G. Smith. Edinburgh: Edinburgh University Press.

Pefanis. Jullian. 1991. Heterology and the Postmodern: Bataille, Baudrillard and Lyotard. Durham: Duke University Press.

Perec, Georges. 1965. *Les choses, une histoire des années soixante*. Paris: Julliard.

Perec, Georges. 1967. *Things: A Story of the Sixties*, translated by Helen R. Lane. New York: Grove Press.

Peruso, Thomas F. 1985. "Madame Bovary in the Consumer Society". *Ça Parle*, Vol. 1, No. 1, the representation of otherness (Fall). Duke University Press.

Peyre, Henri. 1966. "Review: Les choses by Georges Perec". *Books Abroad*, Vol. 40, No. 3 (Summer, 1966). Board of Regents of the University of Oklahoma.

Plato. 1961. *Collected Dialogues*, edited by Edith Hamilton and Huntington Cairns. Bollingen Series 71. Princeton: Princeton University Press.

Plato. 2000. *The Republic*, translated by Tom Griffin, edited by G. R. F. Ferrari. Cambridge: Cambridge University Press.

Polt, Richard. 1999. *Heidegger. An Introduction*. New York: Cornell University Press.

Poster, Mark. 1981. "Technology and Culture in Habermas and Baudrillard". *Contemporary Literature*. Vol. 22, No. 4 (Autumn pp. 456-476). University of Wisconsin Press.

Poster, Mark. 1988. 'Introduction'. In *Jean Baudrillard. Selected Writings*, edited by Mike Poster. Sage Publications.

Racevskis, Karl. 1979. "Theoretical Violence of a Catastrophic Strategy". *Diacritics* (September).

Rajan, Tilotama. 2002. *Deconstruction and the Remainders of Phenomenology*. Stanford: Stanford University Press.

Ramirez, Álvaro. 2005. "Don Quijote" and the Age of Simulacra. *Hispania*. Vol. 88, No 1. March. pp. 82-90.

Ridley, Aaron. 2000. 'Science in the Service of Life'. In *The Proper Ambition of Science*, edited by M.W.F. Stone & J. Wolff, 91-101. London: Routledge.

Ritzer, George. 1998. 'Introduction'. In *Consumer Society* by Jean Baudrillard. Sage Publications.

Roodt, Vasti. 1996. "Nietzsche, Genealogy and the Politics of Communality". *South Africa Journal of Philosophy*. Vol. 15 Issue 1.

Saar, Martin. 2009. "Genealogische Kritik". In *Was ist Kritik?*, edited by Rahel Jaeggi and Tilo Wesche. Frankfurt Am Main: Surkamp Verlag.

Saar, Martin. 2009b. "Forces and Power in Nietzsche's *Genealogy of Morals*". In *Nietzsche, Power and Politics: Rethinking Nietzsche's Legacy for Political Thought*, edited by Herman W. Siemens and Vasti Roodt. De Gruyter.

Sahlins, Marshall. 1972. *Stone Age Economics*. New York: Aldine De Gruyter.

Sallis, John. 1996. *Being and Logic: Reading the Platonic Dialogues*, 3rd Edition. Bloomington and Indianapolis: Indiana University Press.

Sartre. Jean-Paul. 1943. *L'être et le néant*. Paris: Gallimard.

Sartre, Jean Paul. 1946. *L'existentialisme est un humanisme*. Paris: Nagel.

Saussure, Ferdinand de. 1966. *Course in General Linguistics*, edited by Charles Bally and Albert Sechehaye. New York, First Mc Graw-Hill Book Company.

Saussure, Ferdinand de. 1983. *Course in General Linguistics*, translated by Roy Harris, London: La Salle III Open Court.

Schoonmaker, Sara. 1994. "Capitalism and the Code: A Critique of Baudrillard's Third Order Simulacrum". In *Baudrillard: A Critical Reader*, edited by Douglas Kellner, Cambridge: Blackwell.

Schrift, Alan D. 1995. *Nietzsche's French Legacy. A Genealogy of Poststructuralism*. London: Routledge.

Schrift, Alan D. 1990. *Nietzsche and the Question of Interpretation. Between Hermeneutics and Deconstruction*. London: Routledge.

Schwarz, Paul. 1988. *Georges Perec: Traces of his Passage*. Birmingham, Alabama: Summa Publications.

Sheppard, D. J. 2009. *Plato's Republic. An Edinburgh Philosophical Guide*. Edinburgh: Edinburgh University Press.

Simmel, Georg. 1986. *Schopenhauer and Nietzsche*. Translated H. Loiskandt et al. Amherst: University of Massachusetts Press.

Slocombe, Will. 2006. *Nihilism and the Sublime Post Modern: The (Hi) Story of a Difficult Relationship from Romanticism to Postmodernism*. Routledge. New York.

Sloterdijk, Peter. 1987. *Critique of Cynical Reason*. Minneapolis: University of Minnesota Press.

Smith, Daniel W. 2005. "Klossowski's Reading of Nietzsche: Impulses, Phantasms, Simulacra, Stereotypes". *Diacritics*, 35 (1) (Spring). John Hopkins University Press.

Smith, Daniel W. 2006. "The Concept of the Simulacrum: Deleuze and the Overturning of Platonism". *Continental Philosophy Review*, 38: 89-123.

Sokal, Alan and Jean Bricmont. 1998. *Intellectual Imposters*. Picador.

Sokal, Alan and Jean Bricmont. 2000. "Jean Baudrillard". In *Jean Baudrillard*, edited by Mike Gane. Part 8: Baudrillard and Other Theorists. Sage Publications.

Spiller, R. E., 1962. 'Reviewed works: The Image: or What Happened to the American Dream, by Daniel Boorstin'. *American Quarterly*, Vol, 14. No. 2, Part 1 (Summer), p. 216. The John Hopkins University Press.

Strehle, Samuel. 2012. *Zur Aktualität von Jean Baudrillard: Einleitung in sein Werk. VS Verlag für Sozialwissenschaften*. Wiesbaden: VS Verlag für Sozialwissenschaften. Springer Fachmedien, GmbH.

Sukla, Anata Charana. 2001. *Art and Representation: Contributions to Contemporary Aesthetics*. Westport: Praeger Publishers.

Thom, Paul. 1993. *For an Audience: A Philosophy of the Performing Arts*. Philadelphia: Temple University Press.

Tseëlon, Efrat. 1992. "Fashion and the signification of social order". *Semiotica*, 91. 1-14

Tseëlon, Efrat. 1994. "Fashion and the signification in Baudrillard". In *Baudrillard: A Critical Reader*, edited by Douglas Kellner.

Tseëlon, Efrat. 2000. "Postmodernism and the Clothed Meaning". In *Jean Baudrillard*. Ed. Mike Gane. Vol. III. Sage Publications.

Van Tongeren. J.M., 2000. *Reinterpreting Modern Culture: An Introduction to Friedrich Nietzsche's Philosophy*. Indiana: Perdue University Press.

Venus, Jochen. 2001. *Referenzlose Simulation?*. Königshausen u. Neumann.

Walters, James. 2012. *Baudrillard and Theology*. Continuum.

White, Richard. 1988. "The Return of the Master: An Interpretation of Nietzsche's Genealogy". *Philosophy and Phenomenological Research*. Vol. 48. No. 4.

Whitfield, S. J. 1991. 'Review: The Image: The Lost World of Daniel Boorstin'. *Reviews in American History*. Vol 19, No. 2 (June), pp. 302-312. John Hopkins University Press.

Wilk, Richard and Lisa C. Cliggett. 2009. *Economies and Culture: Foundations of Economic Anthropology*. Westview Press.

Winkler, Rafael. 2007. "I Owe You: Nietzsche, Mauss". *Journal of the British Society for Phenomenology*. Vol. 38, No. 1, January.

Winkler, Rafael. 2016. "Time, Singularity and the Impossible: Heidegger and Derrida on Dying." *Research in Phenomenology*. Vol, 46. Issue 3.

Winkler, Rafael. 2018. *Philosophy of Finitude: Heidegger, Levinas and Nietzsche*. New York: Bloomsbury Publishing Inc.

Woodward, Ashley. 2008. "Was Baudrillard A Nihilist?" *International Journal of Baudrillard Studies*. Vol. 5, No. 1 (January).

Woodward, Ashley. 2009. *Nihilism in Postmodernity: Lyotard, Baudrillard, Vattimo*. Davis Group Publishers.

Zapf, Holger. 2010. *Jenseits der Simulation – Das Radikale Denken Jean Baudrillards als Politische Theorie*. Berlin: Lit. Verlag.

Zeitlin, Irving. 1994. *Nietzsche, A Re-examination*. Cambridge: Polity Press.

Ziegler, Jean. 1975. *Die Lebenden und der Tod*. Berlin: Ullstein.

Zima, Peter W. 2010. *Modern/Postmodern. Society, Philosophy, Literature*. Bloomsbury.

Index

Aesthetics of appearance, 106
Allison, David, 21, 119,122, 130, 151, 189, 194
Allsobrook, 10, 38, 39, 194
Anderson, R.I., 6
Arendt, Hannah, 11
ascetic, 192
    consumption, 75
    ideal, vii, ix, 12, 46, 51, 56-61, 65-69, 74-75, 79, 80, 82, 89, 93-94, 97, 102, 167, 186-187, 200
    priest, vii, ix, 12, 42-44, 46-47, 55-61, 63-67, 86, 97, 102, 167, 186
    procedure, 56
    requirements, 59
asceticism, 60

Barthes, Roland, 107, 137, 194

Bataille, Georges, 8, 21, 65, 67, 69, 72, 74, 76, 88, 111, 174, 176, 187, 194
Baudrillard, Jean, v, vii, ix-x, 1-32, 39-45, 47, 50, 52-55, 57, 61-99, 102, 105-107, 110-153, 155-160, 162-164, 166-192
Benabou, Marcel and Bruno Marcenac, 90
Bolt-Irons, Leslie-Anne, 21
Boorstin, Daniel, 82-86, 196, 205
Borges, Jorge Luis, 107, 110, 196
Botha, Catherine, 21
Boulter, Jonathan, 110
Breton, André, 106

Butler, Rex, 5-8, 28, 85, 110-112, 117-118, 134-137, 152, 169, 178-179, 196
Butterfield, Bradley, 182

Callinicos, Alex, 3

consommation, 52, 194
consumer society, vii, ix, 1, 10, 12, 16, 19-21, 23-24, 28-30, 40-44, 50, 52, 54, 57, 61-62, 64-69, 73, 75-87, 89-94, 97, 114, 140, 145, 147, 167, 185-187, 195, 203

consummation, 72, 76, 88
consumption, vii, ix, 10-12, 19-20, 23-25, 27-28, 32, 41, 43-45, 52-54, 62-64, 67-68, 73, 75-81, 87-88, 91-93, 97-98, 157, 186, 200

death, v, vii, x,1,5, 7, 8, 11,13-15, 17, 71, 83, 106, 112, 117-118, 121-123, 128, 130, 141, 143, 146, 150-153, 155-164, 166-179, 181-183, 188-191, 195, 196, 197
Debord, Guy, 146
debt, ix, 42, 44, 49, 50-52, 54-55, 64-65, 68-72, 170, 192, 199
Deleuze, Gilles, 8, 13, 21-23, 29, 32, 35, 81, 94, 95, 98-99, 105-112, 119-123, 132, 188, 196-198, 200, 204
Deleuze, Gilles et Félix Guattari, 107,197

Derrida, Jacques, 69, 72, 112, 152, 160, 162, 166, 196
de Saussure, *see* Saussure

Éluard, Paul, 106
Essbach Karpenstein Christa, 124
expenditure, iv, 34, 40, 68-69, 71-74, 76-77, 175
Foucault, Michel, 15, 22, 32, 111, 123-124, 132, 156, 164-166, 196

genealogy, v, vii, ix-x, 1-2, 4, 8, 10-12, 14-17, 19-24, 31-35, 38, 41-46, 49-50, 55, 60, 66, 68, 75, 89, 93, 100-102, 111-112, 121-122, 130, 133, 144, 151, 155-157, 163-168, 171, 175, 180-181, 183, 186, 188-192, 194
Gane, Mike, 7, 129, 143, 195-196
Genosko, 4, 82, 124, 171, 174, 182, 198
gift, 39, 62, 65, 67, 69-73, 75-76, 88, 169-170, 172, 175, 177, 182, 191, 201
Graeber, 170
Guignon, Charles, 176
Gungov, Alexander, v, 117, 199
Habermas, Jürgen, 21

Hanlon, Nick, 13-14, 155-156, 158-160, 168, 175-182, 191, 199
Hegarty, 22-23, 115, 123, 131, 132, 174, 175, 199

Heidegger, Martin, v, vii, x, 1, 13-14, 16, 21, 71, 100-101, 139, 151, 153, 155-164, 166, 170, 175-180, 182, 190-192
Hoffmann, Piotr, 176
Hyland, Drew A, 113, 199
hyperreal, 13, 99, 113, 118, 121, 123, 130, 138, 141, 144-145, 150-152, 188-189
hyperreality, x, 5-6, 16, 101, 111, 113-114, 116, 119, 121, 130, 137-140, 144, 148, 151, 153, 190, 201

image, 1, 6, 11, 24, 30, 39, 52, 63, 81-84, 86, 87, 95, 98-100, 104, 106, 108, 112-113, 115-119, 121-122, 124, 125, 135, 148-150, 160, 165, 188, 196, 201, 205

Jarry, Alfred, 142, 175, 199

Kellner, Douglas, v, 39-41, 66, 80, 124, 143-143, 161, 173, 200
King, Anthony, 3, 9, 10, 137, 144, 148, 173, 200
Klossowski, Pierre, 110, 116, 200, 204
Koopman, Colin, 156, 165, 166, 173, 200

Lacan, Jacques, 124, 171, 200
Lacoue-Labarthe, Philippe, 105, 199-200
language, vii, 11, 15, 20, 24-26, 28-30, 32-33, 37, 41, 62, 91, 100, 103-104, 106, 114, 129-130, 132, 137, 174, 178, 185, 194

La Rocca, David, 111
law of value, 126, 128-130, 146, 189
Leiris, Michel, 106, 200
Lepers, Philippe, 1, 8-9, 201
Levin, Charles, 4, 7-8, 29, 40, 72, 79-80, 82, 94, 97, 111, 116-117, 129, 135, 139, 143-147, 173, 180, 195
Levinas, Emmanuel, 159-160, 177, 197, 201, 205
Lévi-Strauss, Claude, 25
linguistics, vii, 11, 20, 24-25, 31, 32, 113-114, 121-123, 129-130, 146, 185-186, 189, 197
Lotringer, Sylvère, 111, 201
L'Yvonnet, François, 1, 22, 195

Marcuse, Herbert, 80
Marxism, 3, 80, 128, 200
Mauss, Marcel, 4, 39, 65-76, 169, 187, 201
Maussean potlatch, 74, 76
media, 63, 82-84, 86, 97, 133-135, 141, 147-150, 194
Metz, Thaddeus, v, 155
morality of consumption, vii, 10-12, 19-20, 25, 32, 43, 88, 186

Nehamas, Alexander, 41
Nietzsche, Friedrich, vii, 1-61, 63-82, 85-86, 89, 93-94, 97-113, 115-119, 121-122, 129-132, 138, 143-145, 150-153, 156-157, 163, 167, 171, 173, 176, 180-181, 185-193
nihilism, 5, 10, 60, 75, 79, 81, 94, 101, 117-119, 121, 123, 137, 200

Norris, Christopher, 6, 113, 202

objective irony, 153
Oniki, Yuji, 92-93

Pawlett, William, 1, 3, 21-22, 30-31, 39, 63, 69-70, 73, 75, 116, 125, 137, 157-158, 165, 171, 173
Pefanis, Julian, 21, 72, 111, 142
Petruso, Thomas, 90, 91-92
Perec, Georges, 68, 89-93, 187,
Plato, 7, 12, 13, 16, 67, 98, 100, 104-113, 116, 119, 121-122, 152, 180
Platonism, vii, x, 5-7, 13, 28, 94, 97, 99-101, 105, 110, 117, 121, 187-188
Poster, Mark, 11, 24-25, 31, 32
pseudo-events, ix, 68, 82-83, 86, 97, 187

reality, 3, 5-6, 8, 10, 13, 16, 33, 43, 54, 63, 79-80, 82, 84-85, 87, 92, 94-95, 98-99, 101-102, 104-106, 112-117, 119-122, 125-127, 129-132, 136-137, 139, 141, 145-146, 148-150, 152, 153, 163, 165, 169, 180, 188-189

ressentiment, 36, 45-46, 50, 56-58, 60, 186, 197
reversibility, 4-5, 14, 117-118, 123, 152-153, 170, 190
Ritzer, Georges, 23-24, 52, 65, 67, 77, 87, 203
Rockmore, Tom, 159

Saar, Martin, 38, 65, 203

Saussure, Ferdinand de, vii, 4-5, 11, 20, 24-25, 30, 32, 113-114, 117, 121, 123, 171, 185, 204

Sahlins, Marshall, 39, 73, 77-78, 169, 204

Schrift, Alan D, 21-22, 49-50, 101, 115, 120

semiological paradigm, 24, 113

semiology, 4, 24-25, 32, 71, 114, 137

simulacra, vii, 1, 5, 13, 29, 53, 89, 95, 97-100, 105-137, 143, 148, 152, 163, 187-189

simulacrum, 6, 13, 29, 95, 98, 99, 105, 106-113, 115- 117, 120, 124- 125, 127, 130, 135, 136, 138, 143, 144, 145, 151, 163, 188

simulation, 1, 11-13, 68, 71, 82, 83, 85-87, 89, 95, 97-99, 101, 107, 111- 124, 128-137, 139, 141-150, 187-189, 194-195, 199

Smith, Daniel, 107, 108, 110

Sokal, Alan and Jean Bricmont, 143

solicitude, ix, 55, 62, 86

Spinoza, Baruch, 39

subjectivity, 13-14, 17, 23, 25, 41-42, 50, 66, 139, 155-157, 160, 162, 175-179, 182, 191

theory, vii, 3-4, 7-8, 11, 15, 17, 21-22, 24-25, 30, 41, 57, 72, 76, 79-80, 98, 106, 113, 114, 116-117, 129-130, 133, 135, 137, 140, 142-143, 146-148, 150, 177, 185

time, 4, 25-26, 36, 38, 44, 51-52, 54, 69-70, 73, 76, 87, 88, 92, 98, 99, 126, 141, 147, 149, 155, 158-167, 172, 190

transcendence, vii, ix, 67, 80

transhumanism, 168

value, 2, 5, 10, 12, 15-16, 19-20, 23, 25-29, 33, 35-38, 43, 61, 67, 73-76, 79, 80, 86-88, 90, 93, 94, 97, 101-104, 118-122, 124, 126, 128-130, 135, 139, 146, 153, 157, 175, 185, 187

Van Tongeren, Paul J. M, 34, 43, 45, 47, 49

Virilio, Paul, 148

Walters, James, 4

White, Richard, 35, 37

Winkler, Rafael, v, 5, 14, 16, 51, 61, 65, 67-72, 118, 162, 178, 180, 205

Woodward, Ashley, 79, 94, 205

Zapf, Holger, 3-4, 7, 83, 124, 147, 206

Zima, Peter W, 3, 143, 206

ibidem.eu